Theatre and the Virtual

Theatre and the Virtual lays out a set of conceptual instruments for the articulation and engendering of the forces of theatrical potentiality.

Creating a passage towards a reconstitution of the given, a theatre of the virtual opens bodies in motion to a region of an ongoing genesis of forces. The outcome: regimes of constraint are abandoned through a radical practice of ecological attunement. Violence is eschewed through an onto-ecology of touch. Closed systems are repotentialised to become co-constitutive of their environments. A logic of spectrality settles in—not so much entities as atmospheres, not so much a being as a style of being, not so much a body as multitudinous milieus of response. This is the task of a theatre of the virtual—to safeguard the possibility of the extra-epistemological and uphold one's right to offer accounts of oneself from outside of being, all the while creating a fractured record of the wondrous mutations of a moving, gesturing body.

This book will be of great interest to students and scholars in theatre, philosophy, new materialisms, environmental humanities, gesture, and the ontology of response.

Zornitsa Dimitrova is a theatre researcher focusing on the philosophy of technology, the ecological turn, vulnerability studies, and the aesthetics of the Anthropocene. She holds a PhD in English Literature from the University of Münster. Research monographs include *Literary Worlds and Deleuze: Expression and Mimesis and Event* (2017) and the present book, *Theatre and the Virtual: Genesis, Touch, Gesture* (2022). Pieces on theatre have appeared in *Deleuze Studies*, *The New Theatre Quarterly*, *The Journal of Dramatic Theory and Criticism*, *Performance Philosophy*, and *Skenè. Journal of Theatre and Drama Studies*.

Routledge Advances in Theatre & Performance Studies

This series is our home for cutting-edge, upper-level scholarly studies and edited collections. Considering theatre and performance alongside topics such as religion, politics, gender, race, ecology, and the avant-garde, titles are characterized by dynamic interventions into established subjects and innovative studies on emerging topics.

ASHÉ
Ritual Poetics in African Diasporic Expression
Paul Cater Harrison, Michael D. Harris, Pellom McDaniels

Dancehall In/Securities
Perspectives on Caribbean Expressive Life
Patricia Noxolo, 'H' Patten, and Sonjah Stanley Niaah

Circus and the Avant-Gardes
History, Imaginary, Innovation
Anna-Sophie Jürgens and Mirjam Hildbrand

Aesthetic Collectives
On the Nature of Collectivity in Cultural Performance
Andrew Wiskowski

Dance Data, Cognition and Multimodal Communication
Carla Fernandes, Vito Evola and Cláudia Ribeiro

Theatre and the Virtual
Genesis, Touch, Gesture
Zornitsa Dimitrova

For more information about this series, please visit: https://www.routledge.com/Routledge-Advances-in-Theatre-Performance-Studies/book-series/RATPS

Theatre and the Virtual
Genesis, Touch, Gesture

Zornitsa Dimitrova

Routledge
Taylor & Francis Group
LONDON AND NEW YORK

First published 2022
by Routledge
4 Park Square, Milton Park, Abingdon, Oxon OX14 4RN

and by Routledge
605 Third Avenue, New York, NY 10158

Routledge is an imprint of the Taylor & Francis Group, an informa business

© 2022 Zornitsa Dimitrova

The right of Zornitsa Dimitrova to be identified as the author of this work has been asserted in accordance with sections 77 and 78 of the Copyright, Designs and Patents Act 1988.

All rights reserved. No part of this book may be reprinted or reproduced or utilised in any form or by any electronic, mechanical, or other means, now known or hereafter invented, including photocopying and recording, or in any information storage or retrieval system, without permission in writing from the publishers.

Trademark notice: Product or corporate names may be trademarks or registered trademarks, and are used only for identification and explanation without intent to infringe.

British Library Cataloguing-in-Publication Data
A catalogue record for this book is available from the British Library

Library of Congress Cataloging-in-Publication Data
A catalog record has been requested for this book

ISBN: 978-1-032-13767-4 (hbk)
ISBN: 978-1-032-13845-9 (pbk)
ISBN: 978-1-003-23108-0 (ebk)

DOI: 10.4324/9781003231080

Typeset in Bembo
by codeMantra

Contents

Acknowledgements — vii

Introduction: the Virtual as a Theatrical Force — 1
Motion 3
Ontology 4
Body 4
Environment 4
Ecology 5

1 Potentiality and the Virtual — 6
The Depletion of Potentiality: Motion and Action 9
Motion and Growth in the Poetics *and* Nāṭyaśāstra *14*
Other Forms 19
Actual and Virtual 22
Potentiality as an Ontological Horizon 27

2 Genesis and the Virtual — 35
Strandbeests 41
Interfusing 46
Theatre as a Technical Object 52
Gestural Potentiality 57
The Transducer 64

3 Violence and Touch — 72
Land of Palms 74
The Technicity of Touch 79
Violent Conditions 83
Touch and Event 90
Repotentialising Matter 95
Engendering Practice: On Environmentality 98

4 Organism and Gesture 107
Organism and the Field of Potentiality 109
Diaphanous Organismicity 114
Organism and Machine 117
Omnia 123
Response: Against Communication 128

Conclusion 141

Glossary 147
Index 153

Acknowledgements

Chapter I contains material that first appeared in the article Dimitrova, Zornitsa. 2015. "Aesthetic Codification of the Unsavoury from *Nāṭyaśāstra* and the *Poetics* to Postdramatic Theatre." *New Theatre Quarterly* 31 (4): 399–411, reproduced with permission by Cambridge University Press.

Equally so, some of the work on potentiality and the virtual in Chapter I is based on material first presented in the article Dimitrova, Zornitsa. 2016. "A Drama of Potentialities—Toward an Ontology." *Journal of Dramatic Theory and Criticism* 31 (1): 65–87, hereby acknowledged as the first place of publication of this material.

Initial work on response, now substantially modified and expanded to form a subsection of Chapter IV, was first presented in the article Dimitrova, Zornitsa. 2017. "Robotic Performance: An Ecology of Response." *Performance Philosophy* 3 (1): 162–177, which is hereby acknowledged as the initial place of publication.

At Routledge, I thank the series editor Laura Hussey, the editorial team, represented by Swati Hindwan, and the production team represented by Kathrin Immanuel for overseeing the manuscript through completion and publication. I also thank Sebastian J. Golla and the anonymous reviewers for their insightful and timely interventions.

Introduction
The Virtual as a Theatrical Force

This book examines the concept of the virtual as a theatrical force. More than ever before, we are surrounded with myriad examples of virtuality, becoming acutely aware of the manifold spectral presences that traverse our being. It is becoming increasingly difficult to perceive anything whatsoever as a solid, finite, discrete object walled off from its multiple environments and fields of interaction. Our awareness of the pervasive force of the virtual is growing. The increased evanescence of our being compels us to seek different ontologies and novel systems of valorisation that can do justice to our changing condition. The virtual is everywhere in theatre, yet there are preciously few conceptual instruments to help us excavate this ontological manifold and examine its work. The present book sees its task in presenting the first sketches of a theatrical ontology of the virtual, one that vicariously considers its multiple environmental, political, and social incarnations. For the virtual to show its mettle, we are in need of novel conceptual instruments that give shape to this complex and pervasive phenomenon. Equally so, we are in need of revised concepts of body, environment, and ecology—such that are capable of accommodating the force of the virtual and making its work palpable.

The virtual thrives on motion. This kinetic foundation tells us yet again that we can no longer rely on statism, notions of immobile being, and a perception of bodies as sedentary. Our very systems of thought need to be refigured to make tangible the fully permeable, spectral, and kinetic virtual. This is how we can bear witness to whole new conceptual landscapes in theatre that coalesce out of the atmospheres surrounding bodies, dispersive gestures, and continuous motion. Our first task is to reinstate ontologies of expansion and incessant multidirectional movement over ontologies of boundary-forming. Within this initial scaffold, we will begin to speak of the force of the virtual—an underlying region of perpetual enmeshment that has the power to repotentialise the given.

We define the virtual as a nonlocal force, continually shifting and fundamentally kinetic. This is a primary constitutive region of infinite potentiality. This region permeates the given and is fundamental in relation to it. Yet the virtual only remains a clandestine inherence if we assume the vantage that our worlds are composed of finite and discrete actual objects. Another point

DOI: 10.4324/9781003231080-1

of access and another vocabulary are needed to reach towards this region and illuminate the various ways in which the theatrical is perturbed by it. If we seek to comprehend these through the logic of solid actuality, we will come to realise that the virtual is nowhere to be found. But then again, a look at the regions of ontological constitution will reveal a landscape of incessant motion, traversed by grades of potentiality and actuality. Once we have assumed this vantage, we witness multiple theatres of individuation, multi-local and infused with a visceral spectrality.

Artistic practice has this force—it informs the given in novel ways. It drafts out trajectories for the possible and gives us the conceptual fuel to refigure existing notions of bodies, environments, and ecologies. We begin to see how performance work does not simply expose and critique practices of injustice or adherences to obsolete orders. Rather, what we witness is how theatrical ontologies themselves already contain the blueprint for taking on different trajectories and different forms of world-making. And this possibility is given to us not through descriptions or ethical imperatives but in and through performance. It is the task of this book to delve into the possibilities that open up in exploring the virtual as a theatrical force. And we may even go as far as to say that the force of the virtual is equally the force of the theatrical—both make us aware of a vast multifarious creation that cannot be exhausted through a mere inquiry into the given.

The present book drafts out a theatre of the virtual using three points of inflection: genesis, touch, and gesture. In taking these three inflections into account, we want to show that the virtual is manifold and capable of taking on a variety of conceptual clusters within its domain. When we speak of genesis, we address the elaborate theatre of individuation that the virtual stages at every step of the way. That is to say, we emphasise the generative conditioning of the virtual, its capacity as a force that both individuates and causes infinitesimal individuations. Chapter 1 will help us to see theatrical works as kinetic systems that thrive on a productive enmeshment of grades of potentiality and grades of actuality. Unlike the Aristotelian system wherein potentiality is exhausted in the actual, we propose a continual genesis of forms that does not cease. This means that we begin to see theatrical works as generative matter that folds and refolds as it shapes new ontologies along the way. In Chapter 2, we will see how this will have repercussions for the very formations of individuals within the theatrical. We will also begin to flesh out the consequences of one such change of vantage. Apart from an altered perspective on theatrical ontologies, we will see how this generative streak adds to the concepts of body, environment, the living, and the non-living.

When we speak of touch, we introduce an inflection within the virtual that carries the force to repotentialise the given. In Chapter 3, we position touch as a technique for the engendering of bodies and of introducing novel variation. Within perpetual bodily individuation, touch becomes a chancy encounter with the virtual. Touch, however, is not to be aligned with the physical activity of touching. This is an abstract operation that can be more aptly described as "the state and condition of being perturbed". That is, touch has the characteristic of an event inasmuch as it precipitates a change of state, an alteration of trajectories, and a reorientation of the given. In this sense, we could go as far as to say that the touch-event is the enabling condition for the generation of bodies and their worlds as it continually seeks to remodulate. As an ontogenetic operation for the creation of novel variation, the touch-event is not necessarily radical. It may not signal the complete overhaul of an existing system but will introduce an inflection within the given, a change in tonality. Such inflections signal the foregrounding of an attitude—not simply a change in one's fundamental modes of attunement but a reorientation that is directed and deliberate in its aesthetic, environmental, or political zest.

When we speak of gesture, we conceptualise operations for expanding potentiality. Because of their capacity for infinite gesturely expression, bodies can no longer be confined to their status as mere organisms—it is gesture that safeguards the possibility for continual bodily expansion. In gesture, bodies open towards the virtual and draft out novel environments within existing peripheries, continually enlarging the spectral atmospheres that surround them. A theatre of the virtual thrives on this generative dimension of gesture—we witness how it derives its force from ambiences. Throughout the pages of this book, we position gesture as an operation that is precarious and minor, indeterminate, and without directionality. Still, as a locale at the threshold of the body, a gesture holds the power to form new bodily alliances and alter the ecologies that bodies form in their co-enmeshments. As we will discover in Chapter 4, a gesture equally so becomes a compositional force as it opens up a territory for the work of response—a practice of visceral attunement that is the very beginning of co-creation.

The concept of the virtual developed in this book is an ontological concept. It explores a reorientation of being from solid, static, local, and definitive to spectral, kinetic, multi-local, and generative. And for this exploration to take place, we have to see how our concepts of motion, body, environment, and ecology are also changing. Further, our very definition of ontology undergoes alterations—it does not seek to evade matter but is immersed in material conditions. In lieu of preparation for reading this book, below are some preliminary definitions of the concepts that intersect with the virtual. Once we have set the ground in this way, we can begin to speak of the virtual without reservation.

Motion

If we want to understand the work of the virtual, we need to begin our inquiry with the constitutive force of motion. Motion is multi-directional, dispersive, and constitutive of beings and their milieus of interaction. It has even been defined as the primary ontological category, one that comes before being, signalling "the invention of a new conceptual and ontological framework of analysis that begins with the primacy of motion" (Nail 2019, 517).

One such vantage is necessary if we are to perceive the theatrical through concepts such as spectrality, non-locality, or entanglement.

Ontology

Ontology is no longer the philosophical description of being as such. When we speak of being, we speak of the ongoing, motioning-forward performance of matter. This performance of matter encompasses not only bodily movement but the entirety of milieus and fields of interaction. This material embeddedness of ontology makes it reliant on material conditions and the practices surrounding them. Further still, material conditions, practices, and ontologies are co-emergent and co-dependent. So ontologies are no longer static and historically fixed world description regimes but expansive actional realities that remain in the making. The good news is that ontologies are not fixed and universal—we do not speak of the ontology of this and that but of "ontologies" to indicate that there are many. And just like anything else, ontologies are fluxional and capable of change.

Body

Equally so, the concept of the body undergoes a dispersal to incorporate bodily peripheries. This is no longer a discrete entity that easily aligns with the concepts of organism or individual but a threshold, an instrument for entering the virtual. A body is a momentary capture of a state, a brittle composition shot through by potentials. Our concept of the body does not recognise the distinction between the living and the non-living, nor does it entail an exclusive discussion of simian bodies—within the pages of this book, a body is an inflection within the virtual, a point of perturbation that has become singular. Yet these points of perturbation within the continuous virtual field are incapable of seclusion as they are fully responsive and entirely shot through by other bodily peripheries. Perhaps it is no surprise that within a theatre of the virtual, bodies are spectral and non-local. These are maximally open and expressive systems best described as gesturely atmospheres.

Environment

An environment is a bodily surrounding, a fluid field of interaction. Environments are not necessarily local but encompass the entirety of relations that a body creates in its various enmeshments with other materials. An environment is ever-expanding as a body reasserts its existence by continually building novel relations. In a sense, we could imagine environments as perpetual clouds of virtualities hovering over bodies. At the same time, environments are concrete. Unlike milieus, which designate the pre-existing material climates and conditions into which bodies are invariably immersed, environments are the relationalities emanating from bodies and generated by them. That is to say, whereas milieus can exist without a given body, environments only subsist in tandem with their bodies. Within the pages of this book, we think bodies and environments as co-extensive and co-constitutive. At times, the interpermeation between bodies and environments will compel us to speak about bodies–environments.

Ecology

The term ecology dates back to the nineteenth century when Ernst Haeckel defined it as the totality of relations between a living being and its environment (Haeckel 1866). And even though this initial definition has been refined and enriched in a variety of ways, we still have the presence of a living being and a separate physical environment as the conceptual core of that term. The persistence of the dyad "being and world" cannot be retained within a theatre of the virtual. The very concept of the virtual precludes the possibility of thinking of entities as entirely discrete. The virtual, rather, will see individuals as nonlocal atmospheres—not entirely stable bundles of potentiality. Their environments, in turn, become porous peripheries as we begin to see how bodies stretch out to incorporate the entirety of their milieus of interaction. Further still, within the pages of this book, ecology cannot remain a biological concept as the virtual region does not distinguish between living and non-living, biological object, and artefact. The concept of ecology that pervades the pages of this book has overcome the fascination with the fact that there are vast multifarious forms of existence beyond the biological and the "living" and incorporates these without reservation. Ecology is expansive and deals with the expressions of being in its various practices of world-making. It seeks to examine these practices and flesh out the significance of the various bodily enmeshments therein.

Work Cited

Haeckel, Ernst. 1866. *Generelle Morphologie der Organismen*. Berlin: Georg Reimer.
Nail, Thomas. 2019. *Being and Motion*. Oxford: Oxford University Press.

1 Potentiality and the Virtual

This section takes a closer look at the concept of potentiality and its implications for the work of performing. This should be understood in Aristotle's sense, but not quite. Potentiality is, first of all, openness. Traditionally, potentiality's counterpart—the concept of actuality—pertains to entities that are fully available to recognition, fully formed, and known as such to the senses. When we speak of potentiality, we choose to foreplay indeterminacy—that which has not been made final yet. With the introduction of indeterminacy, we shift to a region that has little to do with things available to the cognitive faculties. This region is more speculative than epistemologically informed. It busies itself with that which can be—not even in the sense of forming an entity but in the sense of generating various networks of ecological attunement. Speaking of this region is an exercise in ontology. It is yet to be seen how this region relates to the concept of being.

At the same time, a departure from the actual shows something extra-ontological—even more difficult than dealing with "being" is this touch of an atmosphere that is not even an "is" anymore. Hardly is it solely a matter of genesis, of an individuation as a being yet to be. Within this region,

> potentiality does not become actuality, because in that case one would have an infinite reduplication of the potentiality actuality relation. Rather, it is the entity that actualizes potentiality, or that expresses its own potentialities. Potentiality and actuality are not entities in a reciprocal, intrinsic, and necessary relation; rather, they are principles of the entity that are really distinct, so that their ontological consistency is their relation. They are, therefore, transcendental relations: actuality is a determining and determined principle, whereas potentiality is a determinable and undetermined principle.
>
> (Diodato 2012, 88)

In order to show how this concept of potentiality is shaped, I begin with the classical ontology of drama. Here we still deal with something familiar—albeit complex—the actual. Classical dramatic theory has the actual as its goal. Its stuff is motion, but at the same time, it foreplays the extinguishment

DOI: 10.4324/9781003231080-2

of motion in reaching a formal attainment, a final cause. The drama comes to be because of motion, interweaving potentiality and actuality. There is openness, chance, and shifts of extreme intensity. In the end, however, it turns out that the drama is crystallised in the actual. The concept of drama, across a variety of traditions, appears to maintain an ambiguous relationship to potentiality. Aristotle, whose views on tragedy are tightly related to the cosmological scenarios sketched out in *Physics* and the prescriptive ones presented in the *Ethics*, shows us how the classical plot thrives on the emancipation of potentiality. This, however, has one actual goal: completion and attainment. The concept of potentiality is thus accessory to that of the actual, a stepping stone—that which is habitually called "development". A "situation" "develops" in order to be properly "realised", that is to say, in order to yield a result. In accordance with the ontology of the *Poetics*, the drama is constructed around entelechial scenarios whereby potentiality is largely exhausted in the actual. This ontological practicality is everywhere to be encountered in classical examples of dramatic theory.

Even at the level of its very ontology, that is to say, at the level of its relationship to being, dramatic theory is permeated with such practicality. The plot has a purpose—the extinguishment of potentiality—and it works in its orderly fashion to achieve this purpose. It is the concepts of action and motion, as defined in the *Physics*, that carry the plot and help it to express this purposiveness. Both action and motion are, to certain degrees, defined by the ambiguity within and juxtaposition of the concepts of potentiality and actuality. The *Poetics* is permeated with the ideas articulated in the *Physics* to such an extent that it can be said to exemplify Aristotle's understanding of natural science. And Aristotle does trust "the subject matter of natural science to be motion ... any transition from potential to actual being" (Schmitt 1987, 3). Even more so, the *Poetics* expresses and extends Aristotle's views on the very processes of nature marked by growth, decay, extinguishment, and an irreversible determinism—one thing can only become that one certain thing. In short, we have the view that there is a natural substance characterised by an inner principle of change and stasis (Waterlow 1982). Motion is the expression of change; action is its carrier.

The very fabric of the drama is permeated with action and motion of the most complex type, suitable only to beings "living and knowing". In a manner of speaking, drama is among the most anthropocentric of the arts as it makes "human nature" its sole subject—all the while knowingly showing that "humanness is profoundly unnatural" (Kirby 2011, 74). But then again, we also have a certain extra-personal thrust within this highly personal engagement with the human. The evolvement—or motion—of "human" "action" is realised through the advancement of a plot. The plot itself, however, follows an extra-human entelechy that, in turn, exerts its doings on the drama. One can speculate that, because of this complexity, the plot itself becomes an agency in its own right. It is an entity in action, a separate being of a peculiar formal sentience, one that motions away towards a final cause. Perhaps because of this constructed proximity to the "living", Aristotle declared the drama to be "the most satisfying of the arts" (Schmitt 1987, 5)—we have the principle of entelechy at work, and then again, there is the concept of motion that allows us to express this principle.

Because of the principles of action and motion, the drama achieves its entelechial end. This "end", however, also means a depletion of potentiality. Motion carries potentiality only up to a certain point. Even more so, motion incessantly works towards the exhaustion of potentiality. Potentiality, however, is the distinguishing condition of motion. Because of this, the cessation of potentiality—while it may contain attainment—simultaneously becomes the cessation of motion. It is interesting to observe how the scenarios sketched out in *Physics*, mostly observations from the natural world, have left their imprint on the way Aristotle constructs a dramatic theory. The Aristotelian ontology is entelechial at its core. And accordingly, the drama at its most abstract becomes a motion coming to an end. This motion, starting from a wealth of potentialities, becomes the transition from the potential to the actual. And the actual signals the maximal depletion of potentiality in an outcome.

This book sets out to speak of a theatrical ontology that relies on an intensive engagement with potentiality for its effects to take place. Cases of postdramatic theatres of the 1990s and beyond as well as New European Drama are already classic examples of a more thorough engagement with the productive zest of potentiality. At the same time, there are both far less conspicuous and far more exuberant instances of performances that are entirely constructed around and thriving on an engagement with a fundamental openness. This openness signals a radical orientation towards an ongoing genesis of forces that simply does not cease. In such cases, we observe an engagement of potentiality with actuality that plays itself out in such a way that potentiality enfolds to become ever more varied. Actuality is retained in the shape of little islands of consistency within an overarching conceptual field of potentiality. This field of potentiality operates as an ongoing individuation occurring at various localities at different speeds and within multiple levels of intensity. Actuality is still there, but now, it primarily points to the overarching constitutive region; it becomes a gesture leading beyond itself. The field of potentiality becomes an "atmosphere" of ontological constitution. This playground for the tensions between tendencies appears to generate a region of actuality while the various tendencies persevere in their own constitutive processes yet not leading anywhere in particular. In denying themselves an outcome, these forces and tendencies become profoundly "nonsensical", supreme examples of ontological impracticality.

So we have a concept of actuality that is not self-contained but continually gestures beyond itself. But then again, we also have a potentiality that is infinitely dissipative yet self-contained insofar as it thrives within its own processes of constitution. These latter tendencies cannot so easily be pronounced to be "unreal" as they press their reality status on any "spectator" and, in a manner of speaking, appear to put on display a "reality" more candid in its senseless arbitrariness. The field of tendencies generates atmospheres of potentiality that do not move from the potential to the actual. The movement, rather, is dispersive, taking place from all directions and in all directions. Its course, to the extent that we can speak of one, is extra-linear.

Yet the qualification "extra-linear" is not an apt way to describe a motion that is, indeed, "spectral"—overlapping several localities and times simultaneously, retroactive and proactive at once, zigzagging between levels of being as well as across thresholds of nonbeing. Gilbert Simondon has a way of describing one such situation as "metastability" (Simondon 1992, 300–303). A metastable locale is a region that is dynamic and ever-shifting in its internal structure yet "solid" and "fixed" enough to allow us to speak of a quasi-entity. The presence of a metastable entity invariably invokes a cognitive dissonance as we deal with something lucid and available to our cognitive faculties yet ever so slippery. When I speak of potentiality, I think in terms of this productive relation between an entity and a nonentity, between being and the extra-ontological, outside of being yet real. The theatre of the virtual plays itself out at this very interface between the actual and this region of tendencies and forces, between the almost fully formed and the dynamic multiplicities.

The Depletion of Potentiality: Motion and Action

Let us take a closer look at the classical ontology of drama. Aristotle is at the core of the development of a wealth of dramatic traditions and, for this reason, I take a moment to summarise some of the points put on display in the *Poetics*. These include the concept of plot, the concepts of motion and action, and the concept of entelechy. These concepts are seen to form "a systematic doctrinal whole, marked as Aristotelian by a core of pervasive substantive methodological conceptual constants" (Husain 2002, 3) elucidated in the *Metaphysics* and shaping a particular concept of being and categories of being. The latter entail the categorial priority of *ousia*, immanent causal form-matter constitution in the category of *ousia*, and the ontological and cognitive priority of the object (Husain 2002, 10–17).

"Plot" is the overarching term weaved out of intricate interrelations between motion, action, and entelechy, whereas these, in turn, are composed of ever-changing grades of potentiality and actuality. Traditionally, the plot is a progression of incidents built up according to laws of probability and necessity. The unfolding of a plot is expressed, in turn, by motion, action, and entelechy. First, motion is the interplay of various levels of potentiality and actuality. Second, we have the concept of action as the driving force within the plot. Third, the plot advances not only by dint of laws of potentiality and actuality but also because potentiality and actuality interweave in such a way that the plot moves towards a purpose, towards its own unravelling. The *Physics* already defines entelechy as actuality and completion, the bringing to a close of a certain motion. Even the most radical transformations and events that are difficult to pin or fathom have an orderly place within this cosmology and are made lucid: "'change is the entelechy of that which is potentially' ... for as long as the potentiality is preserved, so also is the change which completes the potentiality" (Edwards 2014, 14). That is to say, that which is *potentially* has one purpose and its purpose is to be transformed into something else, non-potential. The concept of entelechy entails an annihilation of potentiality and the bringing forth of a purpose that is part of the nature of every entity.

In Aristotle, an outcome determines the plot and functions as the system's final cause, the being-at-an-end. The concept of entelechy is fundamental to plot mechanics, and many scenarios put on display exactly the realisation that each being always already contains its purpose within itself. Because of this, entelechy is often described with another term, "teleology"—suggested by Christian Wolff in *Philosophia Rationalis* (1732 [1728]) and derived from *telos* (purpose). The process of actualisation is that of becoming what something already is. The plot is constructed around the metaphysical concept of *entelecheia* and puts forward the assertion that each thing contains its purpose within itself. But Aristotle's dramatic theory also asserts that it takes a movement towards this purpose to bring forth the full actualisation of a thing. What Aristotle defines as the "final cause" is also the purpose of actualisation and the goal of tragedy. That view from the *Physics*—that each entity has its own immanent entelechy and naturally strives towards a self-completion—is transferred to the drama.

Let us see how the process of actualisation is enacted in tragedy. The outcome of the drama is not apparent in the early stages of the plot but is foreshadowed in *hamartia*, the tragic error in judgement that issues from one's ignorance or awareness of a certain state of affairs. At this point, we still have a wealth of potentiality and things have ever so slightly begun to shift towards actualisation. Then, we have *peripeteia*, the tragic turn of events, the turning juncture, or the point of no return that marks the irreversible transition from potentiality to the beginnings of the actualisation of *hamartia*. In the *Poetics*, Aristotle describes this as a shift from probability to (tragic) necessity, "a change by which the action veers round to its opposite, subject always to our rule of probability and necessity" (1902, 1452a22–23). Apart from the turning (*peripeteia*), the plot also evokes another component of change, recognition (*anagnorisis*). The tragic awareness marks an even more pronounced invasion of the actual within the plot. *Anagnorisis* is "a change from ignorance to knowledge, producing love or hate between the persons destined by the poet for good or bad fortune" (1452a29–31). *Hamartia*, *peripeteia*, and *anagnorisis* serve as stepping stones marking levels of transition from potentiality to actuality, from a range of possibilities to a definitive outcome, and thus contribute to the formal becoming of the drama.

Again, the dramatic plot relies on action for its unfolding. Action is drama's motion, "the actuality of that which potentially is, *qua* such" (Aristotle 1984, *Physics* III.1, 201a10–11). As Kosman argues, when we speak of motion in Aristotle, we more or less speak about the constitutive quality of actuality. Motion has no other purpose but to carry a potentiality towards the actual; the entelechy of potentiality is the actual: "Motion, in other words, is not the actuality of a potentiality in the sense of an actuality that results *from* a potentiality, but rather in the sense of an actuality which *is* a potentiality in its full manifestation" (Kosman 1969, 50). According to this view, being can be thought of as a continuum of ever-moving grades of potentiality and actuality. At the same time, however, actuality is not simply an extension of potentiality—in a way similar to that in which Aristotle took infinity to be an expandable finitude—but also the full explication of the previously known as potential. This potential unfolds according to predefined laws of causality: "Everything should follow necessarily or probably; art should be controlled as if by a ruling force of nature" (Schmitt 1987, 4). The unfolding, in turn, takes place in such a manner so as to continue to reveal more and more in the generalised milieu of motion: "the actuality of what is potential, when it is fully real and functioning, not in this, that, or some other respect, but just as movable, is motion" (*Physics* III.1 201a16).

Motion progresses towards an end that is external to it (Kosman 1969, 57). Similarly, the action in the drama is not a purpose but a means to this end as it strives towards the necessary completion of a plot. Unlike the constitutive actuality (motion), the ultimate actuality of completion is static:

> motion is the actuality of a potentiality which is aimed ultimately at an actuality other than the motion and fatal to it. Motion does not, therefore, just happen to cease, its essential activity is devoted to ceasing. Its being is auto-subversive, for its whole purpose and project is one of self-annihilation.
>
> (Kosman 1969, 57)

Motion carries the plot yet motion is not an end in itself. Rather, motion precipitates its own cessation, the conversion of potentiality into actuality. In order to have an impact, the exemplification of a change of state in the drama follows a mechanics aided by the employment of the concept of attainment. Attainment is marked by the complete exhaustion of potentiality and the consolidation of a region that is fully actual yet static. While Aristotle sees drama as a story of purposive becoming, this purposive becoming has a goal that coincides with the depletion of potentiality.

Here one can speak of a tendency to think classical drama in terms of a plot understood as a causal, entelechial motion carried by action. Deuber-Mankowsky illustrates this shift from potentiality to actuality through the gesture of painting as presented by Merleau-Ponty. The artist is captured in a moment of drawing invisible circles in the air above the canvas, "a scanning of possible lines in order to realize, out of an infinite number of possibilities, the one, optimal line" (Deuber-Mankowsky 2017, 57). The artist is likened to the God of Leibniz:

> following the rule that the greatest variety of things must be combined with the greatest order, he chooses, out of an infinite number of

possibilities, the best one. The choice ... is not predetermined, but it is nonetheless necessary, and can, at least in principle, be predicted.

(ibid., 57)

This principle of thought is present in Aristotle's views on both nature and the dramatic plot. The classical ontology of drama offers a mechanics of purposiveness and a linear progression from potentiality to actuality. Across specificities, the ontology of the drama engenders a scenario of becoming through the exhaustion of potentiality. In the *Poetics*, an interweaving of potentiality and actuality precipitates motion. The work of potentiality cannot be underestimated: the plot in its entirety subsists because of potentiality's ontological status as an ongoing gesture of becoming. This difference between the actual and interweaving grades of potentiality is also expressed in the language of the *Poetics*:

> in chapter 14, when describing the plot-type in which an intended act of violence towards unrecognised kin is averted by recognition, he [Aristotle] uses the aorist when speaking of its averted accomplishment (πρὶν ποιῆσαι), but a present infinitive when speaking of the act as imminent but as yet unfulfilled (τὸ μέλλοντα ποιεῖν). So the persistent use of present participles and infinitives when speaking of the change of fortune must be significant. Aristotle is commenting on the process of change, not its completion: the trajectory of the change, rather than its outcome.
>
> (Heath 2017, 346)

Concepts found in the *Metaphysics* and *Physics* are employed in favour of the being status of change but also its precarious relation to something extra-ontological:

> In defining change as a kind of actuality, he [Aristotle] is making the point that change is something that is: it is a part of reality. In defining change as an actuality of what potentially is qua such, he is bringing out the relation between change and what is not.
>
> (Coope 2009, 278)

In line with this is the contention that "there are no bodies alive *purely* potentially" (Freeland 1987, 406). The plot becomes the very playground for this interweave of being and the extra-ontological. Yet the plot motions forward until it arrives at a point where potentiality is at a minimum of being and actuality becomes maximal. From this point on, the plot veers towards one particular outcome. Once a level of maximal actuality is reached, actions and events within the drama begin to work towards the realisation of a singular purpose. These are mirrored in the very design of the dramatic plot insofar as the plot is defined by motion (*kinêsis*) and motion is defined by change. In the *Poetics*, the authority of the plot ascertains that the network of probability and necessity steers the action towards one particular and already definite outcome.

Apart from this formal shift from potentiality to actuality, one observes how the plot begins to strive towards the attainment of an affective constituent, *katharsis*, the "proper purgation" of emotion (1449b21–28). An element here is *pathos* as it additionally marks the orientation of potentiality towards actuality—this time on the emotive level of the plot. *Pathos*, "the thing suffered" (Else 1957) or "suffering" (Heath 1987), is described as "a destructive or painful action, such as death on the stage, bodily agony, wounds and the like" (1452b10–11). In terms of the emotive becoming of drama, the presence of *pathos* shows that the plot has begun to shift towards necessity. With the conversion of *pathos* into *katharsis*, the goal of tragedy is achieved inasmuch as *katharsis* has the nature of an emotional attunement. So, we have the formal entelechial goal of tragedy achieved through the plot. And then, we also have the phenomenon of *katharsis* that engenders a concept of emotive entelechy— hereby suffering is converted into an impassive constituent that can be said to be the emotive end of tragedy. Attainment propels the drama both as an emotive and a formal principle.

Tragedy shows us events that can take place at various levels of probability as the results of possible actions. At the heart of this assumption, we find an actional constituent that causes particular individuals to act in particular ways and not in others. Entelechy pushes its actants towards an outcome. As entelechy seeks its full realisation, germinal dispositions become actions, potentiality becomes actual, and a plot arrives at its completion. Again, this assumption is directly linked to Aristotle's metaphysical concepts of *energeia* and *entelechia*—concepts traditionally associated with activity and translated with the verb *agere* (lit. "to push forward"). By means of action, the tragic plot arrives at its entelechial goal:

> Dramatic action, therefore, is not with a view to the representation of character: character comes in as the means by which action is embodied and made specific. Hence the incidents and the plot are the end of a tragedy; and the end is the chief thing of all. Again, without action there cannot be a tragedy; there may be without character.
> (1450a20–25)

Aristotle's contention that "the power of the tragedy, we may be sure, is felt even apart from representation and actors" (1450b18–19) supplements the definition of Greek tragedy as "the mimesis of an action" (1449b30).

Mimesis puts action on display. Entelechial motion is made palpable through mimesis. In Aristotle, there cannot be a plot without action (*praxis*)—the *telos* of the drama cannot be achieved without it. Action carries the drama and expresses its entelechy; the (tragic) hero is the vehicle which makes action palpable. The definition of tragedy and the concept of mimesis are direct consequences of the view that

> Tragedy, ... is an imitation of an action that is serious, complete, and of a certain magnitude; in language embellished with each kind of artistic

ornament, the several kinds being found in separate part of the play in the form of action, not of narrative; through pity and fear effecting the proper purgation of these emotions.

(1449b30)

In the *Poetics*, we encounter two dramatic traditions, a formalist and an affective one, that define the drama in similarly entelechial terms.

The formal unfolding of the drama is shown in the evolvement of an entelechial plot out of a transition from potentiality to actuality. An emotive entelechy is shown in the motion towards an aesthetic response (*katharsis*) distilled out of suffering (*pathos*). These concepts, in turn, are entwined with the definition of motion in the *Physics* and the assertion that *motion has its own being*, that is to say, motion is a reality in its own right. Aristotle's very definition of motion as the actuality of potentiality *qua* such informs both the insistence on entelechy as a process of actualisation and the emphasis on action in the Greek drama. Action, however, is not to be understood as something personal initiated by a knowing subject in possession of one's intentionality. Action is to be seen as an impersonal force that only has the plot, the tragic hero, and the general milieu of the drama as placeholders that allow it to flow forth.

Motion and Growth in the *Poetics* and *Nāṭyaśāstra*

Aristotle thinks of being in terms of two types of actuality, a processual and a final one, *energeia* (being-at-work) and *entelechia* (being-at-an-end) (Aristotle 2002, *Metaphysics* 1050a20–23). The idea of the plot as motion (*kinêsis*), "the actuality of that which potentially is, *qua* such" (*Physics* III.1 201a10–11), corresponds to the first actuality in its capacity as "being-at-work". At the same time, Aristotle differentiates between two corresponding types of potentiality: an inactive and an active potentiality, that is to say, the potentially potential and the actually potential. In terms of the drama, this shift from potentiality to actuality amounts to the formal and the emotive becoming of the dramatic plot. Accordingly, the plot structure is defined by motion (*kinêsis*) and change. It employs two components defined by change—reversal (*peripeteia*) and recognition (*anagnorisis*). *Peripeteia* is the plot device that effects the unfolding of the tragic. In the *Poetics*, it is described as "a change by which the action veers round to its opposite, subject always to our rule of probability and necessity" (1452a22–23). *Anagnorisis* is "a change from ignorance to knowledge, producing love or hate between the persons destined by the poet for good or bad fortune" (1452a29–31), and *pathos* can be (a) intended with full awareness; (b) intended with full awareness, then not performed; (c) an act done unwittingly; (d) intended out of ignorance, then not performed (1453b30–33).

Herein the notion of plot advancement through purposive action remains of priority. In insisting on the primacy of action (*praxis*), Greek poetics puts forward an autonomous subject. This subject is characterised by free will and uses one's capacity for action to propel the dramatic plot. What is foregrounded is exactly "action" as it is by action that the plot follows its entelechial path:

> Dramatic action, therefore, is not with a view to the representation of character: character comes in as subsidiary to the actions. Hence the incidents and the plot are the end of a tragedy; and the end is the chief thing of all. Again, without action there cannot be a tragedy; there may be without character.
> (1450a20–25)

The classical definition of tragedy and the adjacent concept of mimesis are direct consequences of this view:

> Tragedy, then, is an imitation of an action that is serious, complete, and of a certain magnitude; in language embellished with each kind of artistic ornament, the several kinds being found in separate part of the play in the form of action, not of narrative; through pity and fear effecting the proper purgation of these emotions.
> (1449b30)

One observes how the plot governed by entelechy begins to strive towards the attainment of an affective constituent, *katharsis* (1449b21–28), the extinguishing of emotion. At this moment, *pathos*, the scene of suffering, comes to the fore. *Pathos* has the quality of a pacifying ritual. In purging the emotions of a spectatorship, it restores equilibrium. Just as the complete unfolding of the plot is the formal entelechial goal of tragedy, so does *katharsis* embody a concept of emotive entelechy.

Aristotle's *Poetics* (335 BC) is not the only early text of dramatic criticism concerned with entelechial mechanics, however. Bharata's *Nāṭyaśāstra* (second century BC—second century), albeit a product of a different dramatic tradition, partakes in building a similar ontology. Both works put on display the importance of plot and insist on its mechanics. Even more so, both rely on the entelechial nature of the dramatic plot. The *Poetics* and *Nāṭyaśāstra* pertain to an analogical ontology that works by means of linear progression, purposiveness, and a causal arrangement derived from the interaction of grades of probability and necessity. The dramatic plot becomes the very embodiment of this ontological design. First, the formal becoming of the drama is shown in the evolvement of an entelechial plot out of a transition from potentiality to actuality. Second, the emotive becoming of drama is shown in the congealing of an impersonal aesthetic state (*katharsis*, *ananda*).

In the *Poetics*, the entelechy of the plot ascertains that the causal network of probability and necessity veers the action towards one particular—and ultimately tragic—outcome. *Nāṭyaśāstra* equally foregrounds the element of action and focuses on the exertions of a protagonist. With this emphasis on action, the paradigmatic scenario of the Sanskrit drama assumes the shape of a quest narrative composed of five successive stages and culminating in attainment. The five junctures of the plot enumerated in Chapter XXI.8 of *Nāṭyaśāstra* are beginning (*ārmbha*), effort (*prayatna*), possibility of attainment (*prāpti-sabhava*), certainty of attainment (*niyatāpti*), and attainment (*phalaprāpti*). Five thematic plot elements (XXI.20–1) correspond to these, namely, the seed (*bīja*), the point of junction (*bindu*), the episode (*pātakā*), the incident (*prakari*), and the denouement (*kārya*). Their formal counterparts are as follows: the opening (*mukha*), progression (*pratimukha*), development (*garbha*), pause (*vimarśa*), and conclusion (*nirvahaṇa*). It is an attainment that infuses the dramatic action with subject matter (*vastu*).

As laid out in Chapter XXI of *Nāṭyaśāstra*, the whole composed of the five junctures of the plot (*itivṛta*) is called the body of the drama. It is divided into five junctures (*sandhi*) (Ghosh 1951, 380). The five successive stages of action—the beginning, effort, possibility of attainment, certainty of attainment, and attainment of the result—are defined as follows. Whereas a beginning is associated with an "eagerness about the final attainment with reference to the Germ (*bīja*)" (XXI.9), under "effort", one understands a "striving towards attainment when the result is not in view" (XXI.10). The possibility of attainment is a thing "slightly suggested by an idea" (XXI.11), certainty of attainment occurs when "one visualizes in an idea a sure attainment" (XXI.12), and attainment takes place "when the intended result appears in full" (XXI.13) (Ghosh 1951, 381). One observes a motion from potentiality to actuality, from probability to necessity. In the exposition of the five junctures of the plot, there prevails an entelechial tinge. The latter is to be understood as a thing directed, purposive, striving towards, and revealing a certain tension because of this purposiveness.

Whereas the five stages of the plot exhibit the dominance of motion, the five corresponding plot elements (*arthaprakṛti*) clearly demonstrate a prevalence of the notion of growth. What both foreground, then, is the becoming of an entity which already contains its purpose within itself. Whereas *bīja* (lit. "seed") is "that which scattered in small measure expands itself and ends in fruition" (XXI.22), the prominent point (*bindu*) is "that which sustains the continuity (lit. non-separation) till the end of the play" (XX.23). We have the seed of an action and the condition allowing us to speak of the same entity at each stage of its evolvement, regardless of the metamorphoses it undergoes. The two elements that follow present us with the stages of this metamorphosis that are available to the viewer. The episode (*pātakā*) exemplifies "the event introduced in the interest of the principal plot" (XXI.24) and the episodic incident (*prakarī*) occurs "when merely the result of such an event is presented for the purpose of another and it has no Secondary Juncture" (XXI.25). *Kārya*, or the action in its entirety, is defined as "the efforts made for the purpose of the Principal Plot" (XXI.26).

The Sanskrit notion of drama (*nāṭya*) manifests the primacy of attainment (*phala*) arising out of a concoction of intricately welded formal elements (*rūpaka*). A resolution is already contained in the drama in the form of a seed (*bīja*), and a prominent point (*bindu*) marks the transitions from one state to another. In addition, the so-called elements of the spectacle—decoration, costumes, and makeup—as well as the presentation of gesture (*āṅgika*), words (*vācika*), and the representation of the four principal temperaments (*sattva*) gain significance. Out of these elements, the Sanskrit drama distils a wider concept of representation (*anukaraṇa*) that incorporates interactionist and affective constituents. Aristotle's contention that "the power of the tragedy, we may be sure, is felt even apart from representation and actors" (*Poetics*, 1450b18–19) feeds into the definition of Greek tragedy as "the imitation of an action that is serious, complete, and of a certain magnitude" (1449b30). Here a theory of mimesis based on action (*mimema*) comes to the fore to be supplemented by the notion of emotive entelechy. The Sanskrit drama with its principle of *anukaraṇa* (lit. "doing after") even more pronouncedly focuses on the impact and heavily relies on an interaction with a spectatorship.

In this way, the Sanskrit drama retains the Greek notion of mimesis with its actional focus and yet surpasses it. The definition of *anukaraṇa* can be found in the very definition of drama at the outset of *Nāṭyaśāstra*. Here the representational and narrative character of a performance gains primacy. Yet Section I.121 already shows that the principle of *anukaraṇa* in the Sanskrit drama intertwines with the capacity of drama to impart sentiment:

> 119. Stories taken out of Vedic works as well as Semi-historical tales (*itihāsa*) [so embellished that they are] capable of giving pleasure, is called drama (*nāṭya*). 120. A mimicry (*anukaraṇa*) of the exploits of gods, Asuras, kings as well as house-holders in this world, is called drama.
>
> 121. And when human nature with its joys and sorrows, is depicted by means of Representation through Gestures, and the like (i.c. Words, Costume, and Temperament or *sattva*), it is called drama.
>
> (I.119–21)

Sentiment within this tradition is an element that is non-representational and supra-narrational. It works entirely by means of suggestion. To this end, Bharata introduces a catalogue of eight *bhāva* or principal states (lit. "feelings") and eight aesthetic sentiments, *rasa* (lit. "taste", "juice"), distilled out of *bhāva*. Each *rasa* represents the consolidation of a permanent sentiment, or a *sthāyibhāva*, and exemplifies eight principal moods enumerated in *Nāṭyaśāstra*. The eight *rasa*, or principal aesthetic moods, are *Śṛṅgāram* (love), *hāsyam* (humour, laughter), *raudram* (rage, fury), *kāruṇyam* (compassion), *bībhatsam* (disgust), *bhayānakam* (fear), *vīram* (heroic), and *adbhutam* (amazement). The *bhavas* or transient feelings out of which *rasa* arises are, accordingly, *rati* (love), *hasya* (laughter), *soka* (sadness), *krodha* (anger), *utsaha* (vigour), *bhaya* (fear), *jugupsa* (disgust), and *vismaya* (astonishment). The eight *rasa* have the status of aesthetic emotions of quality and composition that is deemed "universal". Their ideal recipient, the spectator best equipped to taste a particular aesthetic emotion, is called *sahṛdaya*, "the like-hearted one". Only a *sahṛdaya* is perfectly attuned to relishing the dramatic performance and the congealing of *rasa* out of *bhāva* in its fullest flavour. It is in this interaction—the savouring of the ideal recipient and their registering of a certain aesthetic emotion—that *anukaraṇa* is achieved.

The concept of *anukaraṇa* in the Sanskrit drama does not entirely conform to the notion of representation, that is, the life-emulating depiction of a given actional reality. Rather, it presents us with a concoction of conceptual groupings that has its roots in the very idea of dramatic convention ubiquitous in the Sanskrit drama. That is to say, it not only pertains to the plot but also touches on notions of spectatorial success. *Anukaraṇa*, thus, is both actional *and* interactionist as it pertains to the special type of entelechial congealment that arises out of the communication between the aesthetic emotion represented on stage and the receptive activity of a *sahṛdaya*. To this end, *anukaraṇa* produces aesthetic effects as different as the recipients that have come under the influence of the drama:

> This (the *Nāṭya*) teaches duty to those bent on doing their duty, love to those who are eager for its fulfillment, and it chastises those who are ill-bred or unruly, promotes self-restraint in those who are disciplined, gives courage to cowards, energy to heroic persons, enlightens men of poor intellect, and gives wisdom to the learned. This gives diversion to kings, firmness [of mind] to persons afflicted with sorrow, and [hints of acquiring] wealth to those who are for earning it, and it brings composure to persons agitated in mind. The drama which I have devised, is a mimicry of actions and conducts of people, which is rich in various emotions and which depicts different situations. This will relate to actions of men good, bad and indifferent, and will give courage, amusement and happiness as well as counsel to them all.
>
> (I.108–12)

This interaction assumes the shape of selective "contagion" as each spectator receives that to which they are best attuned. The dominant notion here, as in the Greek drama, remains the uplifting and redeeming quality of *nāṭya*. Its role, roughly stated, is to present us with various actional and emotive scenarios, show us what it is like to be a human being, and suggestively teach us to be better ones. In both the Greek and Sanskrit traditions, the dramatic plot traces the coming to fruition of a situation. This process inheres in both the Aristotelian transition from potentiality to actuality and in the presence of plot elements such as *bīja* (lit. "seed") and *phala* (lit. "fruit") in the Sanskrit drama.

At this point, it becomes clear that the traditions of the Aristotelian and the Sanskrit drama rely on a concept of transformation grounded in the notion of entelechy. Both employ a calculated concoction of formal elements to instruct audiences about the nature of action and glean insights about the causal network of probability and necessity. Further, both exemplify a change of state, yet with heavy reliance on purposiveness. In order to have an impact, this exemplification follows a mechanics aided by the employment of motion and growth. Both Aristotle and Bharata Muni see drama as a narrative of becoming that is strictly entelechial.

Other Forms

True, "even audiences wholly innocent of theoretical consciousness continue to demonstrate Aristotelian expectations" (Schmitt 1990, 1). And still, we have variations within the theatrical that are not simply different in form but also rely on different types of ontology. As a response to this diversification, the study of theatre becomes compartmentalised. Drama Studies gets associated with textual scholarship—meaning largely but not entirely variations and transformations of Aristotelian drama—whereas Theatre Studies covers the domain of the stage. Performance Studies, in turn, becomes an overarching discipline that encompasses any live or semi-live event of a theatrical allure—not necessarily staged, not necessarily verbal, and not necessarily witnessed by an audience. Further, Performance Philosophy signals not only a turn towards philosophy in performance but also a productive alliance and a "mutually transformative encounter" (Cull 2012, 23) of the two disciplines. Yet beyond these formal arrangements, we can look at the very ontology of form as it emerges. Within the present inquiry, we rather speak of "forms of the theatrical" as events confronting us with the force of potentiality. And we arrive at "a drama of potentialities" (Dimitrova 2016). A drama of potentialities is not necessarily a "work" for the theatre but operates within a maximally inclusive definition that incorporates performance, dance, and art installation. It directs us towards *the enaction of a concept*; its structure is compact and veers towards maximal abstraction. A drama of potentialities is a witnessing of the unfolding and refolding of the ontological and extra-ontological, and as such, is expressive without the necessity of communication.

One turning point in dramatic theory and a gesture towards the generative zest of potentiality has been the shift from the ontology of classical drama (action) to that of postdramatic theatre (event). The concept of postdramatic theatre relies on a single event rather than on an action-driven plot. It does not follow an entelechial mechanics, nor is dialogue necessarily there. Interaction on stage, characters, and time progression are optional. We have a "development towards a theatre which is no longer even based on 'drama' … open or closed, pyramidal or circular, epic or lyrical, focused more on character or more on plot" (Lehmann 2006, 30):

> When it is obviously no longer simply a matter of broken dramatic illusion or epicizing distance; when obviously neither plots, nor plastically shaped dramatic personae are needed; when neither dramatic-dialectical collision of values or even identifiable figures are necessary to produce

"theatre" ... then the concept of drama—however differentiated, all-embracing and watered down it may become—retains so little substance that it loses its cognitive value.

(Lehmann 2006, 34)

Postdramatic theatre, known for its qualification as "theatre without drama" (Lehmann 2006, 30), establishes itself as a reaction to the written text. Yet "postdramatic theatre ... does not mean a theatre that exists 'beyond' drama, without any relation to it" but is more of an "unfolding and blossoming of a potential of disintegration, dismantling and deconstruction within drama itself" (ibid., 44).

The distinguishing condition of postdramatic theatre is a shift from work to event. *An event alone is the necessary and sufficient condition for the emergence of the theatrical* whereby the "coherent formation" of a "work" becomes redundant. Postdramatic theatre works not so much with action as with "states" (Lehmann 2006, 68), relies on a "scenic dynamic instead of a dramatic dynamic" (ibid., 69), and shows "a formation rather than a story" (ibid., 69). Further, postdramatic theatre is more attuned to "presence than representation, more shared than communicated experience, more process than product, more manifestation than signification, more energetic impulse than information" (ibid., 85). Lehmann observes that postdramatic theatre "is defined as a process and not as a finished result, as the activity of production and action instead of as a product, as an active force (*energeia*) and not as a work (*ergon*)" (ibid., 104). This intuition leads to a shift towards an energetic aesthetics of theatre whereby the aesthetic dimension is tightly interwoven with an ontological landscape. Even more so, one could say that it is the specific ontological landscape of potentiality, the shift—in both philosophy and art—from meta-discipline towards practice, along with a heightened sensitivity towards what Deleuze calls "the virtual", that shape its aesthetics. One witnesses an affinity towards the very gesture of ontological constitution.

Classical dramatic theory relies on a motion from potentiality to actuality whereby potentiality becomes fully exhausted in the actual. In postdramatic forms of the theatrical, potentiality rarely becomes fully actual. Rather, we have an engagement with the very interweave of potentiality and actuality. Caryl Churchill's *A Mouthful of Birds* (1986) documents this interplay. The dance of Dionysus, performed at the play's opening and final scene, foreshadows and frames a series of transformations. The dance activates the various ways in which the play's eight figures respond to Dionysian intoxication, breaking open and becoming sensitive to their innermost longings. Inasmuch as stories are discernible, these are patterned in exactly the same way. We begin with a character performing trivial tasks in mundane surroundings, then there is an ecstatic rupture as a response to Dionysus's dance, and, finally, we are shown the traces left on a character once the intoxication has subsided. Churchill scaffolds a mock version of an Aristotelian plot with a beginning, middle, and an end. But everything is multi-local and organised around the moments of recognition (Churchill's somewhat irreverent versions of Aristotle's *anagnorisis*); that is, the moments of encountering one's innermost longing and responding to it. The events of *anagnorisis* thus coincide with the play's figures' disruptive self-realisation. Rather than supplying us with a fully fledged version of an entelechial scenario, Churchill focuses on a singular event—an episode of transformation—and orients the entire play around it. This moment of transformation is the organising engine of the play's eight separate vignettes. It captures an energetic process of becoming wherein potentiality and actuality entwine and continually pass into one another. Let's look at the possession of one character, Lena, by an ancient spirit:

> He is a frog. She approaches threateningly as a snake. He seizes her arm and becomes a lover. She responds but as he embraces her he becomes an animal and attacks the back of her neck. She puts him down to crawl and he becomes a train. As he chugs under the table she blocks the tunnel with a chair and he rolls out as a threatening bird. She becomes a baby bird asking to be fed and he feeds her. As he goes to get more food she becomes a panther, knocks him to the ground and starts to eat him. After a moment he leaps up with a fierce roar. She goes into the next scene.
> (Churchill 1997, 11)

In employing such examples of transformational acting, Churchill's play shows how motion does not result in the exhaustion of potentiality but in an infinite proliferation of the virtual wherein each gesture brings forth a new form in an endless unfolding of a previously discrete form. Potentiality and actuality do not subsist in a relation of cause and effect but include both a motion towards actuality and the endless capacity of form to reconfigure and to fold back into potentiality. One is confronted with various gradations of individuation that may just as well recede into potentiality yet again. Here the actual is not irreversible but can recompose and present us with a completely different shape. Instead of the depletion of potentiality in an act of conversion of probability into a necessity, we have an entwinement of potentialities. We no longer deal with the entelechial dimension of a plot, but shift our focus towards the very interplay of potentiality and actuality, towards the motion as such. It is the motion that becomes primary and not entelechy.

Another Churchill piece, *Blue Kettle* (1997), shows us this non-purposive and self-annihilating side of motion, putting on display the reversibility of the motion from potentiality to actuality. The play presents us with a 40-year-old man pretending to be the lost son of various women, given for adoption decades ago (see Churchill 1998). The entire play is organised around this emotional fraud. One could envision the play as a singular organism attacked by a predatory presence that causes it to disintegrate. As the play progresses, a parasitic phrase affects its language. Here words are arbitrarily replaced by "blue" or "kettle"—at first still allowing us to discern what a sentence is about and gradually beginning to frustrate any sense-making effort—until the play collapses under the impossibility to remain communicative. Rather than motioning towards an entelechial end, the play begins to generate potentiality—a productive field of forces and relations that constitute the given. In struggling to neutralise the predator and deal with an emotion that cannot be articulated, *Blue Kettle* takes us to the constitutive chaos of potentiality that is pre-personal and even pre-linguistic. The play's language is reduced to syllables and isolated letters, and its characters—unwilling to confront a reality—dissolve their stature as subjects capable of action.

As postdramatic theatre refigures its ontological portrait, mimesis can no longer remain solely a reality defined by the concept of action. Rather, mimesis in postdramatic theatre is of an immanent cast and of generative character (Dimitrova 2017). It does not necessarily deal with actional scenarios grounded in subjectivity but also addresses a surplus that cannot be exhausted with the work of reason and does not necessarily entail a rational grounding. The strong logicality of the plot is replaced by an interweave of forces. Just as Lehmann relates postdramatic theatre to "energetic theatre" (Lehmann 2006, 38), so does this interweave of potentialities relate to *forms capable of accounting for their ontology* yet does not become exhausted with this role. The turn to potentiality foregrounds becoming yet dispenses with concepts of purposiveness. A processual non-purposive scenario replaces models dependent on entelechy. Instead, one has encounter-dependent motilities open to a plenitude of extra-human forces. We not only become aware of the variety of forces at play within a play but can also observe how a play makes visible its very ontological armature, making exactly this perpetual interweave of contingencies its subject. Because of this, a postdramatic play can be likened to an instrument no longer in command of its own function, one whose thrusts of becoming spring out in unorchestrated ways.

And now, we are better attuned to encounter "those bodies whose favored vehicle of affectivity is less wordy: plants, animals, blades of grass, household objects, trash" (Bennett 2015, 235). This vantage point uncovers ontological regions within the theatrical that are supra-anthropomorphic, constellatory rather than depending on linear causality, extra-actional, indifferent to subjectivity, extra-temporal, and non-spatial. Next, I explain how this interweave can be recast in terms of the concepts of "the virtual" and "the actual" (Deleuze and Parnet 2002, 148–152). Our focus remains the generative divide between the virtual and the actual: the very zest of potentiality, the very work of constitution.

Actual and Virtual

We should not align the virtual with the possible. Removing the category of the possible as an ontological persistence pre-existing the real and ontologically inferior to it allows us to think further than simply theorising the real as something more than the possible and qualifying items in terms of their status as existents or non-existents. The virtual, as something of the order of the real and with the status of an existent, does not consist of numerous possibilities that become actual. The virtual cannot be understood as a bundle of different possible situations of which one is realised: "the virtual is not opposed to the real; it possesses a full reality by itself" (Deleuze 2001a, 211). The virtual and the possible belong to different regimes of world-making, one delimited and finite, the other plural and in a continual state of emergence (Ansell-Pearson 2002, 72). We speak of an "autonomy of the virtual" (Shields 2002, 73) in such a way that the virtual is "real without being actual, ideal without being abstract" (Deleuze 1991, 96).

The actual is marked by continual formation. The virtual differentiates. This is "a force freely structured by divergence and separation thus complicating the identity of objects" (Meiner 1998, 166) inasmuch as it does precipitate change but not in a formative way. Choices are open and differences are included. The virtual works as an envelopment instead of development, an involution instead of an evolution, and an implication instead of an explication:

> In one sense the entity conveys and produces its virtualities. ... In another sense the virtual constitutes the entity. The virtualities inherent in a being, its problematic, the knot of tensions, constraints, and projects that animates it, the questions that move it forward, are an essential element of its determination.
>
> (Lévy 1998, 24–25)

The virtual can be likened to Simone Weil's "decreation", the process of making "something created pass into the uncreated" (Weil 2002, 32). At the same time, this is not an invitation to engage in a "fleshless ontology" (Brians 2011, 119). Instead, the virtual persists in parallel with and permeates the realm of finished products—it offers a conceptual apparatus meant to make us sensitive to the openness of finitude, to the divergent and infinite disparities within a being. The virtual is *an engagement with a manner, an inquiry into a style*. And it is best understood in terms of potentiality (Deleuze 2001a).

"Virtual" derives from *virtualis*, itself derived from *virtus*, meaning power—

> the virtual is that which has potential rather than actual existence. The virtual tends toward actualization, without undergoing any form of effective or formal concretization. ... Strictly speaking, the virtual should not be compared with the real but the actual, for virtuality and actuality are merely two different ways of being.
>
> (Lévy 1998, 23)

A philosophy of the virtual is an inquiry into the very dynamics of creation. The virtual pertains to a region of ontological constitution that is generative and just as real as the region of fully constituted entities. While an ideal region, the virtual has reality status equal to that of the actual and is defined in terms of its capacity for continuous creation. Equally so, the virtual does not precede the actual. Both regimes persist simultaneously—"actual and virtual are contemporary" (Piatti 2016, 52). The dyad virtual and actual allows us to overcome the divide between existence and nonexistence inasmuch as the concept of the virtual allows us to grant reality status to all things all the way down, without recourse to any entity that might be construed as "unreal". And while the virtual can be seen as "a spectrum of potentialities with various distance to actuality" (Kalaga 2003, 102), this does not entail any gradation in the reality of things. We cannot refer to certain constituents as less real or somewhat real. Again, reality status is granted to all things all the way down. And as an extra-ontological region, the region of the event is not to be understood as unreal or as not properly real simply because it is outside of being.

In the Aristotelian system, we have an entelechial motion and a transition from potentiality to the maximally actual. In line with Aristotle's view from the *Physics*, creation is not infinite and motion is not reversible: "Art does not infinitely evolve because, according to Aristotle, nature does not. The idea of motion entails the idea of development and change, but the motions are finite ... Art cannot consist of perpetually new creation ..." (Schmitt 1987, 7). Within the logic of the theatrical event, the emphasis falls on virtual processuality. The actual and the virtual persist in a relationship that makes them two inextricable entities conditioning each other simultaneously. The virtual is not exhausted in its actualisation. Nor is the actual fully freed from the pull of the virtual. The actual can return to the field of constitutive forces and relations. At the same time, each actual entity is never entirely separated from the region of the virtual and remains invariably coloured by it.

Within this interweave, singularity is a term that captures the motion towards actualisation. This entails the various "dramatisations of the virtual's dynamism" (Widder 2012, 40) together with the simultaneity of various degrees of actual and virtual within an entity. The actual itself, on the other hand, pertains to an already formed individual that, nevertheless, remains infinitely open to the virtual: "The actual is the complement of the product, the object of actualisation, which has nothing but the virtual as its subject" (Deleuze and Parnet 2007, 149). Actualisation belongs to the virtual because it is entirely dependent on the interplay of constitutive forces that permeate the given. The virtual alone is constitutive of the actual. At the same time, as shown in the examples from Churchill's plays, the actual can gesture back to the region of virtuality at any time. This gesturing, however, is not to be likened to Bene's subtraction as a "negative and finite becoming toward extinction as de-individuation" (Chiesa 2012, 179). Without recourse to positivity or negativity, it simply "is".

Creative differentiation is capable of shaping conditions for the emergence of novelty in a process of individuation, with the orientation towards the virtual bearing a special relation to chaos. In Deleuze and Guattari's words,

> Chaos is characterized less by the absence of determinations than by the infinite speed with which they take shape and vanish. This is not

a movement from one determination to the other but, on the contrary, the impossibility of connection ... chaos undoes every consistency in the infinite.

(Deleuze and Guattari 1994, 42)

Creation, then, is a matter of inventing forms of consistency that can serve as counterparts to chaos. Science, art, and philosophy become the three variants of thought that are capable of such creation: "the three Chaoids, realities produced on the plane that cut through chaos in different ways" (Deleuze and Guattari 1994, 208). And within the theatrical, we can conceive of the difference between science, art, and philosophy not so much as a difference in nature as a difference in orientation with regard to the virtual and the actual. Science signals an orientation towards the actual, that which already is. Art is also concerned with the actual but allows for counter-actualisation. That is to say, while of the actual, it also turns towards the constitutive virtual region and opens up the actual towards the virtual. Philosophy, then, is maximally oriented towards the virtual and has a most intimate relation to chaos.

Let us have a closer look at these three inflections within the theatrical: science, art, and philosophy. Science is concerned with the domain of the actual. It

> passes from chaotic virtuality to the states of affairs and bodies that actualise it ... As if on top of the virtual plane of constant variation, science lays out an empirical plane through which actual movements and propositions can be distinguished.
>
> (Deleuze and Guattari 1994, 197)

Science can be said to take the metaphysical reality of the virtual and turn it into an epistemological reality that is available to cognition. Out of its infinite chaotic multiplicity, it extracts entities that can be given to our cognitive faculties. In this way, science "relinquishes the infinite, infinite speed, in order to gain a reference able to actualise the virtual" (Deleuze and Guattari 1994, 197). As a medium oriented towards the actual, science signals a depletion of the virtual and a preoccupation with actuality. One could say that entelechial plot mechanics bear something of this "scientific" take on the world—we have a theory oriented towards the cognitive value or epistemological queries associated with a given state of affairs but also a theory demonstrating that "a state of affairs cannot be separated from the potential through which it takes effect" (Deleuze and Guattari 1994, 153).

With art, we have a motion of "counter-effectuation" (Deleuze and Guattari 1994, 159) showing the "pressure" of the virtual on actual states of affairs. If the orientation of science is from the virtual to the actual, art signals a gesture from the actual back to the virtual. Within this region, one can move freely between the virtual and the actual, passing through the finite in order to bring forth the infinite, yet an infinity always already within finitude: "Art does not actualise the event but embodies it, it gives it a body, a life, a universe" (Deleuze and Guattari 1994, 177). Postdramatic theatre carries something of this reorientation towards the virtual. Rather than busying itself with states of affairs or with the task of emulating a literary reality based on action, causality, or grades of probability and necessity, it gestures towards "the pressure of the virtual" (Deleuze and Guattari 1994, 156). This is an ontological surplus that is energetic. Potentiality becomes the leading category, and the interplay of potentiality and actuality becomes of primary heuristic value.

And if science is concerned with the actualisation of an event, and art with its incarnation and relationship to the virtual, then philosophy is mostly interested in *an event's abstraction*. Philosophy "wants to save the infinite by giving it consistency" (Deleuze and Guattari 1994, 197) through the invention of concepts: "the task of philosophy is always to extract the event from things and beings..." (Deleuze and Guattari 1994, 126). As the discipline closest to the virtual, philosophy is also the discipline that is closest to chaos. Philosophical concepts are chaoid states, captures of chaos that have become consistent. Chaos creates infinite variations. One such abstraction of an event can be said to persist in virtual theatricality as the enaction of concepts. Out of a motion that is entirely composed of middles, without a beginning or an end, it distils regions of consistency while yet on the brink of chaos. The pull of the virtual precipitates a balancing act between a state of infinite difference—as the condition of the new can only be found in a principle of difference—and a state of partial determination. Such is the virtual–actual interweave, inasmuch as each actualisation produces the new and, therefore, new difference and a novel virtual.

This is also the place of a theatre of the virtual. Herein science with its affiliation to reference, art as the counter-actualisation of the infinite within finitude, and philosophy with its orientation towards the virtual equally partake in the emergence of the new. Novelty, or the creative refiguration of the given, is possible because of the potential of the actual to remain permeable and open towards the virtual. A theatre of the virtual plays itself out at the interface between virtual and actual. It is at once the abstraction of an event and an opening towards an event's virtual side, all the while remaining linked to the region of actualisation. Because of its orientation towards the virtual, the theatrical becomes both art and a philosophy of creation but also a science in its creative reorientation of the actual.

Actualisation becomes thinkable because of a virtual dimension that sustains the actual. Whereas the actual encompasses states of affairs accountable in epistemological terms, the virtual is a region of ontological constitution that, albeit equally real, is composed of incorporeal events and singularities on their way to actualisation. The virtual, thus, is the mirror image of the actual—it conditions and constitutes states of affairs while remaining of a completely different ontological texture.

This model suggests that becoming is not a linear progression from virtual to actual but rather a tendency and an inflection, a moving-towards that may or may not be a motion towards actualisation. The motion from virtual to actual is seldom unilateral and deterministic. Here a counter-motion from actual to virtual, a counter-actualisation, can freely appear and recompose existing scenarios. A theatre of the virtual would be just that—a focus on the divide between the actual and the virtual. The difference between the two is not so much a difference in "the real" as opposed to "the unreal" or actuality as opposed to potentiality as a productive alignment of two sides of being that are equally real. Such forms of the theatrical are primarily interested in thresholds of becoming. It is this interfusion of the actual and the virtual that becomes their playground. The theatrical becomes not so much a matter of careful design as a phenomenon of intensity. Further still, this intensive interfusion of disparate ontological regions is also where art becomes philosophy and philosophy is entwined with art.

And just as virtualities are always already embodied in part, so are actualities never entirely in possession of their "actual" faces:

> Purely actual objects do not exist. Every actual surrounds itself with a cloud of virtual images. This cloud is composed of a series of more or less extensive coexisting circuits, along which the virtual images are distributed, and around which they run. These virtuals vary in kind as well as in their degree of proximity from the actual particles by which they are both emitted and absorbed. They are called virtual insofar as their emission and absorption, creation and destruction, occur in a period of time shorter than the shortest continuous period imaginable; it is this brevity that keeps them subject to a principle of uncertainty or indetermination.
> (Deleuze and Parnet 2002, 148)

Since the actual is already permeated by the virtual, it is motion that sustains the actual and allows it to persevere in being but also that which carries the proliferation of the virtual. In this way, neither the virtual nor the actual can be seen as an aberration, as a deviation from an overarching order. Rather, both are seen as equally partaking in the complex assembly of a being-region. We observe how two actors without existence precipitate the formation of an existent—something that has the status of a being. Within a theatre of the virtual, not only do we have to consider the fragility of momentary captures but we also get to witness how a multitude of entities without embodiment preside over the actual. And each actual entity is merely a transitory fixture on the brink of becoming something else or of dissolving altogether.

Potentiality as an Ontological Horizon

Aristotle differentiates between two types of actuality, a processual and a final one, *energeia* (being-at-work) and *entelechia* (being-at-an-end). The former is an actuality in the sense of a process and the latter—in the sense of a product. When I speak of the plot as motion (*kinêsis*)—the actuality of x as potentiality—I adopt the first actuality as "being-at-work". Motion can be interpreted as the state of a potential's being actual, or as the manifestation of potentiality. At the same time, there are two types of potentiality: inactive and active. The former applies to the state in which an entity has not yet initiated a change, that is, in which it is still *potentially* something that can be potentially changed. In the latter case, we have a change that has already been initiated so that we encounter something that *actually* is being potentially changed (Witt 2003, 38–49).

If one is to arrange the motion from potentiality to actuality on an imaginary scale, we begin with the first, maximally indeterminate potentiality that is inactively potential, and then shift towards the second potentiality, the actually potential one. Whereas the first potentiality is purely potential, the second is actively potential in that it has begun to shift towards actuality. From here on, the transition from potentiality to actuality takes the form of *energeia*, a being-at-work, to find its completion in the final actuality, the being-at-an-end. Our theatre of the virtual attests to the capture, between potentiality and actuality, wherein motion is simultaneously rest and potentiality is actuality.

On an imaginary scale, this will take place in the middle wherein the very interplay of the second potentiality and the first actuality takes place. This is the locale of the transition, if not the overlap, between the processual, actually potential potentiality and the processual, potentially actual actuality. As the space where the second potentiality and the first actuality meet, this "middle" is the very enaction of becoming: "wherever something capable of acting and something capable of being acted on are together, what is potential becomes actual" (*Physics* VIII.4 255a30-b3). If one is to articulate the distinguishing condition of such theatrical forms, one could say it is a protocol for the passage wherein potentiality = actuality. In entelechial scenarios, the motion from potentiality to actuality translates into a causal motion that forwards both the formal and emotive becoming of a plot. One could speak of immanent causality and immanent individuation. As the plot motions forward, it retains its purpose within itself. That is to say, the purpose, being-at-an-end, inheres within the plot. But a theatre of the virtual sees entities and their interaction in such a way that the difference between bodies is a difference in intensity. There is a different type of causality at work here, one that explicates how the "crucial factor is to recognize that it is not things that differ in kind but rather tendencies; a thing in itself and in its true nature is the expression of a tendency before being the effect of a cause" (Ansell-Pearson 2015, 90).

Bodies fuse into one another and interact only inasmuch as they attune to the intensities of adjacent aggregates. This concept of interaction carries an ethical dimension whereby one is invited to open one's territory to the intensities of others. Herein a body is a momentary composition shot through with worlds, a world's inhabitants, and multilayered fields of continually shifting forces. A body becomes a locale wherein multitudes of intensive states continually pass through. Similarly, its position in a world becomes an ethical task:

> It is no longer a matter of utilisations or captures, but of sociabilities and communities. How do individuals enter in composition with one another in order to form a higher individual, ad infinitum? How can a being take another being into its world, but while preserving and respecting the other's own relations and world? Now we are concerned, not with a relation from point to counterpoint, nor with the selection of a world, but with a symphony of Nature, the composition of a world that is increasingly wide and intense. In what order and in what manner will the powers, speeds, and slownesses be composed?
> (Deleuze 2001b, 126)

This almost marks a return to the *Poetics* wherein the interplay of potentiality and actuality propels the tragic action, allows it to veer towards a certain outcome, and all the while retains an emphasis on an energetic processuality. Aristotle's concern, "what it is to be an actuality (*energeia* in the nominative) as opposed to a mere change (*kinesis*)" (Burnyeat 2008, 226), is found everywhere in the *Poetics*. In seeing change as "closely connected to privation and what is not, and because of this .... 'incomplete'" (201b31–32), Aristotle works to create an account of change that can "explain its connection with what is not, while showing how it can be among the things that are" (Coope 2009, 277). Here, however, it becomes possible to view the theatrical as something enjoying various degrees of intensity wherein action—or what Aristotle called *praxis*—is governed by multiple, encounter-dependent, and utterly contingent flows. While foregrounding becoming, the simultaneity of potentiality and actuality, this ontology dispenses with notions of purposiveness. A processual scenario governed by contingency replaces entelechy. Actors, rather than inherently actantial, are poised at the conjunction points of formative forces and chance. A theatre of the virtual thus has no interest in actual entities, nor does it solely occupy itself with the realm of the virtual as the condition of possibility of its own dynamic genesis. Between the virtual and the actual, it busies itself with the intensive. The intensive is that which has the characteristic of an encounter.

The region potentiality = actuality is the domain of singularities or entities on the threshold of individuation. In this capacity, a singularity simultaneously gestures towards two realms: that of universals and that of particulars. By describing singularities as "bottleneck, knots, foyers" (Deleuze 1990, 52), Deleuze likens them to a place of transition in the process of individuation wherein a potentiality has begun to show its actual face, yet an entity still subsists as "*a* thing" and not as "*this* thing". This is a state of continual emergence that is immanent in things yet points back to the virtual:

> Singularities are actualized both in a world and in the individuals which are part of the world. To be actualized or to actualize oneself means to

> extend over a series of ordinary points; ... to be incarnated in a body; to become the state of a body; and to be renewed locally for the sake of limited new actualizations and extensions. Not one of these characteristics belongs to singularities as such; they rather belong to the individuated world and to the worldly individuals which envelop them. This is why actualization is always both collective and individual, internal and external, etc. ... The expressed world is made of differential relations and of contiguous singularities.
>
> (Deleuze 1990, 110)

Singularities are the very intermediaries in this process of individuation. While singularities remain impassive and without characteristics *qua* such, they bring a new inflection, a nuance of a novelty into a world. A singularity offers a ground for the co-presence of chance and determination.

This ontological landscape would be impossible to grasp with the instruments of epistemological inquiry. An exuberant display of "the pressure of the virtual" and the ontologically shaky worlds encountered in theatrical alliances undermine any effort to administer habitual cognitive templates. Rather, the allure of potentiality-driven forms of the theatrical and their virtual ontologies lies exactly in the chance to retain a fundamental openness towards that which is not prefigured and to which one has not been trained to respond. Immersion into one such nearly Artaudian experience carries an unmistakable ethical streak in that it clears the ground for the possibility of an infinite openness towards a region of ontological constitution and, therewith, towards the formation of ever new sociabilities within a finite entity. We have not so much fully fledged individuals as singularities on the way to individuation whereby each entity remains maximally open to chance and susceptible to novel encounters.

The transformation that a singularity carries is never pre-established, nor does it promise a foreseeable result. It is encounter-dependent and thus relatively contingent, as we are never certain as to what other entities a body will accommodate within its field of interaction, what regions it will traverse, and what forces will begin to skirt it. In this sense, while a singularity has a dimension that characterises it as a pure potential, it also acts as a region of tension that opens up to that which is strictly actual. This latter dimension, however, becomes encounter-dependent. Only in interaction does a singularity show its mettle. What an "impersonal" singularity precipitates can be nothing but the actualised "personal"—the latter is a response to a very particular set of arrangements and a playground of very particular forces within and without a very particular body. "Pre-individual, non-personal and a-conceptual" (Deleuze 1990, 52) singularities are poised on the groundlessness between the virtual and the actual. Deleuze defines singularities as "quite indifferent to the individual and the collective, the personal and the impersonal, the particular and the general" (Deleuze 1990, 52). Yet it is this impassivity that makes them a condition for the emergence of the new. Even

Potentiality and the Virtual 31

entities, that is, derivative phenomena or secondary occurrences within a world arising out of the plane separating the virtual and the actual, are themselves events endlessly open to other events, entities, and individuals (Deleuze 1990, 177). This motion goes on because the finite is never fully actual but remains "open to further determinations" (Bowden 2011, 81).

Within a theatre of the virtual, the passage between potentiality of the second order and actuality of the first order becomes a motion of individuation. While the individuated or the expressed is maximally personal, the expression itself remains impassive. Singularities, however, exhibit a dual nature. With regard to their enaction or the expressed, they tend towards the personal but remain neutral with regard to the expression. Singularities precipitate the strictly personal, an encounter-dependent constituted finitude. The introduction of chance in individuation guarantees their non-entelechial becoming. A singularity precipitates the emergence of a particular entity only within the milieu of a given encounter; a different encounter moulds a different shape. No form has knowledge of a purpose; each movement of actualisation is contingent upon a collision with other entities and the work of internal processes. On the other side of the mirror, when virtualised, singularities remain pre-individual and neutral.

So a theatre of the virtual is first and foremost a *kinetic system*, that is to say, a system entirely composed of motion. Motion and continuity are the primary distinguishing conditions of the system; individual constituents are its secondary effects:

> a kinetic system is not the same as an assemblage of heterogeneous or even heterogenetic elements. A kinetic system is instead composed of continuities: flows, folds, and fields of kinetic patterns or regimes of circulation through which flows of matter are continuously reproduced and transformed. ... Kinetic systems ... are not defined by their fragments or wholes but by their continuities and folds.
>
> (Nail 2019, 189–190)

And matter, within this system, would operate as "pure potential, as impossible transversal communication, as transpersonal reality, as proliferation of genders and as nomadic populations; ... as that which exceeds all systems of identity and subjectivity" (Moulard-Leonard 2008, 152–153).

Now we have sketched out the beginnings of a theatre of the virtual. We have established potentiality and actuality as distinct, equally real, and thriving on the consistency that is their relation. A theatre of the virtual relies on an intensive engagement with potentiality as a continually ongoing genesis and an infinitely productive zest. Here potentiality does not motion towards depletion but exceeds itself to become more varied, shifts towards a greater opening, and forms an expanding region of incessant constitution. Its generative zest does not cease but overlaps with the actual and permeates its region.

So we have an actuality that begins to gesture beyond itself and a potentiality that becomes increasingly dissipative, thriving on the ongoing processes of ontological constitution that yet do not amount to a "being". The task of a theatre of the virtual, then, is to generate and render palpable such atmospheres of potentiality, put on display a concept of motion that is spectral—encompassing both being and extra-ontological regions simultaneously. Within a theatre of the virtual, potentiality is the persistent frontier between an entity and a nonentity, outside of being but equally real. It is precisely this productive relation between being and the extra-ontological that is viscerally witnessed here as a region of tendencies and forces casts its spectral web on forms and entities.

A theatre of the virtual is gestural, explicating tendencies and styles, abstracting an event out of insipid being. In calling its object "a theatre of the virtual", this chapter drafts out a singular locale between beginnings and ends, a middle ground wherein potentiality and actuality interweave in a two-way motion. This motion's ontological portrait does not contain progression, exhaustion, or irreversibility. Rather, we have a productive alignment of disparate ontological regions whereby "the pressure of the virtual" is just as "real" as any actualisation. A theatre of the virtual extracts an event out of states of affairs and opens up towards a world's spectrality but is yet interwoven with the actual. One such theatre is processual and energetic, and is more interested in singularities than in fully individuated selves. Moving on to Chapter 2, we begin to pay closer attention to the singular interweave between potentiality, the virtual, and the theatrical by turning to Gilbert Simondon's work on individuation. This is how we begin to flesh out a theatrical event of a different ontological cast—not simply something that is non-entelechial, spectral, and attuned to concepts such as genesis and the virtual but also a theatre that carries a tinge of the extra-ontological within itself.

Works Cited

Ansell-Pearson, Keith. 2015. "Beyond the Human Condition: Bergson and Deleuze." In *Deleuze and the Non/Human*, edited by Jon Roffe and Hannah Stark, 81–102. London: Palgrave Macmillan. http://dx.doi.org/10.1057/9781137453693.

Ansell-Pearson, Keith. 2002. *Philosophy and the Adventure of the Virtual*. London: Routledge.

Aristotle. 2002. *Aristotle's Metaphysics*. Translated by Joe Sachs. Santa Fe: Green Lion Press.

Aristotle. 1984. *Physics*. In *The Complete Works of Aristotle: The Revised Oxford Translation*, edited and translated by Jonathan Barnes, 315–447. Princeton, NJ: Princeton University Press.

Aristotle. 1902. *Poetics*. In *The Poetics of Aristotle*, edited and translated by S.H. Butcher. London: Macmillan and Co.

Bennett, Jane. 2015. "Systems and Things: On Vital Materialism and Object-Oriented Philosophy." In *The Nonhuman Turn*, edited by Richard Grusin, 223–241. Minneapolis: The University of Minnesota Press.

Bowden, Sean. 2011. *The Priority of Events*. Edinburgh: Edinburgh University Press.

Brians, Ella. 2011. "The Virtual Body and the Strange Persistence of the Flesh: Deleuze, Cyberspace, and the Posthuman." In *Deleuze and the Body*, edited by Laura Guillaume and Joe Hughes, 117–144. Edinburgh: Edinburgh University Press.

Burnyeat, Myles F. 2008. "Kinesis vs Energeia: A Much-Read Passage in (but not of) Aristotle's *Metaphysics*." In *Oxford Studies in Ancient Philosophy (Volume 34)*, edited by David Sedley, 219–291. Oxford: Clarendon Press.

Chiesa, Lorenzo. 2012. "A Theatre of Subtractive Extinction. Bene without Deleuze." *Mimesis Journal* 1 (2): 176–192. http://dx.doi.org/10.4000/mimesis.248.

Churchill, Caryl. 1998. *Blue Heart*. New York: Theatre Communications Group.

Churchill, Caryl. 1997. *A Mouthful of Birds*. 1987. In *Plays: Three*. London: Nick Hern Books.

Coope, Ursula. 2009. "Change and Its Relation to Actuality and Potentiality." In *A Companion to Aristotle*, edited by Georgios Anagnostopoulos, 277–291. Chichester: Wiley-Blackwell.

Cull, Laura. 2012. "Performance as Philosophy: Responding to the Problem of 'Application.'" *Theatre Research International* 37 (1): 20–27. https://doi.org/10.1017/S0307883311000733.

Deleuze, Gilles and Claire Parnet. 2007. *Dialogues II*. Translated by Hugh Tomlinson and Barbara Habberjam. Rev. ed. New York: Columbia University Press.

Deleuze, Gilles and Claire Parnet. 2002. "The Actual and the Virtual." In *Dialogues II*. Edited and translated by Eliot Ross Albert, 148–152. New York and Chichester: Columbia University Press.

Deleuze, Gilles. 2001a. *Difference and Repetition*. Translated by Paul Patton. London: Continuum.

Deleuze, Gilles. 2001b. *Spinoza: Practical Philosophy*. Translated by Richard Hurley. San Francisco, CA: City Lights.

Deleuze, Gilles and Félix Guattari. 1994. *What Is Philosophy?* Translated by Hugh Tomlinson and Graham Burchell. New York: Columbia University Press.

Deleuze, Gilles. 1991. *Bergsonism*. New York: Zone Books.

Deleuze, Gilles. 1990. *The Logic of Sense*. Translated by Mark Lester and Charles Stivale. Edited by Constantin Boundas. London: The Athlone Press.

Deuber-Mankowsky, Astrid. 2017. "The Paradox of a Gesture, Enlarged by the Distension of Time: Merleau-Ponty and Lacan on a Slow-Motion Picture of Henri Matisse Painting." *Performance Philosophy* 3 (1): 54–66. http://dx.doi.org/10.21476/PP.2017.31164.

Dimitrova, Zornitsa. 2017. *Literary Worlds and Deleuze: Expression as Mimesis and Event*. Lanham, MD: Lexington Books.

Dimitrova, Zornitsa. 2016. "A Drama of Potentialities—Towards an Ontology." *Journal of Dramatic Theory and Criticism* 31 (1): 65–87. http://dx.doi.org/10.1353/dtc.2016.0022.

Diodato, Roberto. 2012. *Aesthetics of the Virtual*. Translated by Justin L. Harmon. Albany: SUNY Press.

Edwards, Mark. 2014. *Philoponus: On Aristotle Physics 3*. London: Bloomsbury.

Else, Gerald. 1957. *Aristotle's Poetics: The Argument*. Cambridge, MA: Harvard University Press.

Freeland, Cynthia A. 1987. "Aristotle on Bodies, Matter, and Potentiality." In *Philosophical Issues in Aristotle's Biology*, edited by Allan Gotthelf and James Lennox, 392–407. Cambridge: Cambridge University Press.

Ghosh, Manomohan. 1951. *The Natyashastra ascribed to Bharata Muni. A Treatise of Hindu Dramaturgy and Historionics*, edited and translated by Manomohan Ghosh. Bibliotheca Indica, Work No. 272. Calcutta: The Royal Asiatic Society of Bengal.

Heath, Malcolm. 2017. "Aristotle on the Best Kind of Tragic Plot: Re-reading Poetics 13–14." In *Reading Aristotle: Argument and Exposition*, edited by R. Polansky and W. Wians, 334–353. Leiden: Brill.

Heath, Malcolm. 1987. *The Poetics of Greek Tragedy*. Stanford, CA: Stanford University Press.

Husain, Martha. 2002. *Ontology and the Art of Tragedy: An approach to Aristotle's Poetics*. Albany: SUNY Press.

Kalaga, Wojciech. 2003. "The Trouble with the Virtual." *Symplokē* 11 (1/2): 96–103. https://www.jstor.org/stable/40536937.

Kirby, Vicki. 2011. *Quantum Anthropologies. Life at Large*. Durham, NC: Duke University Press.

Kosman, Aryeh. 1969. "Aristotle's Definition of Motion." *Phronesis* 14 (1): 40–61. https://doi.org/10.1163/156852869X00037.

Lehmann, Hans-Thies. 2006. *Postdramatic Theatre*. London: Routledge.

Lévy, Pierre. 1998. *Becoming the Virtual*. New York: Basic.

Meiner, Carsten Henrik. 1998. "Deleuze and the Question of Style." *Symplokē* 6 (1–2): 157–173. https://www.jstor.org/stable/40550430.

Moulard-Leonard, Valentine. 2008. *Bergson-Deleuze Encounters: Transcendental Experience and the Thought of the Virtual*. Albany: SUNY Press.

Nail, Thomas. 2019. "Kinopolitics. Borders in Motion." In *Posthuman Ecologies. Complexity and Process after Deleuze*, edited by Rosi Braidotti and Simone Bignall, 183–205. London: Rowman & Littlefield International.

Piatti, Giulio. 2016. "The Life and the Crystal. Paths into the Virtual in Bergson, Simondon and Deleuze." *La Deleuziana, Life and Number* 3: 51–58. http://www.ladeleuziana.org/2016/11/14/3-life-and-number/.

Schmitt, Natalie Crohn. 1990. *Actors and Onlookers: Theatre and Twentieth-Century Scientific Views of Nature*. Evaston: Northwestern University Press.

Schmitt, Natalie Crohn. 1987. "Aristotle's Poetics and Aristotle's Nature." *Journal of Dramatic Theory and Criticism* 1 (2): 3–16.

Shields, Rob. 2002. *The Virtual*. London: Routledge.

Simondon, Gilbert. 1992. "The Genesis of the Individual." In *Incorporations*, edited by Jonathan Crary and Sanford Kwinter, 297–319. New York: Zone Books.

Waterlow, Sarah. 1982. *Nature, Change, and Agency in Aristotle's Physics*. Oxford: Clarendon Press.

Weil, Simone. 2002. *Gravity and Grace*. Translated by Emma Crawford and Mario von der Ruhr. London: Routledge.

Widder, Nathan. 2012. *Political Theory after Deleuze*. London: Continuum.

Witt, Charlotte. 2003. *Ways of Being: Potentiality and Actuality in Aristotle's Metaphysics*. Ithaca, NY: Cornell University Press.

Wolff, Christian. 1732. *Philosophia Rationalis Sive Logica: Methodo Scientifica Pertractata Et Ad Usum Scientiarum Atque Vitae Aptata*. Frankfurt and Leipzig: Renger.

2 Genesis and the Virtual

So far, we have looked at the theatre of the virtual as a kinetic system with potentiality as its ontological horizon. Now, we delve into another of its ontological horizons—individuation, or that which individuates as a perpetual enmeshment of systems of metastability. Let us start from the beginning: Aristotle and the philosophers of the Thomist tradition put forward the concept of hylomorphism. This concept breaks down to the proposition that the universe is composed of finite beings and that each being itself is composed of matter, ὑλο- (hylo-) and form, μορφή (morphē). Matter is an inert receptacle that becomes "lively" because of the organising principle of form. Matter, "which in itself is not a particular 'this'", is defined as "potentiality", "that which is changeable", "that which underlies" (1993, *De Anima*, 2.1. 412a9). Form, on the other hand, is "actuality" (412a10–11). And hylemorphism sustains that changes in substance, that is to say, the conversion from one state to another, can be defined in terms of form and matter. We have a type of cosmology suggesting that a being that has undergone a transformation has only changed its form whereas the matter has remained unaltered. It is a form that defines the being of existent entities as well as their *qualia*. Form operates on matter to shape individuals. When it comes to determining how one being can become another, hylemorphism relies on the active principle of form and maintains that matter as such does not possess an active force of its own and cannot initiate an individuation out of its own resources. Matter can be transformed. But this can only take place because of the determining function of form.

Gilbert Simondon's theory of individuation refigures hylemorphism in stating that form is not a principle of determination and matter is not incapable of genesis and indeterminate. As a process, individuation is concerned with "the genesis and the constitution of forms and how they differ from each other" (Sarti and Piotrowski 2015, 49). It allows us, among other things, to "conceive forms of organisation and 'polarisation' which precede the emergence of the subject …" (Bardin 2015a, 85). In a way, matter is already formed, and form has already been made indeterminate and can itself be seen as matter that undergoes a variety of transmorphoses. Simondon does not gloss over the fact that scholastic theory evades: we cannot know what potentials cause

DOI: 10.4324/9781003231080-3

things to coagulate and present us with a novel entity. Rather, this very encounter becomes the object of inquiry. The process can be described as a dynamic individuation:

> Individuation corresponds to the appearance of stages in the being, which are the stages of the being. It is not a mere isolated consequence arising as a by-product of becoming, but this very process itself as it unfolds; it can be understood only by taking into account this initial supersaturation of the being, at first homogeneous and static [sans devenir], then soon after adopting a certain structure and becoming–and in so doing, bringing about the emergence of both individual and milieu–following a course [devenir] in which preliminary tensions are resolved but also preserved in the shape of the ensuing structure; in a certain sense, it could be said that the sole principle by which we can be guided is that of the conservation of being through becoming.
>
> (Simondon 1992, 301)

This view allows us to think outside of the concept of "form" as a principle operating on matter and outside of the concept of "matter" as a receptacle for the genesis of form. We encounter a "matter" that can participate in the genesis of forms out of its own resources and do so spontaneously, without recourse to an external agency or an external organising principle. Simondon's theatre of individuation becomes "an elaboration of performativity ... that allows matter its due as an active participant..." (Barad 2008, 122) as "the principle of genesis becomes internally generated from within the process of individuation itself" (Scott 2014, 6). Differentiation then takes place not because of an encroachment, that is, because of an agency or a disruptive force that segments a given continuum, but with the help of local and singular discontinuities that emerge within the genesis of matter itself so that "distinct agencies do not precede, but rather emerge through, their intra-action" (Barad 2007, 33).

Aristotle's hylemorphism can be said to be replaced by a morphodynamism where we deal with a multitude and a continuity of metastable states. Metastability becomes the state that "transcends the classical opposition between stability and instability, and that is charged with potentials for a becoming" (Simondon 2005, 26; Barthélémy 2012, 216). The regime of metastability, "more than a unity and more than an identity" (Bardin 2015b, 9), is a guarantee that a system remains "lively" across various "historic" stages, that is, capable of further alteration, response, and attunement to adjacent systems:

> ...matter is not an individually articulated or static entity. Matter is not little bits of nature, or a blank slate, surface, or site passively awaiting signification; ... Matter is not immutable or passive. It does not require the mark of an external force like culture or history to complete it. Matter is always already an ongoing historicity.
>
> (Barad 2008, 139)

This state cannot become available to representation because the intra-dynamics taking place within a form is impossible to represent. At the same time, the definite states exhibit a certain poverty of content. Whereas they can be explained by science, such descriptions remain incomplete as they only encompass the vestiges of an individuation that has already taken place in the metastable state. So a genesis of forms is to be examined from within the individuating process. Yet the operations of individuation involved here cannot be known. That is to say, they cannot make themselves available to one's epistemological capacities as they incorporate non-representable and indeterminate constituents: "the object of knowledge appears only upon the stabilization of the operation of individuation, when the operation, incorporated into its result, disappears" (Combes 2012, 7). The process is based on a constitutive incongruity maintaining the tensions of both being and becoming:

> Individuation must therefore be thought of as a partial and relative resolution manifested in a system that contains latent potentials and harbors a certain incompatibility with itself, an incompatibility due at once to forces in tension as well as to the impossibility of interaction between terms of extremely disparate dimensions.
>
> (Simondon 1992, 300)

A finite and entirely stable state, then, would coincide with the self-annihilation of a system. If a system reaches a state of equilibrium and completion, that is, if an individuating matter becomes fully actual, this would only mean a suspension of the generative capacity of matter. Most systems persist in a regime of a perpetual displacement and disequilibrium—a continuously ongoing individuation. We do not deal with established individuals but with incessantly individuating entities. Any capture of an entity is nothing but the freeze frame of a momentary threshold within a multitude of metastable states. Individuation does not begin with the actual, nor is finitude something self-evident. Rather, we speak of a continual "being toward" that vicariously incorporates degrees of stability. Within this scenario, we never have access to an "individual" as the individual becomes more of an ontological horizon. All we are exposed to are the ongoing dynamics of individuating forces and the metastable states ubiquitous to such infra-individual regions. We rather speak of a dynamic "theatre of individuation" inasmuch as "what divides being into domains is ultimately nothing other than the rhythm of becoming, sometimes speeding through stages, sometimes slowing to resume individuation at the very beginning" (Combes 2012, 23).

Both determinism and indeterminism are similar in their attempt to establish a form and give accounts of the ways in which form comes to be and evolves. What differs is the assumed vantage point and the level of analysis chosen in each approach. And what is gained in the indeterministic approach is the acknowledgement of the high degrees of contingency involved in any genesis. What is vital here is the unrepresentable quality of the process. Let us acknowledge this unrepresentability by focusing on the work of singularities, the latter being the triggers that allow a system to shift towards a novel threshold of individuation. Such virtual inherences are endemic to a very particular system and cannot be thought of in their invariance. Their contingent and indeterminate nature is something that exceeds epistemological access. We have the inclusion of something extra-logical and supra-rational, that is, something indifferent to known logics and definitions of rationality, in the genesis of forms. And we are also exposed to the complexity of the operation. Complexity arises out of the interference of potentials and singularities that encroach on the deterministic processes and elude representation, infusing a system with their contingent dynamics and triggering reactions in ways that cannot be predicted. The only thing available to epistemological access is the finite form, but finite forms continue to individuate as they carry new virtualities and potentials. The task of describing the process of their production within the individuating form begins then anew; we continually and ever confront a form in progress.

This take on the constitution and genesis of forms shows us how a creative differentiation of forms occurs in a fully relational milieu. Primary here is the refiguration of the concept of form and its direct opposition to the concept of structure. Whereas structures are networks of codification that entail pre-existing forms, form is something continually on the brink of emergence and inextricably entwined with the concept of individuation. Strictly speaking, we seldom speak of an "individual". Rather, all form is pre-individual and in a state of growing intensity, defined "in terms of an incompatibility, an imbalance between potentials of energy, from which the constitution of an individual emerges progressively" (de Beistegui 2012, 170). Each form, living and non-living, "maintains its own becoming in terms of an individuation understood as a genesis" (Barthélémy 2015, 22). But also, a form is enmeshed in networks of interaction and information exchanges that supply a necessary amount of chaos within its domain in order to perpetuate the individuation of the form. Individuating entities are seen as spots of intensity within a network that resonate with the network in its entirety. Once a system arrives at disequilibrium, the entire network is mobilised to bring forth the individuation of the consistent forms: "This allows us to think the pre-individual as a heterogeneous continuously changing relational field which is functionally supported by harmonic processes that act to individuate its consistent forms" (Mongini 2015, 76–77).

The perpetually open individual is a form in progress whereby "the preindividual internalizes a difference or potential which the individual will be said to have structured or resolved, although not without remainder, through a process of individuation" (Bowden 2012, 137). Individuation takes place on the fault lines between the intra-genesis of matter and the various networks of interaction that co-constitute its milieu. The process of individuation has two dimensions: that of the individual becoming and that of the becoming of its milieu, these processes being both inseparable from one another and divergent. Ultimately, these processes fulfil an interactive function in bringing together various ontological levels. The individual that is being constituted is not so much something that enters into relations as something that is co-constituted and weaved out of relations. Its very status is that of a threshold that comes to be between disparate layers of being.

Individuation comes to be out of a milieu of relations resonating with different levels of intensity and composed of different potentials and virtualities. This pre-individual state is both "energetic and material" so that "individuation in this sense is both partial and local resolution of these disparate energetic/material fields, one that does not exhaust its ontogenetic possibilities and therefore retains the potential for further development" (Mongini 2015, 78). The way the individual relates to the pre-individual is not straightforward as the generative process constitutes the individual but also continues its activity as it perseveres through an individual's relations. Ontogenesis cannot be exhausted. The contingencies introduced by relations ascertain a continual influx of potentiality. Relations here are not a secondary formation but are shaped together with the genesis of a form and in a way also precipitate this genesis. The created individual cannot be reduced to just one order of being; it is always transversal and carries within itself the imprint of a wealth of systems of interaction: "whatever an individual being becomes, it is only ever incomplete—it is in-between metastabilities, a not-yet individuated 'phase' within the transductive continuum of becoming" (Scott 2014, 180). The ongoing frictions between these systems also guarantee that a form can seldom remain finitely stable because heterogeneity is its productive condition: "Individuation becomes thus the moment of intensity that dramatizes the differential potential of the virtual and accounts for the creation of divergent lines of actualization" (Mongini 2015, 81).

Putting indeterminism at the centre of this description also shows how contingency becomes a constituent of the ontogenetic process and, at the same time, how the transition from the individuating to the individual takes place within an ongoing continuum where entities undergo transformations in ways that cannot be made prescriptive. We have a constant feedback loop between the pre-individual, the ontological horizon which the individual is, and the multitudinous milieus of interaction that permeate a seemingly mono-causal system.

One such concept of individuation is often aligned with the concept of "ontogenesis", albeit an ontogenesis that is radically relational and non-deterministic inasmuch as ontogenesis

> is made to designate the development of the being, or its becoming—in other words, that which makes the being develop or become, insofar as it is, as being. ... it is equally possible to maintain that becoming exists as one of the dimensions of the being, that it corresponds to a capacity beings possess of falling out of step with themselves ... becoming is not

a framework in which the being exists; it is one of the dimensions of the being, a mode of resolving an initial incompatibility that was rife with potentials.

(Simondon 1992, 300–301)

Within this ongoing genesis, we deal with regimes of codetermination at each threshold.

The concept of ontogenesis denies the antagonising of matter and form in the ontogenetic process and dispenses with the notion of a fundamental underlying substance. Any allusion to the concepts of form, matter, and substance distances itself from the classic understanding of the terms and shifts towards generative, immanent, active, and co-mingling concepts. In line with this critique, we take the concept of "individual" to be synonymous with the concept of "being": that which is, that which has already been established. Unlike the Aristotelian model that favours a self-annihilating quality of potentiality—an entelechial motion that has a stasis and a full actualisation as its aim—the ontogenetic model puts forward the capacity of motion to account for that which takes place notwithstanding the actualisation. Here we have an ongoing production that invariably retains a relation to the region of constitution.

Within the regime of ongoing constitution, we have the individuating entity as something that in itself is a metastable system and, at the same time, participates in the ontogenesis of adjacent systems of metastability. Because of these intricate entanglements both within and without an individuating entity, one is also led to resort to non-linear forms of causality. Within such regimes, the system that an individuating entity constitutes is shaped by both processes that engage individuals and milieus of potentials. Inasmuch as we do not have individuals as such but metastable systems composed of thresholds of individuation, anything that comes to be is the result of the mutual interferences of formative forces attracting and fusing together previously independent systems. On top of that, we have the convergences of different systems and the formation of system assemblages out of this convergence. And each individual metastable system encounters a milieu of potentials to form ever-newer partially individuating systems. What is primary is the encounter. The encounter is capable of triggering a sequence that is not to be derived from any of its previously evident constituents. We speak of *affluent emergencies*.

Such dynamics of individuation become our sole point of access in examining an individual. An individual, more of an ontological horizon and a hypothesis than an entity, would always be somewhat ruffled around the edges because of the variety of para-individual inherences that would encroach on its "reality". Rather than something to be seen in isolation, an individual would invariably retain a "trans-dividual" dimension that would attest to a bond with the virtual, an unmediated access to the ontological region of ongoing constitution. Again, we arrive at a refiguration of ontogenesis that takes into account and makes primary a movement; we speak not so much of the actualisation of a form as of the entwinement of energetic multiplicities that co-constitute a form. What is interesting is not the form itself but the entanglements of systems of metastability and their singular ways of co-mingling in the genesis of forms.

Strandbeests

Theo Jansen's *Strandbeests* put on display this very condition of metastability and ongoing individuation at the sway of forces. Jansen's kinetic sculptures are released within environments yet to be interwoven into their own ontological fabric, subsisting within a maximal exposure to forces different than the conditions of their production, and in incessant co-constitution. The wind-propelled kinetic sculptures are often placed within urban, human-populated environments and left on their own devises. In becoming fully exposed to external forces and obstacles to their perseverance in a preordained shape, the *Strandbeests* make us acutely aware that the "Anthropocentric environments that are principally designed to accelerate industrialized human beings and their goods are shared with other species" (Cucuzzella 2021, 12). The *Strandbeests* evoke notions of embodied interaction, the possibility of relating to a milieu, and the question of artefactual autonomy. Such instances of heightened responsivity offer a starting point for a revision of concepts of interaction as a communal activity of "living" beings. The wind-propelled kinetic artefacts move within milieus otherwise reserved for non-artefactual forms to put on display infra-subjective practices of co-alignment. In doing so, they invite us to think of the possibility of an eco-philosophical body stretching across the continuum of what is nominally known as the "living" and the "non-living". Within this scenario of a heightened "acknowledgement of shared vulnerability" (Fishel 2019, 351), it is no longer the organism that determines the formation of a biome but the responsive potential within individuating matter.

In the 1990s, Jansen began creating *Strandbeests*, or "beach creatures"— interactive wind-propelled skeletal sculptures that surpass notions of kinetic art by being given a "freedom" of their own. Once created, the sculptures are released on beaches, in urban areas, or other open spaces to roam within a milieu otherwise populated by non-artefactual forms. The quasi-mechanical large-scale sculptures incorporate years of research into the dynamics of movement; one example is "the Jansen linkage movement in a resisting environment" (Aan and Heinloo 2014, 657). Durability of materials and elasticity of connectors make them minimally susceptible to tear (see Komoda and Wagatsuma 2011, 2009). The sculptures are, oftentimes, aligned with robots and studied for their scalability, energy efficiency, and bio-inspired locomotion (see Nansai et al. 2013). And Jansen too evokes speciest practices in giving the *Strandbeest* elaborate Latin names, producing descriptions reminiscent of scientific lab protocols, and archiving a catalogue of body parts,

Fossils, belonging to "retired" sculptures. But at the same time, the kinetic *Strandbeests* are deeply embedded in and co-dependent with their milieus of interaction, showing how "interdependence re-centres life in all its forms, off-centring the colonial practice of ranking lives according to speciesist, racialized, gendered logics" (Kirbis 2020, 845).

These dynamics in coagulating with an environment are played out in the very figure of the *Strandbeest*—an artefactual kinetic form roaming across landscapes shaped by simians and forming alliances with the forces of the outside. In partaking in conceptual atmospheres of heightened affinity towards the ecological in recent kinetic sculpture and robotic art, the *Strandbeests* (strand = beach; beest = animal) work with the generative zest of movement and the continual individuation taking place within the metastable state. The wind-powered sculptures can move autonomously when perturbed by the wind, being able to function mostly in the outdoors. Jansen often releases them on beaches where they are left to begin their autonomous lives. As they move about and wade into water, the beach beasts come across humans, storms, and other artefacts. They could be blown far into the sea or could bump against rocks as they remain entirely dependent on external forces. In this way, apart from partaking in the tradition of Dutch landscape art, the *Strandbeests*—moving within scenic marine ambience—could also be said to be showcasing the cycles of planetary life. Once they have collapsed, the beasts leave us with a little heap of bleached bones half-buried in the sand—forcing us to "think *with* death, rather than against it", showing how "death is also the already and ontological opening of life" (Hinton 2017, 242).

The focus is on the operations of individuation. In looking at the various *Strandbeests*, each named and with a distinct genealogy, we are exposed to a multitude of metastable systems in interaction, adding up to the structuring of extra-anthropomorphic ontologies. And again, the focus is not on the realities shaped therein but on the operations that make the singular come to be and provide insight into the dynamics of the given. Here the traditional concepts of form and matter are insufficient in explicating the dynamics of a system and the variety of ways in which it interacts with the various thresholds of "reality" that traverse it. Individuation is the articulation or the communication between these thresholds of reality witnessing how form and matter co-mingle. The processes of individuation taking place within rudimentary interactive activity—such as being propelled by the wind or entering the ocean, stumbling upon a pile of rocks on a beach, or falling onto a patch of uneven grass—are immanent to the emerging system and can be said to be the "structuring process of a field of reality, which develops within a system" (Carrozzini 2015, 35). The system must be in a metastable state, that is to say, "a state of equilibrium full of potentials and virtualities" (ibid., 35) whereby we experience the Strandbeests as engaged in a form of "affective witnessing" (Richardson and Schankweiler 2019), as bodies that bear witness to their constitutive state of enmeshment.

Individuation begins from a local but indeterminate trigger, a singularity, and spreads in a progressive way within the system leading to an alteration and generating a new state of equilibrium. That singularity has the shape of an encounter—the wind is an encounter, as well as the foam, water, sand, strollers, pets, and other artefactual forms. Each of these, in entering the ambience of Jansen's *Strandbeest*, alters the fabric of their milieu and repotentialises existent shapes. This is not a simple process of formation but a process of "in-formation, which can develop and arrive to an achievement by means of the presence of potentials and virtualities, which are the internal conditions and properties of the system in which an individuation can be produced" (Carrozzini 2015, 35).

Unlike deterministic theories that describe a certain process "from without" and have a seemingly fixed entity as its object, individuation has the purpose of offering the theoretical instruments for the description of the very process of formation within a metastable system while accounting for these processes from "within". A seemingly fixed form, then, would invariably remain a "partial result" of a process, a vestigial entity. This is why we must insist on a change of vantage, shifting the focus towards that which takes place within operations, all the way down to the enmeshments that constitute the state of metastability.

It is in singularities—repotentialising encounters with the outside—that form and matter are shown in their co-mingling. A dynamic transmorphosis permeates that which individuates. Form cannot be thought of as a transcendent principle that imposes its principle on an inactive substance. Rather, form also comes to be within the morphodynamics of a substance. And these morphodynamics are best shown in responsive entanglements with forces other than one's body, within environments continually co-constituted by dint of encounters. One could align the genesis of an enmeshment with an event, as something that has become individuated (expressed) out of the frictions within the pre-individual spontaneous and undetermined process of the expression of a substance.

Individuation rests upon such frictions and entanglements between metastable systems which at times happen to be ontologically disparate. Because of these frictions and entanglements, the metastable systems are also co-constituted in the process. In this way, metastable systems become susceptible to internal resonances that play a role in their ongoing genesis. Deleuze usually describes the articulation of such resonances as an "event of sense", an auto-generative extra-ontological constituent that is the product and the expressed of the plane of ongoing ontological constitution and yet remains inextricably interwoven with it.

The various traversals of form within this shaky arrangement provide glimpses into the onto-ecology of types of co-habitation that are seemingly extra-anthropomorphic but are yet imbued with anthropomorphic agency at their very core. The *Strandbeests* operate within environments moulded by human intervention. Urban settings, mortar and concrete, winds produced by a climate crisis, the disturbed cycles of an ocean, the micro-pollutants in the soil, the waning amount of vegetation on an abandoned beach, the hazardous particles in the air that propels the kinetic sculptures, the transmissions coming out of phones carried by strollers, are all part of a terra-forming activity that has now added yet another seemingly extra-human yet intensely anthropomorphic intervention within the domain of onto-ecological inquiry.

In order to put on display this seemingly extra-anthropomorphic yet intensely human encroachment, Jansen uses a mix of exclusively synthetic materials. The creatures' skeletal structure is made of recycled yellow plastic tubing used to insulate electric cables. In the section *Fossils* (2018), Jansen showcases some of the joints and body parts of *Strandbeests* that have long since yielded to the forces of nature, albeit a nature oversaturated with human action, and carefully catalogues these as follows: "Fossilium Quidam Flip Flop XVI, Origin: Animaris Umerus 2009, Material: PVC tube, tiewrap, plastic in a small showcase with museum glass, Description: single flip flop, 20 × 31 × 8, 2018", or "Fossilium Toothworth Geneticus-VIII, Origin: Animaris Geneticus 1996, Material: PVC tube in a small showcase with museum glass, Description: paddle root, 31 × 20 × 8, 2018", or "Fossilium Connectens Partes Utres-IV, Origin: Animaris Percipiere Primus 2006, Material: PVC tube, polyurethane, iron wire, plastic in a small showcase with museum glass, Description: connection bottles of a windstomach, 20 × 31 × 8, 2018" (Jansen 2018, n.p.).

Suggesting a genealogy coupled with a naturalist effort to compartmentalise and catalogue the living, this digital natural history museum also looks at an effort to freeze-frame the individuating forces at work. Here Jansen displays the insufficiency of any engagement with the actual—a showcase of synthetic bones and connective tissue—in fully comprehending the incessant cloud of virtualities at sway within the ongoing individuation of a form. The amalgamation of anthropomorphic intervention and the seeming effort to depart from the human within an artefactual universe of movement and co-constitution with an environment become part of the display, mixing the actuality of the synthetic display pieces with the virtual lives once led in the open:

> Not pollen or seeds but plastic yellow tubes are used as the basic material of this new nature. I make skeletons that are able to walk on the wind, so they don't have to eat. Over time, these skeletons have become increasingly better at surviving the elements such as storm and water and eventually I want to put these animals out in herds on the beaches, and they will live their own lives.
>
> (Jansen 2018, n.p.)

The *Strandbeests* are systems for the generation of kinetic resonance. They evoke a corporeal persistence that perturbs the landscapes it inhabits and the multifarious forces that happen to traverse its environments, becoming part of its field of interaction. *Strandbeests* are also little machines for the generation of *feeling*—not epistemologically informed sensing but an operation that makes palpable the very pull of the virtual. *Feeling* is an abstract operation that stands for an incorporeal perturbation, a reordering of forces within the virtual that makes palpable the expansive activity of mattering, "of something far more deeply interfused". Synthetic bodies display novel ways of constructing an organism that are not only congruent with the perturbations coming from an environment but make a body co-extensive with the entirety of a milieu—not an organism but a *diaphanous organismicity*. Matter is repotentialised and placed in conditions of continual forceful virtuality.

Theo Jansen's kinetic sculptures do not bear justice to qualifications such as the "living" and the "non-living". The *Strandbeests* form their own categories of co-alignment in that they almost entirely become co-extensive with their milieus of interaction and interwoven within their environments. One can hardly imagine the works outside of their singular coagulation with sand, wind, waves, strollers, vast cloudy skies, the sonorous features of a landscape, and the multifarious unseen residues of human production that have invariably become a fixture of "natural" landscapes. Again, this is not merely artefactual life but individuating matter that becomes in confluence with its milieus. Movement, shape, skeletal structure, pre-ordained motion patterns, and the verisimilitudinal evocation of an organism do not stand in isolation to emulate the organic. Rather, these constituents are cross-linked and entirely enmeshed in their surroundings. The alliances of synthetic matter, inorganic materials such as rock and sand, actors from the technosphere such as electronic devices, drones, satellites hovering over the landscape from outer space, instances of biological life are all traversals across the virtual canvas of Jansen's work. In short, we have been given an excursus into the status of machines today, insofar as "we are no longer dealing with the mechanistic beings of the nineteenth century … but rather with technical systems becoming organic" (Hui 2021, 211). This confluence of matter and exuberance of co-enmeshments evokes considerations of "Anthropogenic effects at the micro-scale of genomic regulation, neuronal functioning and cellular activity" (Meloni et al. 2021, n.p.), putting on display the "slow violence" (ibid.) of the Anthropocene. So apart from the visceral exposure to kinetic artefactual life, the *Strandbeests* excel in "making visible or audible forces that often lie beyond human perception and transcend a particular location, often devising performances that leave no material trace behind" (Page 2020, 275).

The work that the *Strandbeests* perform in their humble strolls in the wind, feats of perseverance, and eventual expiration is the moulding of conceptual atmospheres—an ongoing exercise in ecospheric belonging. This process shows that an individual cannot be reduced to a fixture of simple organising principles as it is invariably permeated by multitudes of other individuating systems. Rather, we speak of systems of codetermination whereby an individuating entity and the metastable multiplicities partake in the same genesis of forms while in a regime of perpetual co-alignment. An individual form is not the product of a mechanised process, as the classic concept of ontogenesis would imply, but an innovative outcome that incorporates elements which elude prior determination.

Because of this, the concept of an individual remains an unattainable phantasmatic inherence—a perfectly static system and a fully finalised process of individuation cannot be. Any individuation, while seemingly geared towards the consolidation of an individual, continually subverts any consolidation and frustrates the formation of fixed wholes. This take on the concept of individual is somewhat more subtle and ambiguous than the vernacular concept of identity. It implies that an individual is not solely an entity but also an infra-entity that partly resides in the virtual and is continually traversed by processes taking place at different levels. This is also why, within a system of metastability, we have discontinuous processes that change in magnitude, and these processes guarantee that an entity would ever waver between structural stability and degrees of indeterminacy, making its individuation non-linear and trans-causal. The influx of indeterminacy guarantees that we cannot speak of a prefigured outcome when we address matters of ontogenesis. Whereas processes have a tendency towards a certain deterministic outcome, we also equally deal with singular encounters that allow us to take into account the role of potentials in the genesis of forms. We can now speak in terms of dynamically shaped phases that mould and refigure individuating entities. These entities are themselves irregular metastable bundles, indefinitely modifiable, and subsisting in regimes of maximal potentiality.

What definitions of a milieu and an environment can be gleaned from this encounter? Milieu and environment are interchangeable concepts to designate the expansiveness of bodies and the yet only nominal distinction between bodies and their surroundings in the pre-individual. A slight difference between the terms can be introduced, however. "Milieu" can be said to designate the conceptual atmospheres and material climates within which a body is plunged and which co-constitute it. An environment designates the climates and atmospheres emanating from a body, and which, as such, actively co-generate both bodies and the larger perimeters within which bodies operate. In this sense, when we speak of environments, we also speak of co-generative worlds. Across the field of potentialities, bodies and their environments are co-extensive and in perpetual information exchange. "Milieu" and "environment" cannot be thought of in purely spatial terms, and even less so can we think of the virtual as a spatially organised area. These are conceptual apparatuses that evade dimensionality. If they are to be thought in spatial terms at all, they can only be thought in their simultaneity—as layers interpenetrating and built upon one another in such a way that no precedence can be distinguished.

Interfusing

With this in mind, let us turn to the main activity of *Strandbeests*—that of relating. What is the ontological status of the very process of forming a relation? We have a shift of focus towards the forming of a relation as such and towards the philosophical position that the act of relating itself engenders a type of being. Relations are entities in their own right and have the status of existents. The act of relating does not coincide with a mechanical connection between two points that have already been established. A relation has an operative function and participates in the very genesis of things. Every relation should be considered "as having the status of being, and as developing itself within a new individuation" (Simondon 2009, 8). Relation is not secondary to the substance and is not simply one of the qualities of a substance. Rather, substance cannot acquire any properties without the act of relating to a milieu populated by other substances. A being, with its very positing, already presupposes fundamental relationality. This stance feeds into the larger agenda of process philosophies that, rather than replacing being with becoming, the aim is to seek a productive alignment between those two reality regimes, showing the various ways in which different reality regimes determine each other and make each other possible. A relation is the articulation of becoming and the entity which carries the process of the individuation of a being. Yet relation and being cannot be thought as separate realities. One can speak of a certain co-determination whereby being is informed by a process of ongoing ontological constitution and becoming participates in being. The dynamics of transformation and rest are thus interdependent. We have a universe contemplated from two different vantage points that are entwined and equally "real".

We get a similar result when we look at the definition of matter from the vantage of entwinement. The vernacular imagination describes substance or matter as a primordial mush in a more or less amorphous state that requires the ordering function of form. In order for the process of individuation to occur, substance, however, cannot be too stable as then it would not be susceptible to change. But then, change itself remains clandestine and strange as "an attunement to the particulate differences that compose change is difficult because many of them occur at rhythms of transformation that are below the threshold of temporal sensitivity available to human perception" (Smailbegovic 2015, 96).

Again, the state of metastability is the productive state of substance, and substance is endowed with a certain self-ordering capacity that allows it to act as a generative force in its own right and engender a reality actively. The process of individuation is initiated by a singularity, an element which is novel and foreign to a system, and produces a shock, disequilibrium, "a momentary pause in individuation" (Scott 2014, 17). In its efforts to regain equilibrium, a system then produces a novel structure which, in turn, also generates energy needed for the further transformation of substance and for further growth. Here we do not speak in terms of a divide between becoming and being as the two are not seen as two ontologically separate regions but as co-constitutive. Becoming serves as "the relation that constitutes the being as individual" (Chabot 2013, 84) but this is not opposed to the perceived stability of a being. Rather, being and becoming are co-constitutive and aid individuation in equal measure. What is essential is not so much the nominal separation between the two as their singular co-mingling.

All these help us to gain some distance from both essentialist philosophies and the type of vitalism that would maintain that being is entirely composed of interfusing energetic flows. In the connection of being and becoming, we rather speak of something that Deleuze calls a disjunctive synthesis (Deleuze 1990). This is a type of synthesis that allows two beings to coagulate while retaining the entirety of their structure. In this way, we have an individuation that takes place between two realities: that which already is—that which has already been shaped—and a dynamic dimension composed of energies—that which is capable of being shaped. The act of thinking "being" and "becoming" separately leaves us with an insufficient definition of any of the terms. If we choose to foreground being, we will no longer be able to account for the multitudinous traversals and transmorphoses within a substance nor would we be in a position to account for a substance's continual engagement with the virtual. But then, if we focus on becoming entirely, everything turns into an energetic multiplicity. We would have a play of virtualities without measure, worlds that are entirely and only spectral. A focus, then, cannot be retained on anything but coagulating ecosystems, the latter being "communal milieus comprised of interdependent components, both organic and inorganic, networked and communicating through a complex web of feedback loops" (Flaxman 2019, 218).

This spectrality attests to an entwinement of being and becoming. The focus shifts from the state of the substance itself, as alternately being or becoming, to the environments within which substance operates as well as on the operation as such. Individuation takes place at the limit that is indifferent to matters of being and becoming but manifests itself as a responsive interface between ontologically disparate regions. The limit brings together being and becoming. This is exactly the locale wherein being and becoming encounter one another in a milieu that allows them to become responsive to one another. Yet this milieu cannot be characterised as either processual or actual. The milieu itself carries its principle of organisation within itself and can self-generate out of its own resources yet is entirely without form. It cannot be defined in positive terms as it does not have a "reality" of its own; it does not partake in individuation. The milieu is ongoing, a "yet-to-come" extra-ontological inherence. If we are to speak in linear terms, one can call it "pre-individual" to the extent to which it has not been individuated yet. At the same time, the milieu's basic condition is the lack of individuation and the abundance of energetic indeterminacy that define it as such. The milieu is the virtual itself but without the addition of action or motion that would allow it to become expressed.

So here we have "the pressure of the virtual" that is infinitely generative but without action and without motion. If we are to speak in the terms of "being", then, this virtual would always be "negative" as it lacks a distinguishing condition. The virtual would be thought in terms of the absence of action and motion but even more so, in terms of the lack of a singularity. If we think through the concept of becoming, on the other hand, we begin to see the very virtual as generative and as energetic. There is no determination at all as there are no form and no limit. There is no individuated being and the type of reality defined by actualisation cannot yet be thought. Instead of all this, the milieu is unformed, plural, and generative in a productive activity without an object. This, in turn, brings us to a richer concept of matter as energetic. Matter is zest itself—not simply a substance and not merely the energising of a substance but a continual encounter between being and becoming that brings forth the new.

When we speak in terms of mimesis, we speak of irreducibility. We have a finite set of individual items that cannot be partitioned into discrete terms without losing much of their unity. Unity and stability are among the principles of mimesis and these principles ascertain that an individual is always mono-central. Mimesis in its traditional form attests to the finite form achieved in individuation, the full and complete actualisation that marks the exhaustion of potentiality. Mimesis, however, is also aided by a "subterranean" force which allows for the influx of degrees of instability within its texture, the introduction of tensions within its domain, as well as multicentrality. Whereas mimesis deals with already established states of affairs, the level of analysis that genesis offers is that of gradations within the virtual and the ongoing co-constitution of matter and form in shaping the pre-individual. And relating could be said to be a reality in its own right: "the relation ... is in fact a dimension of the individuation in which the individual participates due to its connection to the preindividual reality ..." (Simondon 1992, 309).

The pre-individual contains within itself a maximum of potentials and virtualities. In a sense, the pre-individual is all that there is:

> the virtual is a real relation: a relation of procession, or a relation between a generator and a generated, which is body, that is, individual[ity]. This is a strange ontology: an individual, this individual, with its peculiar features or qualities, which is relation and nothing other than relation.
> (Diodato 2012, 58)

Individuation cannot be complete as each threshold of individuation only opens up towards a system of metastability of a different grade and texture. This incessant motion is twofold as it takes place both within the pre-individual, insofar as one can speak of any discrete shape at all, and in its milieu. This environmental component is reinforced by the fact that there is no clear separation between an individual and a milieu but a sort of a co-extensive co-mingling whereby the milieu permeates an entity. And an entity is an environment itself. Each actualisation of an individual, in this sense, also becomes the actualisation of a world. Actualisation is seldom local and isolated; it carries the entirety of networks within which an individual is enmeshed and co-individuates the wealth of relations that traverse an entity within and without.

As change is the ongoing condition of an environment too, we can view the milieu as something composed of metastable virtualities that resound together with the perturbations within an entity but also co-shape entities that have come into contact with their milieus of interaction. In this way, an individual's adjacent reality also undergoes a virtualisation as it takes on potentials and indeterminacies. Such environments are gradually deindividualised—we lose sight of any identities or anything that would serve as a point of orientation—and thus become open to the influx of multiplicities that populate the pre-individual region. Once these degrees of growing indeterminacy are established, one begins to comprehend that the process of the actualisation of one's adjacent reality is coextensive with the process of its progressive deindividualisation. In opening a reality to the pre-individual field of potentials and virtualities, we can witness the mutual constitution of entities and their milieus.

The concept of environment, then, also undergoes a switch from a systemic to a procedural definition whereby territory, identity, border, and locale undergo a virtualisation. What the generative vantage shows is that an entity and its milieu are not two disparate substances but two co-individuating environments. An individual stretches to encompass the entirety of its milieus and the networks that shoot through an individual. At the core of this change in perception is the view that we cannot speak of a separation of things and relations, of solid entities in space and some sort of vacuity between them. Individuals are the manifestations of a multitude of tensions within the metastable systems that compose a universe.

What does this tell us about the theatrical? The theatre of the virtual engages with a singular event spreading across the fabric of a work and engendering its becoming. Still, a singular event is still mono-causal and mono-central; it functions as a locale of transformation but remains discrete and regional. The scenario offered with Simondon's theory of individuation suggests a multiplicity of centres, a reversibility of causal relations or complete suspension of linear causality, and a departure from the notion of discrete and irreducible individuals. What we have are interwoven systems of metastability, each stretching across the entirety of its milieus of interaction, and multiple becomings that resonate across a work as it undergoes continual transmorphoses. These transmorphoses are not local but reverberate across the entirety of a form.

An arrangement of segments leading to an event that precipitates novel sequences could be said to be the scenario captured in the concept of plot. Within the concept of plot, the generative motion is emergent as it deals with an order which, once a certain component within a system is introduced, produces something new. This production, however, is finite and is there to impart a sense of closure: a virtual that has become maximally actual. But we also do not deal with a singular event structure as in what Lehmann calls "postdramatic theatre"—because an event structure presupposes a single centre from which the entirety of a form begins to recompose. That is to say, the ontology of postdramatic theatre appears to be constructed upon two ontologically disparate regions, that of representation and that of the supra-representational transformative event (see Dimitrova 2017). The latter encroaches on representation and causes an existing ontological scaffold to recompose, reshuffling the constituents of a literary world and causing them to regroup anew. But within a theatre of the virtual, we no longer have a set of isolated segments leading to transformation.

Strandbeests enforce a radicalisation of the concept of the virtual. It is with such forms of the theatrical that we find a way to speak of a theatrical ontology that goes one step further than postdramatic theatre as it *follows a generative trajectory that is multi-centred and can engage in several individuations at once together with the perturbations between them.* This perspective allows us to think in terms of the various intertranslations between layers of reality that are disparate in their ontological makeup yet co-resonate because they are part and parcel of the same regime of enmeshment of individuating networks. The concept of a transformative event in Lehmann is thus also expanded: a theatre of the virtual does not presuppose one such discrete event structure but is pervasive. Apart from this internal generative dimension, there is an additional dimension of co-enmeshment to consider. Once we consider the radical relationality at the heart of individuation, we also arrive at a different concept of transformation. What is initially perceived as identities from the order of representation is, indeed, a bundle of enfleshings and uninterrupted motion composed of thresholds of individuation. Each threshold is defined by its capacity to proliferate and precipitate further mobility within a system.

In postdramatic theatre, we still have a tension between the dramatic and the non-dramatic. Postdramatic theatre at its very core relies on dramatic theatre for its positing as a separate object of examination. The event of sense could only emerge and be made an object of discussion because it invariably arises out of a system that is constitutively different from it. In a manner of speaking, the event has been made possible because of the structure (and not in spite of it) as it is only within the structure that it could perform its disruptive work. The concept of relationality entailed here is such that everything leads back or stems from the clandestine event, it becomes the vanishing point that unites and sustains a constructed theatrical world and carries its ontological armature.

With a theatre of the virtual, we arrive at a relationality that has several centres of interaction at once, is intra-dynamic, and is constitutive of a reality starting from the pre-individual and the indeterminate. Just as transcendence supplies a normative dimension that adds up to the emergence of a form from without, so does a theatre of the virtual imply a self-governed becoming from within. Virtual entanglements take place at several locales simultaneously and are dependent on the co-determination between these locales. These various systems of metastability form a multidimensional field that dynamically incorporates ontologically divergent forms.

So the virtual does not designate the formative stages of a certain finite subject and the multitudinous modalities in which it perseveres. Over and above that, the virtual is the dynamic field of constitution that allows for all these interactions to coagulate in singular ways. As a field of individuation, the virtual is then the milieu within which several co-dependent transformations take place at once whereby each constituent expresses a different level of intensity and resonates with the field's modal power. Individuation can be said to carry the articulation of the dynamics of change within a system. But it also clashes with the trans-individual. The trans-individual is an act of ongoing self-constitution as an ontogenetic multiplicity of networks but also that which carries the imprint of an encounter with a de-individualising event: "Unlike the interindividual, it is therefore not simply a bringing-into-relation of the individuals. The transindividual makes subjects intervene in so far as they carry a charge of preindividual reality" (Barthélémy 2012, 203).

Theatre as a Technical Object

We can refer to the theatre of the virtual not only as an agency in its own right with its own singular ways of organising being and mobilising the resources of non-being but also as a "technical object". If taken in the abstract, the definition of a technical object reads as follows:

> A primitive technical object is an abstract system of isolated partial ways of functioning, without common ground or existence, without reciprocal causality, without internal resonance; a perfected technical object is an individualized technical object in which each structure is pluri-functional, overdetermined; in it each structure exists not only as organ, but as body, as milieu, and as ground for other structures; in this system of compatibility whose systematicity takes form just as an axiomatic saturates, each element fulfills not only a function in the whole but a function of the whole.
>
> (Simondon 2017, xv)

If we look at the theatrical as a non-human agent co-constituted by a wealth of fields of interaction, then we can also begin to think in terms of the isolated ways of functioning of the theatrical together with the multitude of milieus adjacent to it and the systems it includes in its actional field. Rather than what Simondon designates as a "primitive" (local and isolated) technical object, the theatre of the virtual is a complex interweave of systems of codetermination, not so much a "thing" as a "milieu", and a condition for further individuation. A theatre of the virtual not only puts on display ways of being and non-being, manifesting itself as one constituent in a universe of things, but actually expresses this metastable whole in its multifarious modes and stages of interaction. We have an interweave of motion, action, rest, and evolvement with or without an end. This interweave exerts its gravitational pull on a wealth of milieus of interaction, shifting with each perturbation and showing us a slightly different face with each encounter. In this sense, each micro-system within the theatrical, be it the one defined as motion, the one defined as action, or that of a reality commitment, permeates all other structures, co-determines them, and participates in their emergence. A system is co-extensive with its adjacent systems and not only forms a milieu together with them but also is itself an extensive milieu for the work of these adjacent systems.

At moments, each system transcends the remaining ones insofar as it is foregrounded at a time. At the same time, the wealth of systems is an interweave wherein all systems of becoming belong together. In this sense, we can speak of a double take on the theatrical: for one, we are confronted with a most finite, determined, and local engine for the production of events. This is also what Simondon designates as a "primitive" technical object. Each entity is discrete, concrete, and defined in separation from its others. Action, motion, world, and entelechy work in their own individual ways and produce their particular effects. And all the while, the intertranslations which these individual systems undergo are infinitely complex, and they all persist in a regime of interdependence. If taken in isolation, each will only present us with a very truncated concept of theatre. Action, motion, world, plot, entelechy, and so on cannot provide a full account of their own reality within the theatrical without an expansive *feeling* of the intermeshing of adjacent realities, ontological textures, and gradations of being constituting the pressure of the virtual. These systems only become highly articulated when they are envisaged in their genesis, within the very flows of co-engendering with adjacent systems. Whereas the systems in isolation stand for being, this being is only expressed in the systems' becoming together with other generative systems. At the same time, this becoming is not an amorphous undifferentiated flux but something that incorporates being insofar as it continually generates the concrete and the finite while remaining open to further determination.

When we look at the ontology of the theatrical, we see this interplay at work insofar as we are made aware of the interrelation of a variety of systems that weave the given, the various collisions within and outside their fields of interaction, the generation of novelty (theatre as an event engine), and so on. We confront an increased awareness of the radical openness called potentiality, something that evades closure and is not satisfied to simply persist and persevere in its existence, guard its boundaries, and thrive on its own. In this way, because of this openness to a field of ongoing ontological constitution, the theatre of the virtual shows us how a system can evolve to display a certain "originality", a reformulation of the given. We can define the virtual field as

> a complex, multidimensional, and dynamic space which endlessly changes along the diachronic dimension (bildung); in search of metastable equilibrium, and in which hierarchical relations between subspaces, structures, forms, and gestalts, can be considered as a peculiar, transitory, and local reductions of uncertainty.
>
> (Galofaro 2015, 199)

If there is any action within the virtual field, this is not the anthropomorphic action of (human) entities within its fabric but the actional force of the various systems of co-determination that construe both the logic of the virtual and its singular reality. What is called "originality" within a theatre of the virtual is in the singular ways in which such systems will congeal to construct a logic of evolvement and an adjacent reality. This "originality" is responsive in its nature because it only occurs in response to particular milieus of interaction that regroup and coagulate in equally singular ways. A theatre of the virtual evolves spontaneously out of such regroupings. Whereas the various ontological systems within the theatrical (that of action and motion) are already there, the milieus they generate and the alliances they form would be contingent.

And even if we take classical drama ontology as our example, we can observe this principle at work in the moment of reversal or *peripeteia*. Here each decision is a selection within the system that reverberates across the entirety of adjacent systems triggering a wealth of recombinations that, in turn, make a play *turn* in a very particular way. And yet again, rather than of substances, the theatrical is shown to be entirely composed of enmeshments that are pulled in a variety of ways to generate the unforeseen. Because of this dependence on interfusion with various ontological systems, the theatrical event generates a certain "depth". Simultaneously, it not only displays certain qualities and features but also requires a wealth of "subterranean" forces for their unfolding. Because of this, a play invariably projects the existence and importance of a reality that is indifferent to epistemological access. A recipient is presented with a certain state of affairs and given a certain outcome; yet this experience is infinitely insufficient once one is left with the intuition that one has simply reached the limit of one's ability to comprehend and perceive. The reality of the theatrical is thus abyssal as one is invited into regions of forces and relations that evade the possibility of their own description. What one can perceive, albeit ever so slightly, are the incessant affectations that take place among forces that act, move, push forward, and cause to dissolve and, by doing so, generate a multitude of worlds.

Here a system becomes replete with contingency and, at the same time, plenitudinous; everything is overemphasised. We confront a field of constitution that is overpopulated by singularities, things on the brink of emergence evolving in a way that evades reference. This wealth of singularities cannot be captured. The only thing this plenitude puts on display is the fact that no entity can truly disentangle itself from the interweave of co-determinations, affections, and forces that exert their pull on its being.

This heightened engagement with the virtual takes us to a new concept of ecology that foregrounds a supra-human streak within the theatrical. A shift in thinking is called for:

> we need a new theoretical humanities that no longer starts and ends with humans and human systems (language, society, culture, the unconscious, and so on). ... Humans and their social structures are shot through and exceeded by more primary and constitutive material-kinetic processes

and patterns. Humans are thus caught up in much larger meta-stable patterns of motion with their own kind of logic ...

(Nail 2019, 183)

We have the pervasiveness of anthropocentric forms of enaction together with the slight awakening to an awareness of a vast and multifarious life beyond the simian, evoking the question of "how far is it a liberating or a paralyzing thing for new art and criticism to encounter and highlight those structural and embodied limits ... in which even the most intelligent are caught?" (Clark 2015, 192). And further still, how long would it take until we cultivate a certain ontological "embarrassment" (Boysen 2018) of being human and looking no further.

One could speculate that, within a pronouncedly supra-anthropomorphic concept of ecology, we can construct a certain planetary interweave within the theatrical. A theatre of the virtual puts on display the contingent generative streak in the genesis of enaction as we become increasingly aware that "the modern machine is no longer mechanistic and ecology is nothing natural" (Hui 2020, 57). A theatre of the virtual evolves out of coagulations between extra-simian forces, is more involved in the interfused than in that which is immediately available to recognition, and seeks to disclose the very ontological armature of the theatrical event. Aristotle's concept of action begins to expand inasmuch as, if ever there were any actional reality within the theatrical, that would be the reality of collisions or alignments of various ontological systems out of which the theatrical comes to be. In this sense, the observation that "ecology is more like an operation" (Parikka 2019, 44) becomes very much tangible. Even more so, here we begin to shift toward the type of general ecology that Guattari names "ecosophy":

> A new ecosophy, at once applied and theoretical, ethico-political and aesthetic, would have to move away from the old forms of political, religious and associative commitment. Rather than being a discipline of refolding on interiority, or a simple renewal of earlier forms of 'militancy', it will be a multifaceted movement, deploying agencies [instances] and dispositifs that will simultaneously analyse and produce subjectivity. A collective and individual subjectivity that completely exceeds the limits of individualization, stagnation, identificatory closure, and will instead open itself up on all sides to the socius, but also to the machinic Phylum, to techno-scientific Universes of reference, to aesthetic worlds, as well as to a new 'pre-personal' understanding of time, of the body, of sexuality.
>
> (Guattari 2000, 67–68)

We see a perpetuation of an

> aesthetics of the local and the *in situ*, an aesthetics of sensitivity to places and moments, an aesthetics of structures grafted on to reality to give it

form and signification; the aesthetic object depends on the gesture of placing, inscribing, inserting a mark.

(Michaud 2012, 125)

The theatre of the virtual is invariably seen as an expansive milieu. In engaging with an ontology of the virtual, one brings this interplay of virtual forces very close to momentarily constructed beings called "humans", putting them in direct contact with the very "ambience" of the impersonal. In spite of its enmeshment in the human and its doings, the theatre of the virtual creates a heightened sense of the ecology of the extra-human and the non-living.

The very *exposure*, *immersion*, and *attunement* to the impersonal field of ontological constitution already bring us to this interfusion. The theatre of the virtual proposes its ecology not by being prescriptive, that is, by creating an ethical framework and by telling us how to live, but simply by putting different levels of reality in contact and allowing them to enter into various degrees of enmeshment. Again, this type of ecology is not simply environmental in the sense of a terrestrial ecology. This is a mode of thought that aligns with Guattari's ecosophy: "rather than pointing at the urgency and the undeniable evidence, rather than turning ecology into a discipline of redemption, ecosophy would aim at expanding thought throughout the entire phenomenon of life on the planet" (De Fazio and Lévano 2019, 17). The aim would be to enter the extra-human, "as an experimental promise of multiplying the ways of having a body, producing in this process a wider consideration on what life throughout the ecosphere actually is" (ibid., 17).

The impersonal milieu resonates around human subjects, causing them to dissolve, all the while exposing the texture of becoming through them. In these milieus of interaction, the theatre of the virtual confronts us with a dazzling display of otherness. It constructs this otherness as a continually open field of ongoing constitution. We no longer deal with instances of difference, and there is not a particular entity that becomes, at least not so in isolation, but an entirety of ontological systems that traverse one another. The event engine sweeps across what is seemingly foregrounded as "individual" to precipitate shifts that are more global in their reach. There is no gap between individuals. At the same time, entities do not simply disintegrate within the genesis of forces but are shown to be continuously resonating between relative stability and productive multiplicity. So a theatre of the virtual touches upon "a general cosmology and ontology of pervasive and undecidable relation, one that delights in its own paradoxes" (Weinstone 2004, 38). For one, "These are not self-possessed expressions; they come and go, expand and contract, mutate, modulate, *travel* … the categories of self and the other are rendered undecidable, are suspended but not dismissed" (ibid., 41). This type of ontological alignment is related to a certain concept of *conduct* that is best captured in "gestures of opening and holding" (ibid., 41) belonging not so much to a being that begins and ends as to a "virtual self", "an event stretching out …" (ibid., 41).

If we are to conceive of the theatrical through the work that it exerts so as to generate a "virtual self", we begin to see it exactly as

> a coherent global pattern that emerges from the activity of simple local components, which seem to be centrally located, but is nowhere to be found, and yet is essential as a level of interaction for the behaviour of the whole.
>
> (Weinstone 2004, 41)

The categories of self, conduct, and environment coalesce. We do not simply dispose of discrete local components but gesture towards something non-locatable and yet pervasive, non-centralised and yet navigating the movements of the whole. From within the vantage of a theatre of the virtual, we cannot think of autonomous individuals capable of agency but begin to sense a far more multifarious weave of interdependencies.

What was previously "subjectivity" becomes a dissipative system composed of a wealth of responsive locales. As these locales interact, however, they do not aim to lead to an event of signification, nor are they shaped as a reaction to a necessity to signify. The virtual is populated with such responsive thresholds and is continually refigured by local events. This decentralised and non-signifying force cannot be said to be a "system" in the proper sense, however. As "an auto-productive dynamic" (Montanari 2015, 210), the virtual is more of a *texture*, that is to say, the relief, the inflection, or the style in which a world perseveres, and is *gestural*, that is to say, something which is entirely composed of a movement "towards" yet remains contained within itself. Each perturbation resounds across its milieus of interaction, affecting other systems in turn. This is what a theatre of the virtual puts on display—not so much the exposure to gesture as an expression or the agency of the gesturing entity, the separation and striving, the inclination towards an object, and so on—here, we have a conceptual space that opens a ground for "acting otherwise" (Ruprecht 2017, 4). Acting otherwise is an attunement to a different responsiveness and a different logic, that of spectrality.

Gestural Potentiality

Potentiality is gestural not so much in the sense that it gives us a direction to be oriented towards, a deictic event, or the affirmation of an object against the backdrop of a world that is other than oneself. Nothing could be more remote from gestural potentiality than this concept of a gesture as pointing towards an object and, in turn, allowing an object to call us forth out of its depths. There is no need to affirm an object as objects themselves are "too relational to be grasped in coherently governable ways … their distance from us is a product of the richness of the relationality of the world, its infiniteness" (Chandler and Pugh 2020, 70). Potentiality, again, is spectral and expansive to such an extent that it can no longer allow us to think in terms of division.

This is a complete and entire opening; the very distillation of expression yet without an object of attachment.

Here we do not deal with a body that opens itself beyond its confines—in and through movement projecting itself as a not-yet, as something to come. One such gesture is the calling for attention towards the project of oneself, the event of a body's own sketching out and attainment. Even in its most benevolent variants, this scenario is still an entelechial one—it stages a confrontation with a world perceived as a garden of objects. Within the tensions that arise between disparate systems of being, a body projects its own end in the dual sense of finitude and purpose. The virtual thus cannot be thought of in terms of tension and disparity. And the attraction that it engenders is not desiring *per se* but simply expressive. It cannot even affirm a distance as nothing is distant; each event is perturbing and resounding across the field in its entirety, without pre-mediation. Again, the virtual field is an expansive milieu that does not foreground any of its constituents.

Potentiality is the ground providing the occasion—this is the playground for dissonances and perturbations, the triggering, the constituting, the interweaving, and the correlating. Again, potentiality is composed (and simultaneously recomposed) by a wealth of locales, each resounding across the multi-individual environment. Yet this overwhelming connectivity does not make potentiality a whole, an aggregate of parts, or anything that would resemble a "totality". Potentiality is spectral and ruffled, also a bit frowsy—as it contains everything and seldom resolves—but certainly not "total". The concepts of environment and organism are no longer thought in their opposition: we so much rather have "a mesh of virtual selves" (Weinstone 2004, 60) that can be articulated, with equal lucidity, in terms of closure, emergence, dissipation, or emptiness.

Just as a sense of self can be said to arise out of one's capacity to think reflective narration and linguistic closure, so does the sense of potentiality arise out of the event of resounding. The event makes us aware of an expansive habitat; a body that is an environment as such, an organisation that is always already overthrown, an openness that is not so much systemic as an ambience that only becomes palpable when operating through a system. Herein we come to the paradoxical realisation that a body is none of this—neither its environment nor its constituents. A body is entirely empty and spectral and yet spectacularly definite. It continually wavers between a self—as an individual enaction of codes—and a state that is profoundly extra-personal. In spite of the continual exercise in individuation, what is generated here is not so much the emergence of the individual as that of the self-less. As Diodato theorises the virtual body,

> it does not suppress itself as if it were a means, it does not amount to being a means, … it exists so as to act as an entity endowed with a particular relational structure capable of opening up new perceptive, imaginative, and cognitive possibilities.
>
> (Diodato 2012, 36)

Exposure to potentiality allows us to witness an unmediated transmission of energetic flows and their coagulation into more or less definite states. When we speak of transmission, however, we do not mean something directed towards an object external to itself. Because potentiality is not mono-causal, transmission within its domain becomes pervasive. If it is to point to anything at all, it points to the radical connectivity within the field, putting on display the intrinsic intra-transmissions within the expansive environment of movement. The possibility of transmission is everywhere, intrinsic to the field, allowing bodies to become environments themselves. As such, bodies freely partake in the field's connectivity in such a way that the incessant displays of gradations of definiteness—for example, as variants of selfhood or a plenitude of reality constructs—become tangible and become the stuff of the theatrical. What we witness is not so much a play in the classic sense as the enaction of those gradations, something that is maximally conceptual.

Potentiality reveals itself as something that forecloses separation. Potentiality allows us to expand the concept of action to such an extent that the only actional reality remains potentiality itself; yet it also does away with personhood, selfhood, intentionality, and subjectivity in such a way that the myriad tiny individuations taking place within its domain only *allude* to these latter concepts. That is to say, the concepts of action, personhood, selfhood, intentionality, and subjectivity only persevere within potentiality as spectral entities. They are present, paradoxically, only to the extent to which they are to remind us that they do not amount to an individual. Potentiality is more expansive than that and rather points to a "state of heightened involvement" (Weinstone 2004, 140) that posits "a modally differentiated, nonlocal body" (ibid., 141).

This way of approaching the theatrical is different from the model foregrounding theories of action, affect, capital, or cultural production. The latter approaches generate models for drama, theatre, and performance that are grounded in concepts such as entropy (think of debates on destruction, dissolution, recasting), antagonism (shifts in order, conflict between orders, communication), and the machinic (theatres as production engines, capitalism as a theatrical event). These seek an entry point that would allow them to articulate and make sense of action. By proxy, and in the newest debates in performance theory, these efforts have been restyled as the attempt to articulate the less tangible theatrical event. But all of these speak of a separation: a cleft between a body and a world, and a gulf between a selfhood and something other than the self.

Potentiality foregrounds an expansive not-yet that incorporates these constituents in such a way that there is no longer a need to conceive them in terms of distance. The gestural dimension of potentiality shows us how an entity is always already motioning towards its object, perseveres in this motion, yet does not reach that object. At the same time, what is put on display is not so much the distance as the continuum within which all these constituents coalesce. Instead of working towards attainment—the self-annihilation of motion—gestural potentiality resists and perseveres in the indefinite cleft between states. In this way, a theatre of the virtual retains the critical tension of growing. A theatre of the virtual is also the event engine that becomes capable of safeguarding the shift from motion to attainment, a region of a "still" and a "not yet", an openness that does not aim to resolve and does not seek closure. In a manner of speaking, this form of the theatrical secures an opening towards a gesture of creation that is not exhausted in its attainment. But it also shows the resistance of objects, the difficulty of aligning with a world or co-constituting a world as such.

All of this shows how potentiality stretches between a nominal body and its environments but cannot be reduced to a mere movement, nor can it be said to be a mere tendency of bodies towards something external to themselves. We cannot strictly speak of separation because the concept of potentiality forecloses any possibility of introducing the concept of distance at the outset. And when potentiality is described as gestural, one cannot mean the simple activity of reaching out, of living out one's dispositions and expressing one's potentials. Strictly speaking, there is no longer a need to validate the terms "subject" and "object" because entities within the domain of potentiality are rather defined in terms of genesis. In the latter case, we speak of a wealth of gradations and an intricate connectivity.

Potentiality is gestural because it affirms the capacity of forming enmeshments but, at the same time, cuts through this possibility to surpass the event of mere projection. And potentiality is gestural because it posits a body as a case of radical openness, a spectral atmosphere entirely composed of movement—not exactly that which is and not exactly that which is yet to come. Potentiality is profoundly interstitial; it does not uphold a wish to resolve, project a future, communicate, relate through language, or seek a firmer grounding in the flesh. Potentiality does not build a trajectory for the body but rather engages in building "a much larger periphery of the body" (Blanga-Gubbay 2014, 126).

Varro's *De Lingua Latina* shows how the term *gestus* derives from the Latin verb *gerere*. The meaning of this verb—in opposition to more literal actional terms such as *agere* and *facere*—is "*to adopt* a movement". This suggests a different take on the concept of direction in the opening of a body observed in gesture:

> …by achieving the object, the body surrenders to be instrument of something already existing in the world: it is no longer a desiring machine since the movements are no more just expression of a desire of the body, but of instructions of the world.
>
> (Blanga-Gubbay 2014, 126)

Reaching the object would be an entelechial act whereby the body is "revealed as simple instrument of its creation" (ibid., 128). A gesture does something different: it retains the tension—that which has not yet come to

Genesis and the Virtual 61

be. By inhabiting the body, a gesture changes it: "the body can no longer be seen as a transparent instrument ... becoming instead a living body, a matter filled with efforts, failures and unaccomplished *gesture*" (ibid., 129).

Here we speak of a more expansive category of gesture whereby gesture can take place in a variety of "nonspectacular contexts" (Noland 2017, 69)—such as locomotion or steps—hearkening back to Agamben's definition of gesture as something that reveals a power to "express oneself as pure means" (ibid., 69) or further, as that which even forecloses its own expression:

> That which in each act of expression remains unexpressed is gesture ... Gesture is the medium of movement; it is movement *as a medium*, a kind of kinetic surface of inscription, as opposed to other media or supports, such as the painted image or the written word. Gesture exhibits the movement that *is* mediality—crossing over, traversing space, connecting points ...
>
> (ibid., 69)

Bodies become trajectories of movement and force. This force is virtual. It does not seek its cessation but expresses a continuity.

But equally so, this force works with the gesture of discontinuity. Potentiality, then, encompasses phenomena such as limitation, failure, resistance, unwillingness, and incapacity in order to show the very singular type of non-productivity that they engender: "If we ... can have gestures as such, it is precisely because while going toward the object, we meet the limit of the extension of our own body" (Blanga-Gubbay 2014, 130). A gestural potentiality allows a body to encounter its own finitude and foreground its critical "resistance":

> The matter of the body is able with its limit to break the automatic sliding from gesture to action, from the *saying* to the *said*. ... More than a manifestation of weakness, this resistance of the flesh is now a manifestation of freedom, since by preventing the body from the *certainty* of an achievement, it opens it toward the category of *possibility*.
>
> (ibid.)

Potentiality captures a movement at this critical threshold. And again, this is a movement without attainment, still not extinguished in its completion, a motion that has not annihilated itself yet but has entered a region "beyond the body but not already in the world" (ibid.).

And this is the profound ontological impracticality of gesture: a gesture is not efficient, and it does not achieve anything. If it has an existence, it can be said to only persevere in its capacity as an expression, an attitude, a style of being, and an ambience. Gesture, to sum up, shows us the environmentality of a body. Here one is inclined to speak of an ambience, a surrounding, or a periphery. At the same time, however, a gesture does not have a solid and definite existence, is not communicative in the strict sense. It is only very questionable whether a gesture generates meaning or not. A gesture thrives because of this lack of resolve, and remains just that—a cloud of potentialities "on this uncertain threshold of the body".

Thinking along these lines, one can become open to a view on gesture as an art, a mode, a *style*, an inflection within being—

> the word art in German (die Art) continues today to carry one of the earliest meanings of the term: 'manner' or 'mode.' ... To speak of a 'way' is to dwell on the process itself, on its manner of becoming. It is to emphasize that art is before all else a quality, a difference in kind, a technique, that maps the way toward a certain attunement of world and expression. Art, understood along these terms, is not yet about an object, about a form, or a content. It is still on its way, in its manner of becoming.
>
> (Manning 2015, 45)

In spite of varied levels of complexity, theories of style share a common functional trait—they define things in terms of the creative deviation they are capable of engendering—deviating in an individual, therefore, a non-scientific way that makes a thing somewhat inaccessible to the discourse of the general. Style, then, would be the science of difference. It would not seek to establish the general but the local and peculiar (Meiner 1998, 157–159). Along these lines, gesture becomes *the expression of an engagement with a style*.

Within this conceptual landscape, personhood also becomes expansive to encompass a wider range of inherences within a given stretch of a world. A person designates a particular *style of being* and a certain *attitude*, an orientation, and a responsiveness towards an environment stretching out within and without. To this end, within the theatre of the virtual, we cannot think in terms of categories such as consciousness and the unconscious, intentionality and the lack of it, human and non-human, and sentient and non-sentient. Following this line of thought, personhood also becomes part of this gestural aesthetics: a matter of style and expression and a question of subtle gradations of movement.

A theatre of the virtual—of non-scenic, environmental gesture—would also seek to conceptualise touch and its foreclosure. Against the backdrop of a "language of sight" within the theatrical, one such ecological philosophy "needs to generate a whole new language that inclines more toward touch" (Morton 2017b, 112). Actuality coincides with the greatest immediacy of touching. Rather than having the less visceral but more expansive, comprehensive, pervasive moment of seeing, we have something which is local and intimate. Yet touch is also something that can entirely meddle with the dignity of a thing as it abruptly makes an entrance into a thing's field of interaction and aligns its trajectory with that of the touched. Touch as actualisation, be it violent or transformative, unwelcome or welcome, remains part of the ontology of closure. Gesture, on the other hand, forecloses touch. A gesture is moving towards and not attaining.

This line of thought also leads to a "gestural ethic ... based on the posture of inclination: a bending of the body towards those who are vulnerable and dependent" (Ruprecht 2017, 4). Whereas touch presupposes a haptic, non-scenic, visceral engagement with an expansive environment, Ruprecht emphasises that "gesture often avoids touch" (ibid., 4). Gesture as foreclosure and withdrawal allows us to think the possibility of not-accessing and not-exhausting; it is associated with a certain "ethos of restraint" (Butler 2015, 41). Closure can be quite violent. Gesture is the ingredient that continually forecloses. A gesture reminds us that the ontological character of a world is that of the potential. In a visceral way, gesture safeguards the repository of potentiality—the latter, if cast within a different ontology, would perhaps appear as a safe distance. A philosophy of gesture opens towards a conceptual region within which bodies reveal themselves as "splendorous" (Lingis 2011). They are fully open and simmering, still at work yet not reaching a point.

The concept of a world itself would change within the dynamics of gestural potentiality. A world is not only a "manifold that is intrinsically inviting to nonhuman beings" (Morton 2017b, 93) but also not quite there in the first place: "World is always spectral" (ibid., 94). Here a world operates as an impersonal aggregate of forces through which we confront the gestural potentiality of things. And vice versa: it is this potentiality that makes up a world; it is the cloud of virtual inherences and foreclosures that builds up a body all the way down to its ruffled edges. Such bodies are "heaps: ecosystems, boundaries between ecological eras, lifeforms ... To believe in them, we need a logic that allows them to exist" (ibid., 95). This logic could be the logic of the virtual—of worlds composed of thresholds of potentiality—whereby the demarcation between environments and bodies is no longer a matter of distance and alignment but is about a multitude of stages and states of motion.

Throughout the present book, a focus on the mutual enmeshments between potentiality and actuality carries the argument whereby we no longer simply deal with a continuum but with a "perfect overlap" (Morton 2017b, 84) of potentiality and actuality: "To encounter an ecological entity ... is to be haunted" (Morton 2017a, 304) within modes of enmeshment wherein even the actual is "open, spectral, ambiguous" (Morton 2017b, 84). Here we confront an actual that cannot simply be actual and whereby "spectrality, the way a thing keeps exceeding itself" (ibid., 84) is a fundamental condition of all things just as a thing is invariably "haunted—by itself" (ibid., 82). The concept of spectrality (Morton 2017b, 76) becomes significant within a theatre of the virtual and brings forth a crystallisation of the concept of mediality as known from the classic passage, "*The gesture is the exhibition of a mediality: it is the process of making a means visible as such.* It allows the emergence of the being-in-a-medium of human beings and thus it opens the ethical dimension for them" (Agamben 2000, 58).

Along these lines, a theatre of the virtual sees its task as exactly this: the exposure of the spectrality of beings, the logic of ecological attunement, and the kind of thought that becomes a careful pause within an encounter. Here we encounter a type of emanence that incorporates bodies and environments—or bodies–environments—within its domain to put on display the very idea of an expansive planetary enmeshment. A theatre of the virtual exposes attunement and indecision. And in being such, it becomes the conceptual milieu for gestural potentiality:

> When thinking becomes ecological, the beings it encounters cannot be established in advance as living or non-living, sentient or non-sentient, real or epiphenomenal. … What we encounter when we access the symbiotic real are spectral beings whose ontological status is uncertain to the extent that we know them in detail as we never have before. Our experience of these spectral beings is itself spectral …
>
> (Morton 2017b, 69)

The Transducer

Let us have a look at this engagement with spectrality as the effect of theatre's exposure to the virtual. Here the focus is on the very transmission, the movement between states, and the interstitial rests that compose motion. Transmission is energetic and gestural, lays out a virtual field, and plays with the possibility of actualisation without leading to a full articulation of the actual. This is the simultaneity of the mesh wherein concretisation is foreclosed. On this threshold, at the same time, we have to deal with a body: "the main transducer (interface), however, is a human body … a complex living organism inhabited by diverse layers of information and by innumerable drives, which working together shape the actual rendering…" (de Assis 2017, 697). A body participates in the operations of the virtual as a peculiar conduit, a "link between the impersonal and pre-individual diversity of the virtual components of any given work and its actualization in sound and gesture" (ibid., 698) but also as a

> technical object, a continuous electric relay that operates as a modulable resistance between a potential energy and its concrete place of actualization, whereby the resistance can be modulated through the means of information that remains external both to the potential energy and to the actual energy.
>
> (ibid., 698)

A body, in this strict sense, becomes an engine for the production of events; it is the transducer that does not belong to the virtual but has no place in the fully actual either. Its function is to serve as a milieu for the transmission. A body brings forth the virtual within a work for the theatre; the impulse is carried forward and multiplied, or not taken on at all. As an actualisation engine, a body does not have the power to actualise but only to carry forward the impulse of the virtual within a milieu of a different ontological texture. Once transmitted, the impulse of the virtual can thrive (cleaving a fractal multiplicity within the given), not develop at all (cease with its very positing, remaining a petrified capture of that which could have been), or develop only partially.

One could liken a body to an engine for the production of singularities whereby a body in itself does not have any action or movement; it only becomes action and movement through its interstitial entanglement with the virtual. A body carries the transmission of the virtual and interacts with the actual in ways which are multidirectional and non-monocausal. Instead of the mono-local and one-directional progression usually associated with primitive concepts of time and causality, we confront a simultaneity of reverberations across a causal chain that expands in all directions. Albeit spectral, the virtual field is just as real as the actual (Deleuze and Guattari 1994). The effects of a body's encounters with the tensions of the virtual are very much felt. And all the while, the intervention of a body magnifies the force of the virtual, giving it a milieu for interaction and co-immersion, a meeting ground, and a possibility to make an entrance into the actual.

The virtual field is not a unity, nor is it a totality. The virtual is a capture of all that transpires while a body is in motion. This is a juncture for systemic stability and chaotic multifariousness—something that Simondon calls "a metastable system" opening towards the multiplicity of beings and allowing divergent ontological orders to collide with one another at this abyssal interface. Once the system becomes replete with such encounters and produces a surplus, it begins to shift towards a new state. What passes through a body here is a "real potential"—an integral part of the definition of a metastable system because it incorporates the force that enables a becoming but also the very milieu of the becoming as such. And when we speak (through Simondon) of an emergent entity as an amalgamation of body and real potential, we speak first and foremost of its status as a linkage: a

> relation between orders of magnitude. ... relation and not simply in relation to something external. The individual that enables these relations is actually defined by them: it is the relation between different orders of magnitude that make the individual what it is. Thus, any given individual can only emerge in intrinsic articulation with an associated milieu.
> (de Assis 2017, 703)

It is difficult to speak of independent entities as everything subsists in a regime of co-immersion and co-presence. Entities are by definition multiple and non-stable, composed of tension and on the brink of shifting towards an alternate state—sometimes even towards a different order.

Within this model, the virtual is the impersonal force of the field; a body is the trigger-conduit, whereas potentiality itself equally coincides with the entire system at hand but also with the system's energetic dimension, the driving principle. Potentiality is both organisational and forceful in that it continually manages an artful balancing act between structural stability and chaos. Returning to our body within this picture, we encounter the facilitating and dynamising entity that carries forward the genesis of the new. Since a body is interstitial, profoundly gestural in its definition and in the ways it manifests itself, it also becomes the knot, the juncture whereby potentiality pushes through. Just as potentiality is both a system and a systemic force, so is the body a milieu for the interactions of ontological layers. It becomes the forceful push that allows virtual and actual to co-align. A body in the theatre is seldom shown as a stable wholesome "being"—a thing which is so and so—but we are ever so often confronted with bodies that are passages. Such bodies enflesh the zest of the virtual as they drift away from one actualisation to motion towards another.

We are ever in awe in the face of this play: virtual becomes actual and, in a simultaneous sweep, actuality stretches back towards the virtual. All the while, the milieu of the permeable body carries the transition and leaves traces that speak of continuous strings of dissolution and recomposition. For one, we have the body as a systemic stability: this is an entity in motion, carrying itself through time and space. But then again, we just as well have the "energetic" dimension of the system at hand: a bundle of forces that push towards the creation of the new, bringing forth a level of intensity that causes entire environments within and without the body to follow suit. We enter a regime of co-reverberation: as the body enters the virtual, it generates another actuality. In turn, this newly generated actuality is non-total—it is intensive and open, retaining the necessary resource of chaos that would allow the virtual to seep through its permeable boundaries.

Definitions of the body become dissipative within a theatre of the virtual. A body is now defined in terms of dispersive virtuality. Again, a body is invariably a multitudinous phenomenon—inasmuch as certain bodies persist as discrete organisms, the perturbations they unlock in their role as participants in potentiality comes to the fore. So a body is not a question of delimitation but a question of being interfused. As a transducer, a body carries the conducive plasticity that allows the pressure of the virtual to compose and recompose itself, form alliances with the actual, and participate in the formation of multiple ecologies. Within a theatre of the virtual, the body persists as a "transversal" individuality that can be said to be extra-individual not so much in the sense that it precedes, exceeds, or supersedes the individual as in the sense that it incorporates the individual as just one scenario within a situation of multitudinous enmeshments. A body perseveres within its limits with the help of preconstituted iterative arrangements but, at the same time, becomes a conduit for the transversal forces of potentiality.

Within the theatre of the virtual, bodies are not simply the pre-constituted or the already-constituted; bodies are co-compositions. As such, they form a variety of affective ecologies as both the materiality and immateriality of environments are co-shaped in continual becoming. How do they do so and what exactly is this becoming that is so vigorously addressed? Again, becoming is a matter of technique. One might even go on to say that becoming is a technique for survival. In any case, becoming is a certain way of coming to terms with emergent ecologies—both these of one's own body and those of the milieu. At the same time, becoming is not an "inherent" capacity that is somehow ingrained in beings—this is not Aristotle's principle of entelechy that is implanted in and pushed forth through each and every being. Becoming is a movement or a moving-with whereby the focus is on a body's readiness for co-composition. Becoming, however, is not intrinsic the way "entelechy" is thought to be intrinsic. As a technique, becoming is something that can also be felt, cultivated, or affectively received. The push of potentiality is expressed in becoming, becoming is expressed in movement, and movement perturbs bodies. And whereas bodies become through movement and it is movement that sustains potentiality, movement is not inherently ingrained in bodies nor are bodies given to movement in such a way that they do not have any other choice. Movement is not even of the body.

The body as a "transducer" has a crucial role: it carries the gestural force of potentiality and multiplies the movement of the virtual across and through its various milieus of interaction. Upon entering the actual multiple times, a body creates fractally proliferating chains of ever newer virtualities, widening and enlivening the virtual with each participation in the actual. The body becomes an empty middle—not a placeholder for personhood, self, subjectivity, and even less so, intentionality—here we encounter the body as a "nothing but". Nothing but a bundle of forces, a momentary capture of what pre-personal singularities and cosmic games of chance have put together quite arbitrarily, a play of actualisations and a gamble with the abyssal region of the virtual.

Taking on earlier discussions on potentiality and the virtual, this chapter looked at the refleshings and rematterings in individuation. A theatre of the virtual shows how matter spontaneously participates in its own genesis. Herein the principle of genesis is found within individuation itself and we deal with a morphodynamism—interfusing multitudes of metastable states. We begin to speak of processes not readily available to one's epistemological capacities and witness how the theatre of the virtual becomes an exploration of such intra-individual regions. The inclusion of the extra-logical and the supra-rational in the genesis of form allows us to open up to high degrees of contingency within an inexhaustible ontogenesis. Herein individuals are seen as transversal, multidimensional, generative, active, immanent, persistently complicating, and engaging in enmeshments.

And it is here that we begin to speak not so much of individuals as of trans-dividuals, affluent emergencies examined through the intra-dynamics of individuation. So a theatre of the virtual, again, carries an ethical charge as it constructs a perpetually individuating eco-philosophical body indifferent to concepts of the living and the non-living. One such body allows us to get immersed into the responsive potential of matter and engage in *feeling* as an abstract operation for the reordering of forces within the virtual. Within such conceptual atmospheres, individuals become expansive spectralities—irreducible to organising principles and pervaded by multitudes. Trans-dividuals are infra-entities that already inhabit the virtual; their environments are co-generative worlds.

And we arrive at *gesture*—an operation for the multiple engenderings of potentiality. Gesture expresses an engagement with a style and puts on display the spectral atmospheres surrounding a body. A theatre of the virtual thrives on gestural potentiality—a concept that stands for the foreclosing of distances and entities, showing how "entities" are always-already motioning towards and co-enmeshed with their "objects". To say that a theatre of the virtual works through gestural potentiality is to say that it derives its effects from ambiences, surroundings, and peripheries. We expand on these discussions in Chapters 3 and 4.

In fleshing out the workings of the virtual through refleshings, transdividuals, and gestural potentiality, drama and theatre studies become capable of capturing intensive processes and articulating their significance both for the mise-en-page and for the engendering of the theatrical event. To be exposed to a work for the theatre is to enter in agreement with the virtual, become sensitive to the work of spectral forces, co-align with the work of the transducer, enter the milieu of interaction that carries the process, and let that which was formerly known as a (human) body show itself in its emptiness.

Works Cited

Aan, Aare and M. Heinloo. 2014. "Analysis and Synthesis of the Walking Linkage of Theo Jansen with a Flywheel." *Agronomy Research* 12 (2): 657–662.

Agamben, Giorgio. 2000. "Notes on Gesture." In *Means Without End: Notes on Politics*, translated by Vincenzo Binetti and Cesare Casarino, 49–60. Minneapolis: University of Minnesota Press.

Aristotle. 1993. *De Anima*. Translated by David W. Hamlyn. Oxford: Clarendon.

de Assis, Paulo. 2017. "Gilbert Simondon's 'Transduction' as Radical Immanence in Performance." *Performance Philosophy* 3 (3): 695–717. http://dx.doi.org/10.21476/PP.2017.33140.

Barad, Karen. 2008. "Posthumanist Performativity: Toward an Understanding of How Matter Comes to Matter." In *Material Feminisms*, edited by Stacy Alaimo and Susan Hekman, 120–157. Bloomington: Indiana University Press.

Barad, Karen. 2007. *Meeting the Universe Halfway: Quantum Physics and the Entanglement of Matter and Meaning*. Durham, NC: Duke University Press.

Bardin, Andrea. 2015a. *Epistemology and Political Philosophy in Gilbert Simondon. Individuation, Technics, Social Systems*. Heidelberg New York London: Springer.

Bardin, Andrea. 2015b. "On Substances and Causes Again: Simondon's Philosophy of Individuation and the Critique of the Metaphysical Roots of Determinism." In *Morphogenesis and Individuation*, edited by Alessandro Sarti, Federico Montanari,

and Francesco Galofaro, 3–33. Heidelberg, New York, Dodrecht, London: Springer.
Barthélémy, Jean-Hugues. 2015. *Life and Technology: An Inquiry into and Beyond Simondon*. Translated by Barnaby Norman. Lüneburg: Meson Press.
Barthélémy, Jean-Hugues. 2012. "Fifty Key Terms in the Works of Gilbert Simondon." Translated by Arne De Boever. In *Gilbert Simondon: Being and Technology*, edited by Arne De Boever, Alex Murray, Jon Roffe and Ashley Woodward, 203–231. Edinburgh: Edinburgh University Press.
Blanga-Gubbay, Daniel. 2014. "Life on the Threshold of the Body." *Paragrana* 23 (1): 122–131. https://doi.org/10.1515/para-2014-0012.
Bowden, Sean. 2012. "Gilles Deleuze, a Reader of Gilbert Simondon." In *Gilbert Simondon: Being and Technology*, edited by Arne De Boever, Alex Murray, Jon Roffe and Ashley Woodward, 135–53. Edinburgh: Edinburgh University Press.
Boysen, Benjamin. 2018. "The Embarrassment of Being Human. A Critique of New Materialism and Object-oriented Ontology." *Orbis Litterarum* 73 (3): 225–242. https://doi.org/10.1111/oli.12174.
Butler, Judith. 2015. "Theatrical Machines." *Differences: A Journal of Feminist Cultural Studies* 26 (3): 24–42. https://doi.org/10.1215/10407391-3340336.
Carrozzini, Giovanni. 2015. "How to Invent a Form: An Inquiry into Gilbert Simondon's Philosophy of Perception." In *Morphogenesis and Individuation*, edited by Alessandro Sarti, Federico Montanari, and Francesco Galofaro, 33–49. Heidelberg, New York, Dodrecht, London: Springer.
Chabot, Pascal. 2013. *The Philosophy of Simondon. Between Technology and Individuation*. London: Bloomsbury.
Chandler, David and Jonathan Pugh. 2020. "Islands of Relationality and Resilience: The Shifting Stakes of the Anthropocene." *Area* 52: 65–72. https://doi.org/10.1111/area.12459.
Clark, Timothy. 2015. *Ecocriticism on the Edge: The Anthropocene as a Threshold Concept*. London and New York: Bloomsbury.
Combes, Muriel. 2012. *Gilbert Simondon and the Philosophy of the Transindividual*. Translated by Thomas LaMarre. Cambridge, MA: The MIT Press.
Cucuzzella, Carmela. 2021. "Making the Invisible Visible: Eco-Art and Design against the Anthropocene." *Sustainability* 13 (7): 1–16. https://doi.org/10.3390/su13073747.
de Beistegui, Miguel. 2012. "Science and Ontology: From Merleau-Ponty's 'Reduction' to Simondon's 'Transduction'." In *Gilbert Simondon: Being and Technology*, edited by Arne De Boever, Alex Murray, Jon Roffe and Ashley Woodward, 154–176. Edinburgh: Edinburgh University Press.
De Fazio, Gianluca and Paulo Lévano. 2019. "Praktognosia: Ecosophical Remarks on Having a Body." *Revista Tempos e Espaços em Educação* 12 (28): 15–32. http://dx.doi.org/10.20952/revtee.v12i28.10163.
Deleuze, Gilles and Félix Guattari. 1994. *What Is Philosophy?* Translated by Hugh Tomlinson and Graham Burchell. New York: Columbia University Press.
Deleuze, Gilles. 1990. *The Logic of Sense*. Translated by Mark Lester and Charles Stivale. Edited by Constantin Boundas. London: The Athlone Press.
Dimitrova, Zornitsa. 2017. *Literary Worlds and Deleuze: Expression as Mimesis and Event*. Lanham, MD: Lexington Books.
Diodato, Roberto. 2012. *Aesthetics of the Virtual*. Translated by Justin L. Harmon. Albany: SUNY Press.

Fishel, Stefanie R. 2019. "Of Other Movements: Nonhuman Mobility in the Anthropocene." *Mobilities* 14 (3): 351–362. http://dx.doi.org/10.1080/17450101.2019.1611218.

Flaxman, Gregory. 2019. "Out of Control: From Political Economy to Political Ecology." In *Posthuman Ecologies. Complexity and Process after Deleuze*, edited by Rosi Braidotti and Simone Bignall, 205–223. London: Rowman & Littlefield International.

Galofaro, Francesco. 2015. "Structural Syntax and Quantum Computation: A Simondonian Approach." In *Morphogenesis and Individuation*, edited by Alessandro Sarti, Federico Montanari and Francesco Galofaro, 173–203. Heidelberg, New York, Dodrecht, London: Springer.

Guattari, Fèlix. 2000. *The Three Ecologies*. Translated by Ian Pindar and Paul Sutton. London: The Athlone Press.

Hinton, Peta. 2017. "A Sociality of Death: Towards a New Materialist Politics and Ethics of Life Itself." In *What If Culture Was Nature All Along?* edited by Vicki Kirby, 223–247. Edinburgh: Edinburgh University Press.

Hui, Yuk. 2021. *Art and Cosmotechnics*. Minneapolis: University of Minnesota Press.

Hui, Yuk. 2020. "Machine and Ecology." *Angelaki* 25 (4): 54–66. http://dx.doi.org/10.1080/0969725X.2020.1790835.

Jansen, Theo. 2018. *Fossils*. https://www.strandbeest.com/fossils. Accessed August 2, 2021.

Kirbis, Annika. 2020. "Off-centring Empire in the Anthropocene: Towards Multispecies Intimacies and Nonhuman Agents of Survival." *Cultural Studies* 34 (5): 831–850. http://dx.doi.org/10.1080/09502386.2020.1780279.

Komoda, Kazuma and Hiroaki Wagatsuma. 2011. "A Study of Availability and Extensibility of Theo Jansen Mechanism toward Climbing over Bumps." *Proceedings of the 21st Annual Conference of the Japanese Neural Network Society* 21: 192–193. https://jglobal.jst.go.jp/en/detail?JGLOBAL_ID=201202230366714572.

Komoda, Kazuma and Hiroaki Wagatsuma. 2009. "A Proposal of the Extended Mechanism for Theo Jansen Linkage to Modify the Walking Elliptic Orbit and a Study of Cyclic Base Function." https://ihmc.us/dwc2012files/Komoda.pdf.

Lingis, Alphonso. 2011. *Violence and Splendor*. Evanston, IL: Northwestern University Press.

Manning, Erin. 2015. "Artfulness." In *The Nonhuman Turn*, edited by Richard Grusin, 45–81. Minneapolis: The University of Minnesota Press.

Meiner, Carsten Henrik. 1998. "Deleuze and the Question of Style." *Symplokē* 6 (1–2): 157–173. https://www.jstor.org/stable/40550430.

Meloni, Maurizio, Rachael Wakefield-Rann, and Becky Mansfield. 2021. "Bodies of the Anthropocene: On the Interactive Plasticity of Earth Systems and Biological Organisms." *The Anthropocene Review* (April 2021). https://doi.org/10.1177/20530196211001517.

Michaud, Yves. 2012. "The Aesthetics of Gilbert Simondon: Anticipation of the Contemporary Aesthetic Experience." In *Gilbert Simondon: Being and Technology*, edited by Arne De Boever, Alex Murray, Jon Roffe and Ashley Woodward, 121–132. Edinburgh: Edinburgh University Press.

Mongini, Claudia. 2015. "Morphogenesis under Construction: Tracing the Process of Individuation Along Physico-Aesthetic Coordinates." In *Morphogenesis and Individuation*, edited by Alessandro Sarti, Federico Montanari and Francesco Galofaro, 75–93. Heidelberg, New York, Dodrecht, London: Springer.

Montanari, Federico. 2015. "Immanence/Imminence. Thinking About Immanence and Individuation." In *Morphogenesis and Individuation*, edited by Alessandro Sarti, Federico Montanari, and Francesco Galofaro, 203–222. Heidelberg, New York, Dodrecht, London: Springer.
Morton, Timothy. 2017a. "Specters of Ecology." In *General Ecology: The New Ecological Paradigm*, edited by Erich Hörl and James Burton, 303–323. London: Bloomsbury.
Morton, Timothy. 2017b. *Humankind*. London: Verso.
Nail, Thomas. 2019. "Kinopolitics. Borders in Motion." In *Posthuman Ecologies. Complexity and Process after Deleuze*, edited by Rosi Braidotti and Simone Bignall, 183–205. London: Rowman & Littlefield International.
Nansai, Shunsuke, Rajesh Elara, Mohan and Masami Iwase. 2013. "Dynamic Analysis and Modeling of Jansen Mechanism." *Procedia Engineering* 64: 1562–1571. https://doi.org/10.1016/j.proeng.2013.09.238.
Noland, Carrie. 2017. "Ethics, Staged." *Performance Philosophy* 3 (1): 67–91. https://doi.org/10.21476/PP.2017.31165.
Page, Joanna. 2020. "Planetary Art beyond the Human: Rethinking Agency in the Anthropocene." *The Anthropocene Review* 7 (3): 273–94. https://doi.org/10.1177/2053019620916498.
Parikka, Jussi. 2019. "Cartographies of Environmental Arts." In *Posthuman Ecologies. Complexity and Process after Deleuze*, edited by Rosi Braidotti and Simone Bignall, 41–61. London: Rowman & Littlefield International.
Richardson, Michael and Kerstin Schankweiler. 2019. "Affective Witnessing." In *Affective Societies: Key Concepts*, edited by Jan Slaby and Christian von Scheve, 166–177. London: Routledge.
Ruprecht, Lucia. 2017. "Introduction: Towards an Ethics of Gesture." *Performance Philosophy* 3 (1): 4–22. http://dx.doi.org/10.21476/PP.2017.31167.
Sarti, Alessandro and Piotrowski, David. 2015. "Individuation and Semiogenesis: An Interplay Between Geometric Harmonics and Structural Morphodynamics." In *Morphogenesis and Individuation*, edited by Alessandro Sarti, Federico Montanari and Francesco Galofaro, 49–75. Heidelberg, New York, Dodrecht, London: Springer.
Scott, David. 2014. *Gilbert Simondon's Psychic and Collective Individuation. A Critical Introduction and Guide*. Edinburgh: Edinburgh University Press.
Simondon, Gilbert. 2017. *On the Mode of Existence of Technical Objects*. Translated by Cécile Malaspina and John Rogove. Minneapolis, MN: Univocal.
Simondon, Gilbert. 2009. "The Position of the Problem of Ontogenesis." Translated by Gregory Flanders. *Parrhesia* 7: 4–16.
Simondon, Gilbert. 2005. *L'individuation à la lumière des notions de forme et d'information*. Grenoble: Millon.
Simondon, Gilbert. 1992. "The Genesis of the Individual." In *Incorporations*, edited by Jonathan Crary and Sanford Kwinter, 297–317. New York: Zone Books.
Smailbegovic, Ada. 2015. "Cloud Writing: Describing Soft Architectures of Change in the Anthropocene." In *Art in the Anthropocene: Encounters among Aesthetics, Politics, Environments and Epistemologies,* edited by Heather Davis and Etienne Turpin, 93–109. London: Open Humanities Press. http://dx.doi.org/10.26530/OAPEN_560010.
Weinstone, Ann. 2004. *Avatar Bodies: A Tantra for Posthumanism*. Minneapolis: University of Minnesota Press.

3 Violence and Touch

Within the theatre of the virtual, we abandon the scenic and rather work through a logic of touch. Touch is an incorporeality that engenders an event. And "what we call virtual is not something that lacks reality but something that is engaged in a process of actualization following the plane that gives it its particular reality" (Deleuze 2001, 31). From this vantage, touch becomes an operation for the repotentialisation of matter. As such, touch encompasses both *feeling* as a speculative capacity and *sensing* as an epistemological practice. Then, as much as it is a question of technique, touch is also a question of practice. Through negotiating the forces inherent in touch, we articulate operative ways of being within a world. Even more so, we become capable of recognising the effects of touch within a world, showing how touch as practice and technique is environmental in its scope.

Touch introduces a qualitative change within a body. Entanglements become global, comprehensive; a body spills over its edges to enter in recompositions with other materials and environments. Touch, however, is not to be understood as only sensory, experiential, and corporeal. Nor is it to be seen as something adjacent to bodies, a separateness that attaches itself to a body that is already established and aligns itself with that which already is. On the contrary, touch is an ontogenetic operation in its own right, incorporeal and abstract.

Touch directs us towards movement, towards the gesturality of the virtual whereby "the space of the body ... collapses the distinction between a fixed, objectively calculable space and the body as a bounded interiority that moves in that space" (Tiainen and Parikka 2013, 210). This becomes an intensive engagement with novelty, a transversal gliding across concepts so that, in the end, the knower and the known become dissipative; lose both boundaries and established knowledge to stretch across the systems at hand in their entirety. In this way, touch becomes instrumental in engendering new modes of knowing as "we now have to recalibrate our sensorial systems to adjust to contradiction, catastrophe, and ecological volatility born of human activities that override and neutralize long standing histories of local knowledge" (Boetzkes 2015, 272). But even more so, touch also refigures movement itself as it recomposes the ratio between stillness and motion, speed and slowness,

DOI: 10.4324/9781003231080-4

at times triggering entirely novel alliances between materials. The very ontogenesis within the theatrical takes place because of the touch of the virtual, and touch is present at the entire stretch of multitudinous ontological and extra-ontological layers of reality that co-shape the worlds of the site of performance. Bodies intensify or alter the course of their ongoing genesis because of touch. At the same time, the touch of the virtual—as the virtual cannot be thought as mono-causal and one-directional—can make a body re-enter the virtual yet again.

Bodies perturbed by touch are not so much identitarian as global and cosmic. Their engendering is incorporeal and fugitive; their movement is a receptive "toward". The becoming of a body takes place spontaneously and contingently—not because of a project already laid out for its becoming and not because of an ontological imperative. An individuating body is only partly ontological because greater and greater portions of its becoming cannot be captured and articulated from within the politics of being. Individuating bodies are supra-ontological, "in the event". Their prevalent reality is that of an ontogenesis that takes place outside of being and outside of identitarian ways of conceptualising.

Bodies are maximally open systems; their most basic condition is that of gestural expressivity—a body is an engine for the generation of expressions within worlds. Within the theatre of the virtual, bodies downplay their existence and inherence as stabilised entities within proprietary environments. They become dissipative and expansive. Bodily engendering does not take place merely within an individual but is invariably "collective" as it reverberates across the entire chain of co-minglings that involve the individual. Movement individuates; movement causes entire environments to undergo qualitative shifts and transitions towards different regimes of speeds and slownesses. Qualitative changes that occur are changes "in the event" that may not have any corporeal equivalent—we speak of changes that are clandestine and elusive. Change as such is seldom actualised; it forms an alliance with the forces of the virtual and not with the visible world.

And touch is of the domain of the boundary, the region between actual and virtual that coincides with gestural potentiality. Touch is already an event. The movement it carries may not always be in a body's best interest; the reverberations it precipitates across a system may not invariably lead to a system's enhancement and preservation. Touch is a becoming, yet this becoming can even have instrumentality at its core—touch can instrumentalise a body, can lead not to the enhancement but to the lessening of its virtual zest, to the diminishing of its power. Touch can be constraining and incarcerating. Yet a touch invariably is an attempt to reach towards the virtual dimension of a body. But, at the same time, the act of touching, reaching towards and arriving at the frontier, can be an encroachment, a depletion of the event, and the affirming of a violent actualisation. This "affective intensity" of the inherent ambiguities within touch becomes an enabling condition for art (Colman 2007). Because of its already collective quality, touch carries its effects across the systems affected by it, multiplying the actual in its attempt to partake in the powers of the virtual.

Whereas the gestural dimension of touch emphasises the generative, encompassing quality of a body and remains in awe of the virtual without seeking its depletion, we can also speak of a type of touch that is investigative. Touch seeks to determine the frontier of the flesh, to establish the actual, and to "discover" a body in the act of touching. This is where we speak of the violence of touch. A touch that actualises seeks to determine an ontology for bodies; a touch that virtualises acknowledges the unsure metastability of environments. Virtualising touch shows how bodies are always already and not yet at the same time, invariably in excess of themselves, and in an ongoing movement between constitution and re-constitution as they stretch across the interstice between virtual and actual.

Land of Palms

Pindorama (2014) by Lia Rodrigues takes one to a place of water, the forces of a storm. We have phenomena of mobility, moving towards, the showcasing of a simple way to move and bodies being minimalistic in their movement. The performance takes off as audience members are admitted into a darkened black-box space. No windows, no light—or only natural light at first. No boundaries between the spectatorial space and the place of the performance are indicated. Everything is defined by an initial "no"—no indices, no instructions, even the number of audience members is limited. Spectator bodies flow into the space and fill up certain edges spontaneously. There are no seats and no indication as to whether one should sit or remain standing, and where. A seeming organisational intent becomes palpable as bodies begin to regroup in response to other bodies or to shift positions to take up the room's inconspicuous stretches of vacant space. One continues to be quiet even when it becomes clear that it may take a while before everything begins. But in a manner of speaking, "everything" has begun already. Audience members look at one another without expression, arranging themselves around corners. From this vantage, one waits. Everyone is on their own, composing oneself for an encounter without knowing whether the encounter has taken place already.

Spectators begin to step back as two dancers bring a transparent plastic roll into the room. The object is placed in the middle of the floor. As if oblivious to the presence of those who are already there, the dancers begin to unfold the plastic. In doing so, they claim more and more space for themselves, pushing spectators towards the edges of the room and expecting everyone to move over so that the task can be performed without interruption. Audience members uniformly step back, cooperating. The crowd yields to the gesture of territory forming. Soon, the plastic foil covers a whole stretch of the studio floor, demarcating a stage space. Ticket holders appear to recognise this gesture as an invitation to act as an audience and sit down cross-legged around the edges of the foil.

More and more dancers come in, placing small transparent balloons filled with water on the foil. A dancer enters the central space and pours a plastic bottle of water on their head. Without acknowledging the presence of a spectatorship, the dancer slowly begins to roll, glide, and crawl on the plastic surface. Facing the floor, the dancer approaches each of the water orbs. Starting by pressing their torso against the small objects, the dancer becomes increasingly engrossed in the exercise, eventually smashing the orbs. Once an orb is smashed, they move on to the next, repeating the steps of initial fascination, gentle interaction, and escalating violence. Other dancers intervene then—holding the far ends of the plastic foil, they flutter it up and down, disturbing the exercise. The dancer is thrown around into the foil; the orbs begin to roll out of their places. Now, it is the dancer's turn to be vulnerable and exposed as the fluttering gets more vigorous. The remaining dancers make guttural sounds while manipulating the plastic, intensifying their movement as the dancer clings to the foil in a confused effort to regain balance.

As the dancer is flung in all directions, audience members continue to viscerally experience each of the movements on stage. The boundary between stage and spectatorship is liquid. Both stage and spectatorship are placed on the same level, fuse into one another, and are physically exposed to the immediate effects of this co-presence. As a spectator, one feels gushes of air and splashes of water onto one's own skin, the sounds of a body at work to preserve its boundaries and integrity, along with the violent intervention of the crackling waves of plastic. The dancer stumbles down multiple times, rising with greater difficulty each time as their body is relentlessly thrown around at interchanging intervals of increasing speed and accelerating slowness. Instead of precision and calculation, there is vigorous muscle work testing out the endurance of bodies and the stability of surfaces.

Dancers appear without warning from various directions—nobody sees a door opening or another way of indicating that an entrance is being made. It may have been impossible to distinguish performers from spectators if it were not for the fact that the performers' bodies are entirely free of textile. Throughout the duration of the piece, dancers partition the space as they move, slowly carving out a place of performance. In the very beginning, there is chartering and delineating up until a clearing in the centre of the room begins to take shape. Spectators, in turn, are systematically pushed towards the edges of the room and have their perimeter violated in a variety of ways—be it by splashing water or by rolling onto one's shoes if a spectator fails to move over.

The piece of plastic foil carried by the dancers equally participates in the deliberate slow motion, the gestures of enfolding, stretching, acceleration, refolding, and creasing. Reminiscent of Slow Ontology, this

> is a diffraction—a dispersal—of time, space, and matter across different wavelengths, moving in different directions at different speeds. As waves

> travel, they move along the cycles of the sun, moon, water, land, living organisms, and our waking dreams.
>
> (Ulmer 2016, 208)

As dancers crawl, roll, slide, or resist, the surface of the foil is engaged in an elaborate game of foreplaying and withholding. And the numerous transparent balloons filled with water are not so much extensions of the artefactual that encroaches on the space of performing biological bodies as participants in a confluence that exceeds categories such as the living and the non-living, the organic and the artefactual. The spectacle of artefactuality puts on display the arbitrariness of "natural" forces such as waves or gusts of wind. The spectacles of intervention and precarity, in turn, articulate the embeddedness of these forces in bodies, showcasing "a new form of ontological insecurity" (Hamilton 2017, 593) that issues forth out of the enmeshment of humans and synthetic materials.

Swishing and splashing, bodies being slapped against each other or slammed against surfaces, the rustling of the plastic foil, water against bodies—these are the encounters that coagulate to form the soundscape of *Pindorama*. The piece is not accompanied by any sound score other than that which is momentarily and singularly produced by the dancers in their interaction with spilled water, plastic foil, and ground. Plastic, flesh, and water move at various speeds, increasing pace and coming to a lull, intensifying and stopping altogether. The sound that is made therewith is not a "human" sound but the music of forces at work. As the plastic foil is flung and vigorously shaken, the waves get larger—all the while, more dancers roll within the undulating foil, throwing themselves against the floor and into the menacing plastic.

In the second act, the water is mopped up and the plastic sheet is brought in again. Six dancers occupy the performing space—and this time the storm is enacted through the violent motions and collisions of their very bodies. We have an emulated sense of directedness without intentionality, each body groping, catching, or evading its counterparts. The bodies exude a sense of violence performed blindly but in concert. Remarkably uniform, their movements coagulate in a singular twitching organism; a swarm-intelligence-like orb composed of bodies amidst the plastic scenery. This overkill of connectivity does not extend to the performing dancers only but also stretches out to the inadvertently involved spectatorship. Everyone is in the mesh.

Splashing of water and sounds of flesh being slapped against solid surfaces is all we hear. Dancers run into the foil and seem entirely engulfed by it. Writhing, crawling gestures converge up until the point that we begin to see just one unified struggling organism. Boundaries between the individual dancers have vanished as they continually fuse into one another as if diving into each other's bodies. With increased intensity, the dancers swirl and thrash themselves onto their counterparts; the slapping sounds become uncontrollably rapid. The dancers roll in such a way that the plastic foil begins to enwrap them slowly. No sounds come out of the cocoon-like bundle of bodies, water, and plastic. Everything becomes quiet, dancers lying completely still beneath the foil.

In the third act, the plastic foil has disappeared from the scene and we only have the shimmering water balloons dispersed all over the place. As if following an invisible pattern known only to them, the dancers proceed to place the balloons across the room without much attention to audience members. Some of these orbs end up being installed in the laps and on the stretched legs of spectators, making yet again evident that "the things we observe and with which we interact are alive and undeniably expressive" (Oppermann 2018, 9). Again, ticket holders are so urged to abandon their sitting positions. The space previously delineated as a stage is now occupied by a constellatory construct of glistening orbs and human figures standing in the semi-darkness. All 11 dancers come out—their dance, however, is now taking place at the very feet of the spectators. There is slow writhing and crawling. One stands motionless as to not to disturb the fragile coming together of flesh and floor surface.

And anyway, no audience member can reasonably sit anywhere within the room. A thin layer of water has covered the entire surface. Some stand quietly with water splashed all over from previous acts as they have been caught within the dancers' battle with the waves. In this last phase of *Pindorama*, slowness settles in again. The dancers move in deliberate retardation. As the black-box space is darkened, now one observes the shimmering of the plastic together with the calm fruit-like water balloons. As dancers carve their way through this nocturnal garden of flickering plastic, they shift towards the spectators, crawling on a wet floor with their faces turned to the ground. Dancers are either lying still or crawling with extreme slowness, swishing among the clothed spectators and occasionally brushing against leather shoes and pieces of clothing—making these appear inappropriately solid.

At times, the dancers would engage in a racing movement. Then, they would begin to glide with extreme deliberate slowness. It all becomes a mesh of limbs encountering the unyielding surface of the floor, water balloons bursting open, and the abundance of water making its way throughout the scene. Dancers come together and separate; tangled limbs, water, and floor display a wealth of configurations and possibilities of co-mingling. In doing so, the dancers show a remarkable feat of endurance. Some of them remain lying down—facing the floor amidst pools of water—throughout the entire performance. Other dancers remain scrambled together for many minutes underneath the impermeable plastic foil up to the point that one becomes uneasy at the sight. And then again, we have the ceaseless thrashing, splashing, and racing of bodies on the unwelcoming wet surface. All dancers are fully and precariously exposed, one can observe muscles twitching and the skin bristling, chests panting and facial muscles moving not so much with emotion as in reaction to the various acts of physical strain that we observe on stage. All the while, it is questionable whether a line between spectatorship and performers can be drawn. Albeit passive, clothed, and observing, the audience is drawn right into the mesh, amidst the bare bodies; the dancers have penetrated and claimed every corner of the black-boxed space both with their movement and through the impersonal movement of water.

Pindorama was the name given to Brazil in the indigenous Tupí language before Portugal invaded the territory in 1500. "Pindorama", reading literally as "the land of palms", is the third piece in a trilogy that Lia Rodrigues began in 2010 to ask questions concerning the various possible relationships between stage, space, and landscape as well as the interweave of dancers and those who witness the dance. Vicariously, this work touches on questions of withholding and giving in, being resilient and being immersed. Rodrigues delves into the matter of landscape-forming as both a colonising terraforming gesture and a world-shaping spectacle. The complex entanglements of one's connection to "place" come to the fore: "a recognition of the value of a 'human connection to place' … the depth of interrelatedness between human and more-than-human worlds" (Adams 2020, 128). But this is also about claiming a territory while becoming deterritorialised, the stretching of borders, the reactive struggle for containment, and the multifariousness of borderscapes within and without bodies. Lia Rodrigues works at Centro de Artes da Maré, an arts centre in one of Rio's largest favelas.

The 11 dancers of Companhia de Danças look at the concept of landscape with barest and maximally minimalistic means. We have a darkened black-box space, textile-free performers, water, and plastic to tell us about the relationship between landscape, humans, natural forces, and artefactual presence. After *Pororoca* (2009) and *Piracema* (2010), the piece continues the dialogue about water, community, and territory. And whereas *Pororoca* thematises force by putting on display the monster waves of the Amazonas and *Piracema* speaks about swimming against the current, *Pindorama* (2014) concentrates on the very question of movement as a gesture of dissent (migration) or violence (colonising), as a force engendering relationships, enabling emancipatory practices—such as relating and proximity—but also a force that brings forth containment, bordering, and a form of "ecological grief" (Kidner 2021).

Dancers bend their bodies to put on display the very fabric of movement and the very trajectories of ongoing transformation. From within a sparsely demarcated space, one is thrown within a complex interweave of vulnerability and cruelty while dancers shift between fragile individuals exposed to the forces of nature and a swarming crowd—a collectivity that nurtures connection and one that exposes sheer fury. Within these soundscapes and imagescapes entirely composed of bodies and bodily noise, we are immersed in one "living installation" which dancers continue to shape throughout the duration of the performance in a gesture of simultaneous dismantling and building up.

Pindorama is intensely confrontational. It does not leave ticket holders in the inertia of spectatorship. The piece is absolutely not about spectating and not about engaging a gaze. It rather appeals to the faculty of *sensing*—viscerally and through one's own body that is just as vulnerably stretched within the performance space as the bare bodies of dancers crawling through water. We are invited to partake in an immersive sensorial practice that Elizabeth Johnson calls "biosensing ... a way to reconnect with the liveliness of other living things ... A more expansive aesthetic, one that is neither strictly machinic nor biological" (Johnson 2017, 286). And apart from sensing, the piece also gestures towards a certain bodily capacity for *feeling*. Whereas sensing is the physical and cognitively informed manifestation of one's interaction with a clearly delineated outside world, *feeling* is the conceptual counterpart of sensing. *Feeling* expresses a connection to the virtual. Sensing is finite and clearly defined—sensing is tactile, has an identifiable trigger in the outside world, and pertains to the laws of physics. *Feeling* is indefinite and speculative. A *feeling* belongs to the virtual. It is constitutively uncertain inasmuch as it does not seem to have a discrete source but is rather one complex concatenation of multifarious triggers and sources that are not easily disentangled from one another.

Feeling takes place on the threshold between being and extra-being. Feeling is that which is imbued with virtuality but takes place because of the presence of actual existent entities that can serve as the articulations of that "feeling". In other words, "feeling" occurs because of an invasion of the virtual; "feeling" is one way of making the gestural region palpable. The relation between actual and virtual too becomes tangible through one such affective surging—experience stretches towards the unspeakable as the virtual spills over existence. Alternately, movement and sense also find their articulation in "feeling" (the sense of the world can only be felt) and can be made somewhat more available to recognition, albeit as an uncertain cluster of an experiential this and that. "Feeling", then, is an important threshold between ontological and extra-ontological regions. It carries the reciprocity that also defines the relationship between the actual and the virtual. Movement and sense make the work of the virtual felt, that is to say, make the virtual experientially palpable and make it tangible through its appearance as a "feeling" within the world region.

Notwithstanding the limitations of the faculties, "feeling" is the experiential capacity that allows us to surpass experience and to open a door to the virtual forming region. A being region in the making is something that is felt. "Feeling" is the signalling that we have reached a threshold between worlds and between natures—that a change in tonality has occurred. Virtual worldforming becomes available in a this-worldly region through "feeling"; the event is something that can be "felt" as it traverses bodies and interlinks environments.

The Technicity of Touch

Taking the conceptual landscape of *Pindorama* along the way, we turn to a discussion of *touch as a repotentialisation technique*. Within this discussion, the question of touch remains inseparable from the question of technicity:

> As technicity, technology is seen as a mediator, not in the representational sense but in terms of its functioning: technology takes on ontological

> import in and through the forces that it exercises on other beings as well as in and through the new virtualities, and hence realities, it brings into being.
>
> (Hoel and van der Tuin 2013, 190)

Touch shows itself in the activity of its function. Touch, however, does not necessarily mean contact and communication, nor is this a way to account for the work of the senses. We do not turn to the work of touch in order to foreplay experience and encounter a haptic quality in things, or even less so, the haptic as an enhancement of a body and a path towards the making-splendorous of movement.

Within the pages of this book, touch is the carrier of gestural potentiality. That is to say, touch carries the safeguarding of a sufficient resource of the virtual within a system that secures the ongoing play of potentials within the metastable state. From this vantage, touch is not constraining and actualising but rather is the guardian of the virtual. It is an engine for the continual engendering of a body, an ontogenetic operation and the armature that carries the operation. Touch is not something that invades a body from without, encroaches on its prefigured alliances, or violates its code; touch is already inscribed within a body and precipitates change immanently. And again, this change is clandestine and incorporeal because it primarily belongs to the virtual.

This is a way of organising a body and guaranteeing a sufficient resource of plasticity that would allow a body to shift towards further individuation. Not only is the work of touch a means of organisation but also a way to refigure distance and to think the interrelatedness of bodies within and across an environment. Here we cannot speak of contact and communication, at least not from the vantage point of the vernacular understanding of these terms. Contact and communication presuppose a gap, a vacuous region that divides discrete objects arranged within a landscape entirely composed of stretches of vacuity and stretches of objects divided by vacuous regions. Because of this division, one is tempted to establish a pre-ordained difficulty in knowing and reaching towards a given object, a pre-determined need for an object to "communicate" in order to be "understood" by other objects together with a pre-established desire to bring together as many objects as possible. So we operate from within the pre-established value of "contact" and, therefore, from the ethical imperative to create contact.

Contact, when understood in this way, calls forth for a violence of touch—and here we begin to speak of the kind of touch that actualises and depletes gestural potentiality. This is particularly felt if we encounter the violence suffered by bodies that are out of sync or bodies whose rhythms are not those of the majoritarian milieu. In these cases, touch as contact and communication is violent, and it encroaches on the zest of potentiality and reconfigures the distance between bodies in such a way that, instead of a productive co-alignment based on disjunction, it leads to a homogenisation of the field of potentials. We can no longer work with the parameters of style and inflection because the violence of touch has erased them all. What we have, instead, is the complete actualisation that touch has introduced. Rather than a metastable system, we have a totality, and rather than an ontogenetic operation, we have a discrete and particular being that is perfectly in sync with the remaining constituents of that totality. The distance is bridged, the contact is established, and the problem of communication is solved. Now that everything is perfectly in sync, there is no way to communicate a difference in the first place. The cost of this operation, however, is the exhaustion of the virtual and the creation of an environment that fully conforms to the imperatives of being, of that which already is. What can be done, if at all: the response here can only be a "revolutionary negativity" (Culp 2016, 2), a disgruntled voice raised against walls of complacency.

Gestural potentiality entails a completely different definition of touch. Gestural potentiality operates from a vantage point that entails a confluence of things and their environments in a multitudinous interweaving of rhythms and inflections. Here we do not have regions of vacuity and object regions but a continuity as any boundaries between "bodies" and "environments" are maximally permeable. We speak of bodies–environments to capture the increasingly spectral quality of interpenetrating bodies and their milieus. The problem of communication and the need for contact become false problems as bodies–environments are always already and not yet in contact, always already and not yet communicating. The movement from potentiality to actuality is not an exhaustion of the virtual but its intensification. Each passage towards the actual brings forth another inflection from within the virtual field, an enrichment of its thresholds of interaction that, in turn, carry individuation forward. The pull of the virtual is felt every time when a body exceeds itself and begins to spill over its edges; language breaks open to put on display the logic of nonsense that conditions and sustains logical discourse; or when the experiential senses arrive at a frontier that cannot be traversed with the instruments of epistemological inquiry and plunge into a region whose knowing is not a matter of epistemological access.

Touch can also be a mediator, the very interstice that is at stake in the variety of passages between the knowable and the unknown. This is a repository of response that carries within itself an environmental ethics that is cosmic in its scope, "an ecosophical terrain of thought coalescent as material, affective, and activist" (MacCormack 2012, 139). Through touch, bodies become unceasingly. Touch negotiates the brittle boundaries between bodies, creates a site of fluidity wherein one can enter and re-enter the territories of others, and maps out areas of possibility. Touch itself is not primary, nor is the body as a transducer of much significance. It is the potentiality that the gesture of touching perturbs within and upon a body when one is approached as a repository of response.

So apart from the vandalising, disruptive quality that touch brings forth, we also have an operation of engendering. Not exactly the destruction of a body but its unceasing, the opening of a relation to the virtual, the gliding towards something that invariably exceeds itself and becomes part of a cloud of not-quites and not-yets:

> Each opening of one body to another brings into play an inherent intercorporeal susceptibility—with all the risks and possibilities this entails. In so doing, it inevitably articulates a further opening of these bodies to the more extended volatility of the earthly environment.
>
> (Clark 2011, 161)

This focus on engendering allows us to step out of debates on access. Engendering makes it possible to abandon the need to have access to a world because one is already both "in remoteness *and* contact" (Nancy 1997, 59; emphasis added). That is to say, we become open to a mode of enquiry that allows us distinctness and embeddedness at once. One is "among", "between", and "towards"—but not "confronting" discrete objects. The intricate dynamics between seemingly opposing forces such as sense and nonsense, access and impenetrability, are not of interest any longer. Instead of all this, we take a plunge into the multifarious enfleshings of touch.

So touch is not only the annihilation but also the recomposition of a form. This is a scrambling that allows us to make something new out of an existing functional apparatus. In foregrounding the linkage between the generative force of matter and the engendering force of potentiality, touch delivers to us one of those boiling points in the making of a body. It becomes the capture of the virtuality of the actual and the actualising of the virtual. Matter reclaims its generative zest; bodies find a capacity to precipitate structural change out of their own resources and emerge anew out of the depths of their materiality. This is also a way of being "in the event" that guarantees a continued supply of metastability within a system. Just like a body is the transducer in the precipitation of change—the conduit and the vessel through which the force of the virtual can flow—touch is the carrier of the event. The event allows bodies to co-emerge out of the resources of their own potentials and perturbations.

Lia Rodrigues asks: "What are... possible ways of being together? The fusion of individuals until they merge? Asserting our own boundaries and singularity?" (Levy 2016, n.p.). In *Pindorama*, we have the violence of bordering emerging each time that the dancers get caught within the foil—as bodies washed up on a shore or hurled into a mass grave—or delineate a territory within the performing space in deliberate terra-forming gestures. The repotentialising force engendered by the very landscape, then, is re-established through touch. Touching, in an interweave of *sensing* and *feeling*, has the capacity to re-pattern the field of potentiality yet again and cause the virtual to re-enter the expansive land- and soundscape. At the same time, touch exposes the conditions of violence that weave the fabric of *Pindorama*.

Violent Conditions

Violence is to be understood in and through the various conditions it engenders and from which it emerges. Conditions make violence possible and it is conditions that make it thrive. "Violent conditions" (Laurie and Shaw 2018) are not intrinsic to individuals, nor are they homogeneous and atomic. Rather, such conditions can be seen as the "existential climates by which localized subjects and worlds condense into being" (Laurie and Shaw 2018, 8) but also vicariously show how "violence is embedded in the flesh and bones of our worlds" (ibid., 8). Conditions are the starting points of worlding. These conditions can be as vast a spectrum as ecological, economic, psychological, geographic, and physiological. This, in turn, is tightly linked to a definition of violent conditions as the geographies of being that undermine life's flourishing (Tyner 2016) and the very definition of violence put forward by Galtung in the 1960s: "the cause of the difference between the potential and the actual, between what could have been and what is" (Galtung 1969, 168).

Violence operates on the very threshold between actual and virtual acting as a selective sieve that grants or denies access to actualisation. Accordingly, violence can be conceptualised as any force that sustains and perpetuates the threshold of acceptability; that is to say, any force that makes the threshold insurmountable, actively widens the gap, is unable or unwilling to lessen that gap, or simply turns a blind eye to an invariably present discrepancy between "what could be" and "what is". This leads us to a definition of violence that does not have intentionality or a particular discrete human subjectivity at its core. This is, rather, a definition of violence that is *atmospheric*. Here we speak of a dispersive hive-intelligence-like spectral kind of violence that is embedded in a wealth of interweaved practices—ecological, economic, and so on—and carried out by a myriad of knowing and unknowing agents and recipients of agency. Beneath the visible layer of concrete violence manifestations, we have an intricate weave of cultural, infrastructural, and systemic violence—the latter indicating violence-enabling ontological systems—at work:

> Bodies inhabit a world shaped by social ideas and practices. Each body's visible traits, its place in prevailing social hierarchies, affects its exposure to the world—how a body is seen, heard, approached. Visible attributes thus affect how it sees, speaks, and approaches the world. These actions enter into the constitution of the flesh of the world, which in turn coils over each body and weaves its flesh. The social-material world touches upon and folds into even the tiniest element of human carnality.
> (Rivera 2015, 133)

Just like the event in Deleuze, violence does not exist in and for itself but inheres and subsists in states of affairs. It is more of an energetic influx that gives a certain being its texture but only gains an existence in the varieties of practices and structures built in its name. Unlike the event, however, violence is not infinitely open to variation, to a plenitude of mutations within and without being, and to a wealth of modalities. Violence seeks to limit and diminish variation. It seeks to widen and sustain the gap between virtual and actual, that is, between one's felt capacity to fully express oneself in a given world—which is the pull of the virtual—and one's actual conditions that enable or disable this capacity or allow for its enfolding only to a certain extent—which is the pull of the actual. Violence works in the name of actualisation: it seeks to narrow down, impose, and contain possibility. And violence presents us with a "truncated life" (Laurie and Shaw 2018, 8).

Violence, then, also becomes a problem for the virtual and a question of atmospheres and tonalities in practices of matter-forming. Conditions can be conceptualised through the virtual as generative, energetic, thriving on potentiality and the work of transductive powers, co-shaping but also straitjacketing being in its very texture. Here we do not simply have beings shaped by and enmeshed in already existing conditions or pre-determined by a variety of situations. A tradition of violence unmistakably pre-exists and is very much felt in a world. But that which is "handed over" in the form of accepted practices is paired with that which is continually co-constituted and re-negotiated at the very moment of its concrete articulation within a given world. We do not have a scenario in which agents and recipients of agency unwittingly "respond to directives" but a scenario in which agents and recipients continually re-enact their violent conditions.

This reading of violence allows us to speak of worlds actively constituting themselves in ways that may or may not include violence. But the possibility of bending violent conditions exists. "Little public spheres" (Hickey-Moody 2013) and enabling "working recognitions" (Hickey-Moody 2016) can be introduced into an otherwise unyielding milieu. Such discrete enclaves for the work of potentiality subtly alter the ontological fabric of the overarching region of violent conditions. Or we can work within the scope of devastation:

> Devastation does not simply amount to the existence of destructive qualities themselves or destruction per se. Devastation relates to changes in the conditions of becoming and can be of a form of very active production, reconfiguring the relations between stability and change, expansion and contraction, wreaking havoc in chains linking habitats to cosmologies …
>
> (Fuller and Goriunova 2017, 326)

The conditions of a milieu are a matter of a decision made in the act of constitution and engagement—or an unwillingness to engage—with processes of materialisation that carry within themselves the tinge of violence. In this way, violent conditions are

> similar to the climates from which fleeting weather patterns emerge—the atmospheres by which social reality condenses. A condition does not

simply define what is, or what must be, but *what can be*: the fields of potential that nourish the already-existing.

(Laurie and Shaw 2018, 12)

Beings emerge out of conditions and unwittingly co-shape these same conditions in a perpetual co-alignment between condition and world. And whereas discrete practices can alter the texture of violence to a certain extent, a complete reinvigoration of the conceptual atmospheres surrounding those violent conditions is needed to make this change significantly tangible. This is why "learning how materiality's configurations influence the epistemological processes through which we understand and therefore constitute things, our human and non-human relationships, and ourselves, is indeed a matter of urgency" (Battista 2018, 191).

The concept of "world" is at stake here. This is not Heidegger's anthropocentric world in which stones are worldless (Heidegger 1995, 177). Nor is this a world concept that presupposes a strong boundary between the living and the non-living, existent and non-existent, and sentient and non-sentient. The stance that our world concept adopts towards such distinctions, rather, is "you never know"—but also, more fundamentally, "it does not matter". A world is a generative system, a metastable locale somewhere between actual and virtual, immersed in its own practices of engendering and pushing forward choices at each and every step. Violence, in one such world, is the perpetual encroachment of the actual.

It only takes a choice, an active engagement with the practices of limitation, to cause this atmosphere of violence to become dense and become an actual participant in matter-forming. In looking at these conditions and the virtual regions of violence, one becomes capable of seeing how "justice is also material, ecological, geographical, geological, geopolitical, and geophilosophical. Justice is a more-than-human endeavor" (Ulmer 2017, 834). And this definition is already a call for practices of decolonised, participatory, "engendered diverse peace" (Oswald Spring 2021, 25).

One could claim, along these lines, that the question of violence and the problem of conditions are ecological queries. This is not merely a question of enabling, allowing for a force to show its power, of making space and leaving spaces open, but also a question of co-constitution in a quasiverse of conflicting interests and a wealth of limitations to one's ability to cope and thrive:

> … to apprehend violence only with its surface-level expressions is to bypass its subjacent virtuality. Conditions are constituted by the topological circuits between the virtual and the actual: indexed by ancient materialities, emergent events, immanent thresholds, and multiple and decaying bodies. This understanding moves past linear instances of causality between actualized bodies—and thus, of direct, personalized violence. Violence is always bound by, and produced by, conditions: it is not a thing,

person, or event that is hermetically sealed from the world. That is to say, violence is a condition: the condition of truncated life ...

(Laurie and Shaw 2018, 16)

Speaking of violence in terms of the virtual, then, does not only encompass the kind of violence that forecloses perseverance in one's own being, that is, it is not bound to the physical fact of surviving alone, but also touches on questions of flourishing. Truncating a life is not simply equivalent to the practice of "shortening lives" (Di Paola and Garasic 2014) but is weaved into larger questions of sustainability, "inescapably local and particular" (Maggs and Robinson 2016, 184) and emerging out of public practices.

If we turn to *The Nicomachean Ethics* and seek to disentangle Aristotle's definition of happiness as the "highest good" (1094a), we see that this definition is, perhaps unsurprisingly so, linked to the concept of end or a purpose and, directly, to the concepts of potentiality and actuality. Happiness is "unqualifiedly final, chosen only for its own sake and never for the sake of anything else" (Irwin 2012, 508). A "happy life"—that which has been able to flourish—is defined as an end in itself and not as a means. Even though we have an entelechial definition—"happiness is becoming that which one already is"—this definition shows us how flourishing is not simply the perseverance in and enfolding of one's being. In addition to that, we have a connection to the field of potentialities—this connection engenders both a world and an ability to make the resources of potentiality flow. And then again, the concept of violence is related to the broader political question of social equality and egalitarian co-habitation across intersecting forms of world-making. It reiterates Butler's claim that non-violence is a political position found within a political field where violence is most readily exerted on those most severely exposed to its lethal effects. Lives claimed to be ungrievable, and lives that do not even count as lives are those that become the playground for violent acts:

> To be grievable is to be interpellated in such a way that you know your life matters; that the loss of your life would matter; that your body is treated as one that should be able to live and thrive, whose precarity should be minimized, for which provisions for flourishing should be available.
>
> (Butler 2020, 59)

So the question of violence is an ecological question. In and for themselves, the efforts of perseverance, the securing of one's existence, succeeding in remaining alive and other such manifestations of systemic violence are grounded in an organismic concept of ecology. A virtual ecology, however, would see these efforts as part of a more comprehensive paradigm that deals with the *expression* of being and continual—albeit conflicting—practices of world-making across a field of potentialities. Truncated life is not only that which "ends abruptly" because of a variety of material conditions and ways of thinking that suspend mobility across levels and fields of interaction. A truncated life does not necessarily need to be one that is "vitally surrendered" but a life that is not having the conditions allowing it to thrive on the resources of potentiality. Life expectancy is not necessarily measured in years but also incorporates more subtle parameters such as the extent to which a life has been decoupled from its violent conditions or, alternately, is irreparably entangled in them. Perhaps this is why Rodrigues states,

> I believe that in my country the artistic act cannot be restricted to the creation of an artwork; one must at the same time occupy a space, create a territory and provoke the conditions to survive in it. To build a terrain so that the work of art may exist.
>
> (Scott 2016, n.p.)

This, itself, is a practice of engendering that supersedes existing narratives of oppression that compel us, as Simone Weil ruminates, to "have only the choice between surrender and adventure" (Weil 2004, 58). Rodrigues gives us active engendering while being in the mesh of things.

Truncated lives and truncated worlds are those that have not been able to establish a connection with the virtual. Condition and connection are related and mutually determining concepts inasmuch as a condition supplies the locality and the spatial parameters for a body whereas connection supplies the continuity between locales and thresholds of matter. In this way, we never have simply a discrete entity entirely at the sway of highly localised conditions but a quasiverse of virtualities that forecloses the keeping of bodies "in their place". Because of the interplay of condition and connection, we can no longer have a scenario in which "The world watches in agreement as people are told their status—their actuality—is good enough" (Laurie and Shaw 2018, 15). Even if *this* world simply watches in agreement, other worlds *might* not offer their consent. The transformative force of this "might" peers through bodies as a reminder that "this" world cannot be the only one.

Even if bodies are irreparably entangled with local conditions, connectivity within the field of potentiality enables entrance into different practices and modes of relating. This allows us a vantage point from which violence is not continually stable and equally distributed across the field of potentiality. Events of violence, together with their less pronounced yet more pervasive counterparts, structural and systemic violence, are limited and local. They operate at frequencies that may not be shared with the entirety of a field. A shift in register, an alteration of tonality, and a slight dent into the texture of what appears to be the way of things might be enough to introduce change in violent conditions. The vast resource of the virtual may seep through present articulations, altering both existing conditions and tangled connectivities, de-legitimising the perpetuity of violence by decoupling the conditions of a world from violent world-making practices.

As a "transversal" condition and a matter of a trans-subjective ecology (Guattari 1989), violence is something that circulates through subjects, condensing in violent worlds. Looking at bodies through organismic ecologies, though, is not the only legitimate way to disentangle the perpetuity of violent being. Guattari's ecologies of the virtual, too, receive a place within the equation as these put on display a capability to recompose the given and place a new inflection within a world. Violent conditions impose a politics of constraint onto worlds that are at once *conditioned* to accept a tradition of violence as "handed over", perpetually reassuring us that "this is the way" and "things really are so", and, in turn, *conditioning* the perseverance of one such world bearing the shape of violence. From the vantage of the virtual, however, a politics of violence—as defined by Galtung—becomes but one neither particularly competitive nor attractive world model within a multifarious quasiverse. Within this wider quasiverse, a politics of all-connection to the resources of becoming is far more yielding than a politics of restraint and a withholding of these resources. Conditions can ally with connectivities to cause new practices of world-making to coalesce, to come up with ontologies that foreclose violent conditions at the outset, that leave a space for critical openness at every step while moulding bodies at the interstice between actual and virtual.

Eschewing violence is a question of technique. Forming alliances with movement and creating types of motion that evade the organismic translates a body into a rhythmic system of co-determinative practices that can change pace and tonality at any step. We think in terms of a non-entelechial motioning-toward, an approaching of a politics of the "almost", not so much of the "more than" (human, worldly, this) as of the "not quite" and the unresolved. This would not be a politics of overcoming but a politics of engagement with. Even "humans" are not seen as "transitional animals" (Blake et al. 2012, 6) on the way to "becoming-other-than" but as locales of perpetual negotiation maximally receptive to others. Engagement is an attunement towards co-existence, relational traversing, and a shift towards regimes of greater plasticity.

A politics of engagement does not entail movement as striving. Here we would rather conceptualise engagement in terms of enhanced receptivity. Engagement is directionless to the extent that it does not necessarily strive at an arrival. Engagement is matter-forming via a comprehensive receptivity. One such comprehensive receptivity gives one a direct sense of the ways relations are distributed and of the web of relations out of which entities are composed. Also, comprehensive receptivity allows us to sense the relations manifest in the subtle interstitial intervals between stillness and movement. Movement is not an entity distinct from bodies and bodies cannot persist as such without movement. Instead, movement-bodies are environments of receptivity that are only and always *pre-constituted* regardless of the intensity of the movement and the vastness of the environments they make. This state of perpetual pre-constitution allows movement-bodies to remain maximally permeable, maximally open to the virtual, crossing over a variety of practices in pursuit of the "nothing in particular".

Pre-constitution is also that which gives an entity its dynamism. Again, beneath the nominal distinction between form and matter, we have a spontaneous morphogenesis whereby matter becomes generative and forming out of its own resources without an external organising principle. This is a "motionless journey" across the entirety of the spectre of potentiality and yet without ever visibly departing from the actual. Pre-constitution is where the force of the virtual is felt and wherein movement-bodies partake in the morphogenesis materially, intensively, and through unconstrained spontaneous self-forming. The force of the virtual manifests itself where materiality comes to be as various degrees of intensive co-alignments traverse an environment. A "plastic principle" (Hughes 2012, 34) is at play.

Albeit invariably and only in pre-constitution, movement-bodies become the very expressions of this virtual force. Through engagement, one becomes receptive to the various political entanglements that make relations and hence bodies. And violence is foreclosed at the very outset, *in pre-constitution* and at the point where intensities together with their potential entanglements are yet formed and negotiated. As movement-bodies fold and refold, the potentiality of matter becomes manifest. Together with this exposure to the sheer force of matter, one also chooses to arrive at movement-bodies that are entirely alien to violence. A receptive engagement with the virtual has put forward an enhanced sense of relation. And this is a matter of technique: the modelling of one's climates and atmospheres in ways that simply show a full indifference to the politics of repression.

A technique is needed in order to articulate and present the work of moving co-composition as an interweave of iteration and difference. Here the technicity of touch is something that nurtures bodies as matters of collective individuation. What is summoned in the technicity of touch is an event. The brink of novelty, the surge of an affective co-composing within an expansive body, is all the result of becoming and the introduction of an event in the flux of becoming. That which touches is not a body but a co-composition of virtualities. Touch is not inherent and is not to be described in ontological terms as the potentiality of actuality; we have a movement which thrives on the extra-ontological force of the event.

In order to preserve its relative integrity, a body requires this touch-event that adds up to its continual engendering. A genesis is not an assault to integrity but the necessary condition for a body's preservation. That, however, would be an integrity that is constantly being attuned to the emergent ecologies within and without a body. And if one is to speak of integrity as perseverance within one's own boundaries, this perseverance is only enabled through constant moving with. Touch is not a decentring or a productive disorientation. It is the very expression of what an "attunement" might be. This enhanced conceptual receptivity towards the event of attunement makes us very much aware that the body is neither the beginning nor the end of becoming but a fragile intermediary: "the body is a relative fact, a phase of being" (Manning 2013, 16). Even more so, "event and milieu are always

Touch and Event

An engagement with the virtual engenders an event. An event is this evanescent extra-ontological non-entity that has no existence of its own yet changes everything. A decision to touch is a decision to be in the event, to engage, and to enter into a negotiation at the brittle boundary between the infinite and finitude. Opting for the finite also involves a decision to become less, to contract the cloud of virtualities into a manageable shape, and to agree to work with that shape. Yet the touch of actualisation is far more complex and nuanced. The touch of actualisation can ultimately turn out to have been a gesture of abyssal generosity but also, in being transformative, can equally well destroy a given system.

A body is a system for the generation of worlds: "To have a body ... is to be traversed with virtualities" (Alloa 2014, 153). As something that continually sustains an environment, a body only thrives because of the incessant resource of potentiality that the virtual field feeds into it. At the same time, it is not the arrival at the actual but the decision to enter into intentionality that precipitates violence for a body. In entering a region of intentionality, the body is no longer related to virtual becoming—a touch without an object, non-purposive gestural potentiality that only has the touch itself as its teleological aim. In intentionality, one desires an object. There is a striving towards a finality and there is a misrecognition of oneself as self.

Touch incarnates this paradoxical meeting point whereby we encounter both directionality as violence and gestural potentiality as the affirmation of the dissipative character of a system. Violence is directional. It is a precipitator of change that is, in all possible senses, productive. This is why systems of oppression employ violence: it invariably yields results. Gestural potentiality, on the other hand, is a supreme example of ontological impracticality. It does not produce and its movement does not move towards anything in particular. Gestural potentiality is the locale that escapes the violence of directionality, intention, and desire. At the same time, the region of potentiality can be a conduit for encounters of the most violent kind. Potentiality provides an ambience for the recompositions of a body that can be quite fortuitous at times. And touch carries both this violence and an interweave of forces that exceed bodies and their environments, causing actualisations to yet again become dissipative. A touch remains at the interstice of the virtual whereby one can choose in favour of the violence but can also remain ontologically imperceptible, "in the event". This is a locale of entanglements with unknowability but also a chance to engender finitude. The gesture of touching does not simply expose a surfeit of the indefinite but exposes the complexity of the relation between being and becoming, an awakening to a body's entanglements and ecological response where one is approached in relation.

It is bodies that allow for such transitions between worlds. Again, these are conduits for the virtual. At the same time, with their very positing, bodies mark an entrance into the actual. The same goes for violence not only as a rupture but also as a facilitator for the recompositions of a body. Violence shows how a body spills over its edges, is slit open, and exposed to cosmic fortuity. Potentiality reaches a maximum: where violence has been exerted, bodies are perturbed and displaced to such an extent that that they exit finitude. In this sense, violence does not precipitate the cessation of a body, nor does it present us with a body that is petrified in having exhausted the virtual: "Violence always exceeds it-self. In this sense, violence is always witness to the incompleteness of its own project. Violence is the constant reminder of the body's potential for metamorphosis, of its movements of desire and its multiplicitous sensations" (Manning 2007, 66).

The topos of violence allows for another way of looking at the dynamics between touch and potentiality—through the question of the touchable. Touching is making available to the senses, bringing forth into presence, exorcising an entity into visibility, persuading a thing to reveal itself. Yet one's reaching towards an entity does not immediately give one license to perceive of things as touchable. Another mode of co-subsisting in a world, an ethos of not-engaging, of creating space and giving space, and of allowing a thing to remain withdrawn, presents itself with the logic of touch. This is a logic inherent in gestural potentiality as a logic of the perseverance of the irreducible, that is, the safeguarding of distance and retaining the interstice. At the same time, this is also a logic that sustains the unknowable, nurtures the kind of thinking that imposes violence on the known, and maintains the boundary between being and becoming.

"We will not ask therefore what is the sense of the event: the event is sense itself", says Deleuze (1990, 22). And in *The Sense of the World* (1997), Jean-Luc Nancy proposes that a loss of possibility is equivalent to a loss of reality. If we cannot have access to a meaning, then we cannot have access to a world. Optimistically, a withdrawal of meaning is simultaneously a withdrawal of reference and hence a foreclosing of the actual. To make meaning redundant is to cause a world to withdraw. But then again, meaning is also related to classical potentiality. These two constituents are involved in a careful balancing act. A maximum of meaning is a minimum of sense and vice versa. A maximum of sense also alludes to maximum potentiality and, hence, an almost complete withdrawal of a representational "meaningful"' world. Once we have reached a region almost exclusively composed of sense, that region we have in front of us is utterly unrecognisable. This is a region devoid of mimesis and maximally potential. Potentiality, a withdrawal of meaning, an irrelevance of reference: the simultaneous presence of such constituents within a given region tells us that this region has become open to the work of sense.

Where the actual has vanished, we are accustomed to remaining on the lookout for something not quite of the order of meaning. We look for sense. Where the actual has become withdrawn and we no longer deal with reference, we begin to seek potentiality. But then again, Nancy implies something counterintuitive. Where possibility has vanished, we can no longer speak of a reality. Here we move towards the very other end of the scales. What if possibility was completely and entirely depleted? In this case, we would not simply have a "world" that is maximally actual, that is, referential. We would have no world at all. World and sense are each other's doubles: their co-presence cannot be readily negotiated and they seldom operate on the same ontological plane. At the same time, world and sense are mutually inextricable: it is a sense that sustains worlds. A world cannot put on display the work of reference if it were not for a subterranean influx of sense.

Sense cannot be foreclosed and sought in isolation. Sense does not even show itself—unless it begins to exceed meaning. But then again, sense is vicariously constituted, generated in passing, and encountered somewhere in the peripheral visual field but never locatable centrally. Sense cannot be confronted. Full visibility cannot be thought in relation to sense. Sense is a practice of the body and a practice in the genesis of worlds. As such, it can at best be obliquely located in the region of gestural potentiality—a spacing sustained by excess. This is a region outside of being—if there is any existence to be attached to it, this is the very particular *style* in which a sense co-creates and is co-present.

Sense is "neither a property nor a substance" (Nancy 1997, 27), "cannot be produced", "nor does it produce itself, not having the resources of a subject. It is 'produced' in the remarkable sense of 'taking place', 'happening'" (ibid., 28). We have a production without a subject and a creative act that is self-engendered and self-propelled, albeit devoid of intentionality. Across a variety of ontologies of sense, sense is defined as a "non-existent" yet "haunted" by existence. In a way, sense even depends on existents as it is entities that allow sense to perform its work. In terms of gestural potentiality, sense is best described as "a sense", "that which is not *in* its end" but "*toward* itself":

> ... distance, direction, intention, attribution, élan, passage, gift, transport, trance, and touch: sense in all senses, sense of the existent. ... in Aristotle the model of that which is a single act, a single entelechy, even as it differs within itself as one being from another being, is sense as the act of sensing and being sensed: the act of sensing and the act of the sensed are the same. Existence is the act internally differing from its own sense, its self-sensation as its own dehiscence.
>
> (Nancy 1997, 28)

Sense signals a withdrawal of a world, but equally so, this withdrawal could be a spontaneous reopening and becoming susceptible to one's exposure to a world. Sense is not a supplement, nor is it an aftermath of being. It has a far more complex relationship to being, always orienting itself towards a world and composing itself in response to the compositions of the worlds it traverses. A sense cannot be thought as an effect of being or an emanation resulting from a particular concatenation from within being. Sense can rather be described in terms of the excess of the virtual that is inherent in gestural potentiality—of having been "this sense" and becoming "a sense". As sense ensues, it shows us exactly what it is: "the opening of its very supervenience, of being-toward-the-world" (Nancy 1997, 28).

The world cannot be accessed through sense. Rather, worlds become palpable in spite of sense. And what is needed is a certain callousness: a "cold eye, this insensitivity to sense" (Nancy 1997, 38). This condition grants us not only access but also an understanding of a world. If we focus on "the" world itself—not on the "a" and the "towards"—then existence begins to pick up pace. We arrive to a region that is not "extending towards" but "made available". This region is not a concatenation of chance encounters but the work of a decision. In other words, we arrive at a locale where things are "established". Even more so, we begin to have actors. These actors populate the world—not "a" world but "the world"—and exuberantly choose to exist. Further still, they do so in concrete ways—existing as examples of "this" and "that". The world is to be gained by turning a blind eye to sense.

At the same time, saying that sense is "towards a world" may evoke the impression that sense is somehow located outside of a world in a spatial co-composition. But when Nancy speaks of "the sense of the world", the philosopher does not imply a spatial concept that involves sense being located outside of its world. Nor are worlds seen as, strictly speaking, places with a background, that is, places with sense-bestowing external locales. Sense cannot take place "in the outside" unless we speak of a world which "has its outside on the inside" (Nancy 1997, 54). Sense is an "out-of-place instance" that "opens itself up within the world" (ibid., 55). And it is in this manner that we can speak of sense as a "toward" and an orientation without an existence. It is not exactly an additive to existents but more of a super-addition; it is not, strictly speaking, an externality but a "toward" that is already "within". A world, then, is a moving co-genesis of an extra-existent and a more or less constituted environment. The focus is on the immanence of the movement in the kind of an environment that shapes itself prior to actualisation, that is, prior to the point where we would be able to speak of "*the* world".

There is a quality of sense that Nancy calls a "transimmanence"—indissolubly ideal and material at once—and that shows its connection of pervasiveness:

> Quite simply, that the sense of the world is this world here as the place of existence. This 'quite simply' contains the most formidable stake, the one that requires of us, in order to say this absolutely simple *thing, a completely different style or, rather, an interminable alteration of style.*
>
> (Nancy 1997, 56)

If sense is the inflection, then matter also becomes a participant in the intra-manoeuvring of world-forming as "the very difference through which *something* is possible, as *thing* and as *some*" (ibid., 57). On the one hand, we are exposed to the work of the inflection and are, therefore, open to a wealth of modulations that build up the given; on the other hand, we have the connectivity of virtual and actual—of some and thing—that build up matter-differing:

> Matter means here: the reality of the difference ... that is necessary in order for there to be something and some things and not merely the identity of pure inherence ... Matter is a matter of real difference, the difference of the *res*: if there is something, there are several things; otherwise, there is nothing; no 'there is'. Reality is the reality of the several things there are; reality is necessarily a numerous reality.
>
> (Nancy 1997, 58)

Apart from sense as an inherence and an inflection, we have the generative activity of differing, existing, and causing to exist. And then, we have a connection. Gestural potentiality is the region that enables this interfusion, where matter populates environments with things and sense gives them a wealth of modulations.

Sense has the force to repotentialise through the plasticity of movement that is its basic condition. Being defined predominantly through its characteristic as an "orientation", sense displays the entire exuberance of the tension between "this world", "the world", and "a world". In a manner of speaking, this activity of sense touches on another basic condition of the composition of a world—movement. Sense works through movement and its mode is that of the passage. It does not reconfigure and does not recompose but creates conditions and opens up alleys through which worlds can do so.

The opening towards sense gives us one instance of how the concrete is simultaneously the virtual. We have a wealth of potentiality and a multitude of matter-forming activities permeated with sense all the way throughout in such a way that "the outside is on the inside". Speaking of sense also allows us to better articulate the relationship between movement, mattering and forming, acceleration and slowness, the gradations of force, and the generative power of the "not quite". Sense pervades all these components in the genesis of a world to sustain them. It gives a world the solidity required for its stature as a "reality" region within a virtual quasiverse. At the same time, the opening up of sense within an already constituted world also exposes the work of constitutive forces, never quite letting us forget that none of "this" is properly existent and properly solid. Sense reminds us that, even when it is utterly solidified, "this world" is still not so much a matter of being as a "style of being", an orientation and modulation without a subject. What we have been accustomed to call "this world" happens to be an inflection within a quasiverse composed of the movements and cadences of a multifarious "not quite".

Repotentialising Matter

Again, since metastable systems are in a state of continual disequilibrium, we have a surfeit of potentiality and a focus on the very forming of relations within this oversaturated landscape of shimmering selves. The event introduces disequilibrium within a system and the shimmer of potentiality is distributed across its fields of interaction in novel regroupings. In metastability, we do not have a distinction between the formal and the material as both are interwoven in the generative zest of potentiality. Reworking, or better still, rescrambling the connections and formations that have existed so far, the event can even reverse-engineer bodies previously known as "identities" to make them open to flows of an entirely different quality. Nothing is pre-constituted. The work of the event is rather in the finding and probing of a variety of qualities and textures, in trying out different colorations of the given.

To engender does not necessarily entail the radical alteration of a system and the entire regrouping of its constituents in unprecedented ways. Inducing metastability and becoming open to the work of the event can merely mean the introduction of an *inflection* within a system. Such slight refigurations foreground the aspectuality of the virtual. That is to say, they allow us to see the work of the virtual as the introduction of nuanced varieties of ways of being and becoming. What we have here is the foreplaying of the *aspect* of an entity—hence the preoccupation with the forming of relations—and not so much the entity as such. Further still, the engagement with the virtual allows us to see that bodies cannot be solid monolithic things but rather shimmering apparitions entirely composed of the aspects of a form that is never there. In fact, "being in the event" can be seen exactly as the oversaturation of an aspect, the drawing together of the wealth of all possibility into one loaded bundle of chance.

Each engendering participates in the virtual of the system at hand and is involved in the moulding of a multitude of configurations. This surfeit of configurations without a palpable order or logic makes a given form brittle. In thinning out, in entering the multitudinous, a given form also re-enters the play of potentiality and the work of differing. This potentialisation does not operate from within an already-formed body but foregrounds the work of novel configurations. When working through potentialised form, networks of codification are rescrambled anew.

Potentialised form still bears a tinge of the mimetic, however. Even when not pre-formed, potentialised form carries a certain normativity within itself. When we speak of the creative rescrambling of form, we still inadvertently evoke the ideal of a form in its "pre-scrambled" state. With the potentialisation of matter, on the other hand, we encounter an engendering without a point of orientation, a "nomadic normativity" (Braidotti and Pisters 2012). Here we do not have the burden of reference. The potentialisation of matter is also a forming, but this is a forming of a different ontological texture that takes us closer to the extra-ontological work of the event. The operation is atopological and can be likened to an overflowing whereby a body wells over its edges, becomes in surfeit of itself, and confuses the existing parameters of the systems at hand. And as we do not have the external imposition of form, we witness a matter-forming of an immanent cast. This practice of matter-forming has the quality of a force. The potentialisation that ensues cannot be sustained in a normative description. This potentialisation of matter is eruptive and fleeting, and operates in local bursts and spontaneous entanglements. As a variety of bodies populate the system, anybody can become a transducer and can enter this play of individuation.

In *Pindorama*, scarcity of form and a frugality of means is the approach—there is no light, no costumes, and no musical score. Dancers' bodies are raw and exposed; the materials used as props are pointedly insipid. All the while, the confluence created by bodies and materials generates its own musical score that is intensely situational—it involves the phenomena evoked by the very performing bodies in their interactions with non-human materials. We have the voice of flesh slamming against wet floors, the crunching of a plastic water bottle, the smashing of synthetic balloons, guttural vocals, heavy breathing, the swishing sounds of air as dancers are enmeshed in their work, and the sound created by the vigorous movement of the plastic foil. The music score, one could say, is entirely composed of tactile events. These tactile events emerge out of the confluence of bodies and non-biological artefacts—a bodily confluence that takes place in such a way that, together with a soundscape, an ontological landscape is being mapped out.

This is a *sensing* landscape. One is invited to co-shape a connection and experience proximity. While the darkened space discourages the scrutinising gaze, we have an abundance of sensorial stimuli and soundscaping gestures. These, in their entirety, amount to an intricately networked environment of *feeling*. The performing space is carved out of the black-box room through bodily sound and the voices of non-human materials to take on an existence of its own. One such networked landscape exists as both actual (*sensing*) and virtual (*feeling*), as cognitively available and speculative, and as finite and indefinite. The interweave of actual and virtual does not take place in the form of a linear progression but is one of continuous simultaneity. Sensing and feeling overlap—their togetherness is that of continuous mutual repotentialisation whereby those two nominally separate constituents of the landscape are layered onto one another in a spectral confluence. Matter repotentialises environments and environments repotentialise matter.

The repotentialisation of matter as an ontogenetic procedure additionally exposes a different definition of relation. Relation here is an immanent quality that is ubiquitous to the engendering of both form and matter in an extra-normative process. "Relation" does not imply the act of bringing together entities of a different ontological cast and has little to do with the establishing of communication. Rather, a relation triggers reverberations across a system and operates as an event. In relation, we have processes of recodification that help us define relating as a force in its own right.

The work of relation as a tensile force can find a place within a dialogue on an ethics of response and the triggering of responsiveness in systems. Relating is mining for potentiality. The phenomenon of response signals that a system has begun to shift towards this potentiality. This shift is not merely a motion towards emergence but a more intricate aggregate of outward moving and inner reconfiguring that is maximally expansive in its scope. Just as a body is the transducer in a metastable system of multitudinous co-determinations and just as touch is the event that signals the beginnings of the work of the new within a system, so is relating both an aspect of touch that is tensile in its character, and an aspect of response that shows a growing tendency toward potentiality. In the reality of the maximally virtual, we have entrance into new compositions that attest to the phenomenon of the potentialisation of matter and show how this phenomenon is woven within an intricate network of movement, gesture, a body, a touch, relating, and responsiveness. These, however, are stripped of their conventional capacities and senses. They rather serve as placeholders to attest to the infinite zest of the virtual. The virtual brings together potentialised matter and eventful immateriality, bodies that can be both corporeal and incorporeal, cases of engendering that operate "in the event", and operations of actualisation that counter-intuitively make us re-enter the virtual. Even more so, the work of these elements cannot be placed within a hierarchical dependence as each constituent is co-determined by its others in ways that cannot be subjected to a rigorous analysis. Because of their mutual entanglements, it is difficult to tell which initiates which and which triggers which—the regime is not one of mono-causality but of simultaneity.

Touch, seen in this way, is both a movement and a carrier of individuation as it expresses the alteration that a body goes through. At the same time, we cannot think of a body as such but only of a movement, of the type of motioning toward that was previously described as gestural potentiality. We do not deal with an identity and cannot conceptualise in terms of an environment that is separate from the individuating bodies that populate and co-constitute this same environment from within and from without. In a similar manner, we cannot think of touch without the intricate politics of gesture and the potentiality attached to it, nor can we conceive of the procedure of relating without immediately evoking its tangled ethics. Discerning—making any of these procedures separate and distinct—remains an abstract exercise and one can only make distinctions nominally, that is, for the sake of classificatory clarity. In the ontogenetic operation, we can only trace the movements of a genesis that scrambles together the practices of touch, response, and relating to give us glimpses into the very gesture of an object engaged in the task of its continual constitution. The work of individuation is not necessarily epistemologically accessible. It is, among other things, an invitation to think otherwise and seek ways of conceptualising that are indifferent to the tools of epistemology.

The ontogenetic procedure is born in the gesture of relating. Relating is opening oneself to allow the flows of contingency—of ontological vulnerability and of extra-ontological knowability—to enter in composition with a body:

> being together with others in ways that involve a constitutive exposure or vulnerability ... also entails articulations with forces far beyond the human. And not merely in a manner that involves the using or tapping of these forces, but also in ways that apprehend such forcefulness in and through its resurgent exteriority as an excitation, an impetus, an imperative.
>
> (Clark 2011, 143)

In the ontogenetic procedure, we do not think of relations and the terms of a relation but of a co-constitution in the various acts of responding. Bodies as transducers are also receptacles for the swirling of energies and forces that cause multiple entanglements. The repotentialisation of matter thus promises infinite mutation in the best possible sense: motion and pause, interstice and fullness, outward and inward are rescrambled and refracted upon themselves, vanishing and reappearing in mutant configurations.

We cannot think of a divide between matter and form but a composite that in itself is a perpetually constituted engendering, a coexistence of a multiplicity of regimes of being and extra-being. Engendering is a matter of expression. And expression, as we know from Deleuze (1990), is a way to be in connection with the event of sense. An inherence of an extra-ontological order, the event leaves its marks on an existing state of affairs without revealing anything of its nature and without becoming less elusive in the process of having shown itself. The work of engendering is similar to this as it shows us how a body undergoes an alteration and a recomposition that can be quite incorporeal at times. An alteration may not be "visible" or epistemologically accessible as such but can be a recomposition in the aspects of a body, a change in inflection that matters politically, ethically, and environmentally. Touch, engendering, and gestural potentiality create an amalgamation of forces that prompt us to expand expressivity in ways that are no longer self-serving and confined to the mere project of the becoming of a body. Here we deal with ways of potentialising as introducing inflections and aspects within a milieu carrying repercussions that can be planetary in their scope. This is a novel engagement with the expanse of being-becoming that—albeit perfectly open to chance—is informed, committed, and deliberate in its ethical and environmental zest.

Engendering Practice: On Environmentality

The force of a theatre of the virtual lies in its engendering of ethical, aesthetic, environmental, and political practices outside of any claim for epistemological access and outside of any wish to establish mimetic credibility. This is not a practice of persuasion and of gaining the upper hand. It is a practice of engaging and of painstakingly thinking with. The one thing that is at stake within one such landscape is one's intensive engagement with the virtual and one's ability to remain maximally open to its force. That type of engendering—motioning, touching, gesturing, potentialising matter, and entering the virtual—moves across interstices as an elusive simultaneity of disparate regimes. And this is the task of a theatre of the virtual—to safeguard the possibility of the extra-epistemological, uphold one's right to offer accounts of oneself from outside of being, all the while creating a fractured record of the wondrous mutations of a moving, gesturing body.

An experience of touch is also an encounter with the incorporeal. We have dwelt on the double nature of touch—on its capacity as a precipitator of violence and its force to be a carrier of the potentialising of matter. Then, we have touch as the event and the body as the transducer—both entering in a regime that allows them to remain maximally open to the virtual. And then again, we have the impositional quality of touch, the pact with the actual. It seems that entering the territory of touch becomes a careful political and environmental balancing act. We are prompted to move forward, live in the disruption, and remain open to chance. But, at the same time, we speak of withholding. Apart from a restless openness toward the virtual, here one also encounters a subterranean politics inherent in touch: a politics of retreat. Certain things are not to be touched and certain gestures have to pause in the middle, certain bodies should not move in certain directions, and certain becomings are to cease. We now have reached a point in this investigation that makes it possible to pose questions about one such approach to touch within a philosophy of the virtual. What is the significance of such disruptive gestures and sabotaged potentialisations?

A politics of retreat can easily be likened to a practice working in favour of the cessation of movement. Equally so, the force of touch can easily bring forth not liberation but organisation, the becoming-organism of a body. Yet the politics of retreat does not seem to work in favour of security; this is not about the safeguarding of an organism. Nor is it about interrupting individuation. Rather, we have a practice that seeks the retention of movement, a movement stretching out infinitely and withholding finality. The retention of movement can also become a way to multiply movement and make it expansive by momentarily freezing and foregrounding just one discrete aspect of the infinity of motion. A practice of organising, then, cannot be more than a temporary suspension of alteration and a short-lived freeze frame of a continuous invention. It is a different kind of game: not towards a greater articulation but towards the stretching of an articulation. Even a politics of repression reaches towards the same thing: a gestural potentiality.

And even a politics of withholding is susceptible to the work of gestural potentiality. Bodies and environments, environments–bodies, and bodies–environments are not unique identitarian subjects; they, however, become distinct through involvement in the intricate politics of touch. In gesturing, touching, and moving, a body–environment responds to a wealth of reverberations showing us the various mutations of the possible. But even more so, the dynamics within the politics of retreat outlined so far show us how even the impositional, the freezing and stratifying efforts within the work of potentiality carry the virtual within themselves: "Static bodies are a myth, a stabilizing projection of the nation-state's desire to construct an imaginary that can be reproduced only meiotically" (Manning 2009, 146). Even that which has been withheld from becoming is already in the virtual. Impositional scenarios can function only as abstract propositions. Bodies become available to recognition only momentarily, as temporary captures of this and that, and only to the extent that they show themselves in order to be recomposed in a second step. The work of the virtual resists the impulse towards stasis, reinvigorates where bodies become weary, and challenges violence from within a concept of gestural potentiality that is itself very much open to the fortuity of violence but also carries a promise for unforeseen liberation.

What ensues from one such engendering of an event is a becoming-environment. This, however, does not entail losing or dissolving one's otherwise solid boundaries. Here we have a flight from every determination. Such travels occur without a palpable change of locale. Change takes place in a clandestine manner, without altering the substance of the things it perturbs. Such expansion is a vital constituent of one's becoming as it invites an expansive co-alignment whereby a body stretches out to incorporate the entirety of its environment.

Movement appears to be grounded in corporeality and to be one of the many capacities of bodies. Bodies are perceived as primary whereas movement is a secondary, accidental capacity. A body can choose to move or not to move; it can generate motion out of its own resources—think of Aristotle's definition of "the living"—but it can also be perturbed by external forces that direct its motion. And from the vantage of a theatre of the virtual, movement becomes a cosmological category. Movement, rather than a mechanical activity of shifting direction, is the play of the actual and the virtual that brings forth the genesis of bodies. In a manner of speaking, it is movement that generates bodies as individuating environments.

The question of movement can also be posed without reference to a body. What is it that moves? Is movement that which moves or do we speak of an even more abstract event entirely inaccessible to human recognition? Within a theatre of the virtual, we speak of a movement without a body, a movement that may or may not have a body as its field of enaction. Movement is expansive and generative. In a theatre of the virtual, it is movement that we see as the foreground of things. Bodies are downplayed and movement has taken the scene. A theatre of the virtual traces the ways in which movement moves, looks at how movement creates both environments and ecologies, and witnesses how movement generates its own systems of valorisation. Movement, being one of the forces of potentiality, brings forth the politics of response on stage and viscerally demonstrates how response can recompose the given both from within and from without.

At the same time, there is no clear separation between movement, a body, and a world. Processuality pervades them all and gleans various layers of complexity out of their interaction:

> While each energy system is specific to its form, body, and action over time, the understanding of an ontology of body is never a question of singular knowledge but always one of an intra-active, politically situated knowledge performed through a biomaterialized field.
> (Colman 2015, 250)

Whereas movement is not simply the accidence of the body, it also is not separate from bodies and even less so is it detached from bodily environments. A theatre of the virtual gives us access to one such modality of perceiving where one can viscerally experience the generative force of movement while witnessing the becoming-environment of bodies.

A theatre of the virtual opens a door towards a level of perception that is richer in that it simultaneously allows access to the virtual as a speculative reality. This access is enabled by the witnessing of movement as an ecologising force. Movement renders visible the connections of processual pervasiveness that mark the given. It clears the ground for a modality of thought that foreplays not so much the discreteness of objects as the expansiveness of being. Through this focus on movement, a theatre of the virtual clears the ground for a new inflection in our ways of perceiving. This new perception invites us to cultivate a sense for the expanse and an affinity towards the force of the virtual.

Movement is a practice of testing out the virtual field, affectively engaging in various exercises of attunement and rhythmic co-alignment, the creation of an inflection and a tonality that allows us to think beyond the given and, therefore, makes the given richer. There is a sober rigour to movement as its work is that of sustaining the vitality of worlds. Movement itself is continually on the verge of shifting towards something else, working from within a maelstrom of speeds and intensities. It is an unmediated plunge into an expanse and an opening towards *feeling*. Here the conceptual does not disentangle itself from experiential openness but works together with *feeling*—the manifestation of the pressure of the virtual. The visceral and the conceptual do not form a dichotomy but subsist in movement as its two different inflections—as changes in tonality within the virtual field.

The moulding of climates and atmospheres, however, does not entail an engagement with an externality or the reconstitution of one's milieu only. What we have at hand when presented with a body is an "environmentality in the making" (Manning 2013, 32). Environmentality (Foucault 2001) here is not the asymmetrical scaling and management of relationships of power and technologies of knowledge production within human–environment interactions but an expansive practice of co-determination. What is felt in this gesture is how bodies manifest themselves as quasiversal motilities. These motilities represent knots of response varying in intensity and differing in the texture of their being. One does not conceptualise through the apparatus of "inside" and "outside" but through the matter-forming force of the virtual. The force of the virtual is both directionality and a refusal to go in any particular direction. Again, this is the "not quite" and "nothing in particular" of something in the making, that is to say, an expansive environment wherein bodies and movement are interchangeable. And what the pre-constituted accounts for is exactly this wealth and permeability of the passage between virtual and actual, a *feeling* that is continually and only being made, perpetually matter-forming. We cannot encounter the form and the made.

Change here does not necessarily entail anything groundbreaking. Again, a change can be an alteration in tonality, a shift in inflection. At the same time, change spreads across the entirety of an affected system. Even when we do not have an alteration in the substance of things, a subtle modification that is purely of *style* can precipitate tremendous variation. Change, hence, is not something that can be aligned with the substance of things. Rather, change is related to the virtual and carries out its work. Change lives off the permeability of a system, that is, off the inventive zest of an environment that self-constitutes within landscapes of contingency. Through a closer look at the nature of change, we can witness the interchangeability of emptiness and matter-forming, that is, of the virtual and the cornucopia of worlds that the virtual produces. We see how an environment is shaped *rhythmically* and via the work of *style*. We also see how it is coloured through the inflection that engagement introduces within its domain. All of this takes place within the region of the pre-constituted.

Even a minimum of gesture takes us to this pre-constituted region. Here entities do not have an intrinsic value, nor do they become fully formed as entities out of the relations that co-constitute them. Entity-hood is not expressed in a thing's capacity to persevere as a discrete object or as a co-constituting force within an environment. Entity-hood is expressed in the non-entelechial emergence within the field of potentiality, in the *feeling* of a growing edge. If locatable at all, then, entity-hood can be attributed not to discrete objects and their environments but to the passage wherein the forces of potentiality become manifest. The passage, the very figure of gesturing, is that which carries things towards their entity-hood as they are coloured by the pull of the virtual. The passage makes relations *felt*. Gesture, that is to say, the expression of potentiality, signals an opening towards conjunctive thinking. Here entities in the pre-individual region co-determine their limits and the conditions of their existence within a world. We witness the very modes of operations, that is, the crystallisation of the very tonalities of these yet-to-be existences. The taking of form through the spontaneous expression of matter, the abundance of environment, and the lessening of the individual are all phenomena of this passage.

The "pressure of the virtual" is also the force out of which the actual receives concepts to be moulded and engraved into their worlds. The interchangeability of world and concept is most felt at the passage. Here the virtual presses its imprint into the region of the actual and the actual invades the area of pre-constitution. Concepts are articulations of the virtual and as such, also continually remain in the making. One might add: this is why concepts are oftentimes a question of *feeling*—concepts articulate the virtual but cannot be sufficiently articulated in language as such. They carry within themselves a surplus that does not belong to the actual. Concepts are fugitive as they, while being formed in the middle, traverse the regions of pre-individuation and the individual, move across the various layers of actualisation, compose and re-compose themselves, responsively beckon towards their environments. At the same time, concepts are imbued with *feeling*, that is, they maintain a continual relation to the "pressure of the virtual". *Feeling* shifts towards a becoming-environment; a tendency and an inflection brings forth a world. The constitutive forces that they gather with their traversals are such that they express the entity-hood of the passage and they manifest themselves as *felt* sense within worlds.

These approaches offer us access to a conceptual region of permeability and dissolving boundaries, an encompassing arrangement that incorporates environments and layers of being, inflections, modulations, and tonalities within a rhythmically defined substance. In this way, the force of the virtual can become *felt* in an encounter with a body:

> ... it must make the body a force for thought in the moving, unfastening the body from what we perceive as its integrity. It must create a disorientation, an involution, a fold, a setting-to-rhythm not only of this or that body, but of an ecology in co-composition, an ecology that is not only a recomposition of spacetimes bodying, but also is a thinking in act, a movement of thought.
>
> (Manning 2013, 15)

We see that *feeling* and conceptual entanglement are coupled in such a way that there is no clear separation between any of these domains. In the co-composition that a body continually works towards, thinking and movement co-align to create *feeling*. This is how concepts come to be—concepts as a question of *feeling*. And again, the body as an entity is a momentary capture, an arbitrary point of juncture within the field of potentiality. It expands towards a virtual body. Equally so, "ecology" cannot be confined to the concept of a region of nature separate from humans. Nor can it simply be an account of the effects of institutions and infrastructures on bodies or the effects of material geography on social formations. Rather, ecology accounts for the spectrality of bodies, that is, the atmospheres and inflections that bodies generate because of the pull of the virtual.

This chapter showed how a theatre of the virtual does not rely on the logic of the spectacle and the scenic but rather on the visceral tactility that is the logic of touch. We defined touch as an ontogenetic operation, an event-engine for the continuous engendering of a body. In being such, touch is not something that happens to bodies; it is not an encroachment from the outside. Rather, touch is already woven into bodies and carries their emergence immanently. Yet touch has a double nature—it is both an operation for the repotentialisation of bodies and a form of violence. The event of touch supplies a continual engendering, that is, a perpetual repotentialisation of the given. But then again, touch can also re-establish the actual. It can make bodies expansive but can equally so homogenise and deplete. This is the violence of touch: it imposes a politics of constraint, generating truncated lives whose relation to the virtual has been severed. And eschewing violence means evading the creation of environments that fully conform to the imperatives of being, that which already is. One answer to this is *Pindorama*'s movement-bodies, the immanent modelling of one's climates and atmospheres in ways that simply show indifference to the politics of repression.

We touched upon the overlap between event and sense and what it means for touch to be an event: an extra-ontological inherence, self-engendering, and residing within potentiality. Engaging in a brief excursus about the nature of sense, we fleshed out its status as an enabling condition for a world. And then again, we delved into the work of touch as a repotentialising force. As a technique for repotentialisation, the touch-event does not necessarily engender the radical alteration of a system; it rather introduces an inflection. In turn, the foregrounding of such inflections become ethical, aesthetic, environmental, and political gestures of engaging and thinking with. Finally, we showed how a theatre of the virtual opens a door to modes of perceiving through an abstract capacity we called *feeling* and allows us so viscerally experience the individuating zest of movement. And it is in movement that we encounter environmentality—the practice of bodily becoming-environment. In what follows, we continue to work through the logic of the virtual as we begin to see that it is not enough to adopt an "organism-plus-environment mode of thought which takes seriously the entangled and relational constitution of all life on earth" (Wright 2014, n.p.) but that it is necessary to disrupt entire lines of division to arrive at locales of radical response.

Works Cited

Adams, Matthew. 2020. *Anthropocene Psychology: Being Human in a More-than-Human World*. London: Routledge.

Alloa, Emmanuel. 2014. "The Theatre of the Virtual—How to Stage Potentialities with Merleau-Ponty." In *Encounters in Performance Philosophy*, edited by Laura Cull and Alice Lagaay, 147–171. Basingtoke: Palgrave MacMillan.

Aristotle. 2009. *Nicomachean Ethics*. Translated by David Ross. Oxford: Oxford University Press.

Battista, Silvia. 2018. *Posthuman Spiritualities in Contemporary Performance: Politics, Ecologies and Perceptions*. London: Palgrave MacMillan. https://doi.org/10.1007/978-3-319-89758-5.

Blake, Charlie, Claire Molloy, Steven Shakespeare. 2012. "Introduction." In *Beyond Human: From Animality to Transhumanism*, edited by Charlie Blake, Claire Molloy, Steven Shakespeare, 1–11. London: Continuum.

Boetzkes, Amanda. 2015. "Ecologicity, Vision, and the Neurological System." In *Art in the Anthropocene: Encounters among Aesthetics, Politics, Environments and Epistemologies*, edited by Heather Davis and Etienne Turpin, 271–283. London: Open Humanities Press. https://doi.org/10.26530/OAPEN_560010.
Braidotti, Rosi and Patricia Pisters. 2012. "Introduction." In *Revisiting Normativity with Deleuze*, edited by Rosi Braidotti and Patricia Pisters, 1–8. London: Bloomsbury.
Butler, Judith. 2020. *The Force of Nonviolence*. London: Verso.
Clark, Nigel. 2011. *Inhuman Nature: Sociable Life on a Volatile Planet*. London: Sage.
Colman, Felicity. 2015. "Dromospheric Generation: The Things That We Have Learned Are No Longer Enough." *Cultural Politics* 11 (2): 246–259. https://doi.org/10.1215/17432197-2895807.
Colman, Felicity. 2007. "Affective Intensity: Art as Sensorial Form." In *Sensorium: Aesthetics, Art, Life*, edited by Barbara Bolt et al., 64–83. Newcastle: Cambridge Scholars Publishing.
Culp, Andrew. 2016. *Dark Deleuze*. Minneapolis: The University of Minnesota Press.
Deleuze, Gilles. 2001. *Immanence: A Life*. Translated by Anne Boyman. Cambridge, MA: MIT Press.
Deleuze, Gilles. 1990. *The Logic of Sense*. Translated by Mark Lester and Charles Stivale. Edited by Constantin V. Boundas. London: Athlone.
Di Paola, Marcello and Mirco Daniel Garasic. 2014. "The Dark Side of Sustainability: Avoiding and Shortening Lives in the Anthropocene." *RIVISTA DI STUDI SULLA SOSTENIBILITA* 2: 59–81. https://doi.org/10.3280/RISS2013-002004.
Foucault, Michel. 2001. *Power: Essential Works of Foucault, 1954–1984*, edited by James D. Faubion, translated by Robert Hurley. New York: The New Press.
Fuller, Matthew and Goriunova, Olga. 2017. "Devastation." In *General Ecology: The New Ecological Paradigm*. Edited by Erich Hörl and James Burton, 323–345. London: Bloomsbury.
Galtung, Johan. 1969. "Violence, Peace, and Peace Research." *Journal of Peace Research* 6: 167–191. https://doi.org/10.1177/002234336900600301.
Guattari, Félix. 1989. *The Three Ecologies*. Translated by Chris Turner. *New Formations* 8: 131–147. https://www.lwbooks.co.uk/new-formations/8/the-three-ecologies.
Hamilton, Scott. 2017. "Securing Ourselves from Ourselves? The Paradox of 'Entanglement' in the Anthropocene." *Crime, Law and Social Change* 68: 579–595. https://doi.org/10.1007/s10611-017-9704-4.
Heidegger, Martin. 1995. *The Fundamental Concepts of Metaphysics, World, Finitude, Solitude*. Translated by William H. McNeill and Nicholas Walker. Bloomington, IN: Indiana University Press.
Hickey-Moody, Anna and Marshall, D. 2016. "Working Recognitions: An Introduction." *Review of Education, Pedagogy, and Cultural Studies* 38 (1): 3–13. https://doi.org/10.1080/10714413.2016.1119639.
Hickey-Moody, Anna. 2013. "Little Public Spheres." *Performance Paradigm* 9: 1–11. https://www.performanceparadigm.net/index.php/journal/article/view/129.
Hoel, Aud Sissel and Iris van der Tuin. 2013. "The Ontological Force of Technicity: Reading Cassirer and Simondon Diffractively." *Philosophy and Technology* 26 (2): 187–202. https://doi.org/10.1007/s13347-012-0092-5.
Hughes, Joe. 2012. *Philosophy After Deleuze*. London: Bloomsbury.
Irwin, Terrence H. 2012. "Conceptions of Happiness in the Nicomachean Ethics." In *The Oxford Handbook of Aristotle*, edited by Christopher Shields, 495–529. Oxford: Oxford University Press.

Johnson, Elizabeth, R. 2017. "At the Limits of Species Being: Sensing the Anthropocene." *South Atlantic Quarterly* 116 (2): 275–292. https://doi.org/10.1215/00382876-3829401.

Kidner, David W. 2021. "Anthropocene Subjectivity and Environmental Degradation." *Ethics and the Environment* 26 (1): 57–83. https://doi.org/10.2979/ethicsenviro.26.1.03.

Laurie, Emma W. and Ian Shaw. 2018. "Violent Conditions: The Injustices of Being." *Political Geography* 65: 8–16. https://doi.org/10.1016/j.polgeo.2018.03.005.

Levy, Nina. 2016. "Pindorama an Ever-shifting Landscape." *The West Australian*, March 3, 2016. https://thewest.com.au/news/pindorama-an-ever-shifting-landscape-ng-ya-100404.

MacCormack, Patricia. 2012. *Posthuman Ethics: Embodiment and Cultural Theory*. London: Routledge.

Maggs, David and Robinson, John. 2016. "Recalibrating the Anthropocene: Sustainability in an Imaginary World." *Environmental Philosophy* 13 (2): 175–194. https://doi.org/10.5840/envirophil201611740.

Manning, Erin. 2013. *Always More Than One: Individuation's Dance*. Durham, NC: Duke University Press. https://doi.org/10.1215/9780822395829.

Manning, Erin. 2009. *Relationscapes: Movement, Art, Philosophy*. Cambridge, MA: The MIT Press.

Manning, Erin. 2007. *Politics of Touch: Sense, Movement, Sovereignty*. Minneapolis: University of Minnesota Press.

Nancy, Jean-Luc. 1997. *The Sense of the World*. Translated by Jeffrey S. Librett. Minneapolis: University of Minnesota Press.

Oppermann, Serpil. 2018. "The Scale of the Anthropocene. Material Ecocritical Reflections." *Mosaic* 51 (3): 1–17. https://www.jstor.org/stable/26974107.

Oswald Spring, Úrsula. 2021. "Decolonising Peace in the Anthropocene: Towards an Alternative Understanding of Peace and Security." In *Decolonising Conflicts, Security, Peace, Gender, Environment and Development in the Anthropocene*, edited by Ursula Oswald Spring and Hans-Günter Brauch. Cham: Springer, 1–47. https://doi.org/10.1007/978-3-030-62316-6_1.

Rivera, Mayra. 2015. *The Poetics of the Flesh*. Durham, NC: Duke University Press.

Scott, Melissa. 2016. "Review: Pindorama." *Pelican Magazine*, April 10, 2016. http://pelicanmagazine.com.au/2016/04/10/review-pindorama/.

Tiainen, Milla and Jussi Parikka. 2013. "The Primacy of Movement: Variation, Intermediality and Biopolitics in Tero Saarinen's Hunt." In: *Carnal Knowledge: Towards a 'New Materialism' Through the Arts*, edited by Estelle Barrett and Barbara Bolt, 205–225. London and New York: I.B. Taurus.

Tyner, James A. 2016. "Population Geography III: Precarity, Dead Peasants, and Truncated Life." *Progress in Human Geography* 40 (2): 275–289. https://doi.org/10.1177/0309132515569964.

Ulmer, Jasmine. 2017. "Posthumanism as Research Methodology: Inquiry in the Anthropocene." *International Journal of Qualitative Studies in Education* 30 (9): 832–848. https://doi.org/10.1080/09518398.2017.1336806.

Ulmer, Jasmine. 2016. "Writing Slow Ontology." *Qualitative Inquiry* 23 (3): 201–211. https://doi.org/10.1177/1077800416643994.

Weil, Simone. 2004. *Oppression and Liberty*. Translated by Arthur Willis and John Petrie. London: Routledge.

Wright, Kate. 2014. "An Ethics of Entanglement in the Anthropocene." *Journal of Media Arts Culture* 11 (1): n.p. http://scan.net.au/scn/journal/vol11number1/Kate-Wright.html.

4 Organism and Gesture

A gesture is an opening. And a "minor gesture" (Manning 2016, 64–86) carries the possibility to think and act otherwise even if facing the danger of remaining unrecognisable and unperceived. The minor is unshielded. Lives and bodies are enmeshed in this exposure. Even more so, lives and bodies are attuned to the terrestrial biome that itself is ontological vulnerability. Precarity is one crucial theme of the minor, and further still, it is the theme of the region of the virtual. The directionality of a gesture is indeterminate. Its flourishing cannot be ascertained. The processuality of motion is the sole actional reality in the region of the gesture, and this region remains unsettled. At the same time, this is the region in which bodies recompose, form new alliances, and alter the ecologies into which they enter. Within this region, things are not so much a matter of being as a *style* of being. That is to say, instead of things, we have attitudes and inflections, or ways of doing things that, by definition, are minor because of their chancy engagement with the virtual. Through style, the virtual exposes its own singular materiality, the texture of a particular type of non-being replete with singularities, and an atmospheric non-being that is a "not yet". Bodies in motion shift towards ways of showing and performing operations that can be recognisable and trivial but, at the same time, unsettling and strange.

The intervention of style also has its ecological effects as it reverberates across the entire environment of a body. This intervention is not an easing of the difficulties posed by the virtual but their un-easing. The virtual complicates, makes everything more strenuous, and introduces ever-novel entanglements within its field. This builds up toward a "geomorphic aesthetics" (Yusoff 2014, 383) whereby environments and genealogies co-create a spectral non-presence of things in series of not theres and not yets. An inhuman formatting envelops bodies. Things within the field hang by a thread. Entities are enveloped by an unsure environment that flickers and moves with each change of inflection. The virtual does not constitute a cosmos composed of objects with stretches of vacuity between them, unsurpassable passages that call for communication and contact. Nor does it operate from within the vantage point of directionality. The virtual field is composed of expansive movement. Its constituents come together in a disjunctive synthesis—a synthesis

DOI: 10.4324/9781003231080-5

in which each item relates and becomes something else but, at the same time, preserves its structure in its entirety. The virtual field thrives because of the disjunction—the synthesis which interweaves and leaves everything intact. We cannot presuppose a separation between objects and cannot anticipate a need for contact as each constituent is interwoven with the field to such an extent that the field persists in a regime of continual connection to itself. At the same time, each constituent retains a relative autonomy of movement that is fostered through *style*, through the introduction of an *inflection* within the field and the preservation of an *attitude*.

There is no necessity to build bridges between entities conceived as disparate and needing to establish a connection. One is already enmeshed within a landscape of tendencies and the reverberations that these tendencies create. Each bond within the field is fugitive but cosmic in scope as it permanently alters the texture of the given. It carries forward a movement, that is to say, the field's actional reality, and makes it tangible as it is in this movement that the field produces an event. Here one can be actively "in the event" and engender new conditions for living, draw trajectories without directionality, and busy oneself within a motion without intentionality.

Subsisting "in the event" also means exhibiting a movement, making the means "visible as such", and reorienting that same movement in a dynamic remodulation. One can begin to see entities enmeshed into their worlds as passages for the event that, at the same time, are invariably already "in the event" as they put on display their *style* of being. In style, one consists solely of a foreground and of degrees of cleaving. Movement is shown to have its own materiality just as much as it is interstitial. And movement can often go against the determinations of a body, drifting off in directions that are unplanned or outside of the scope of a body's self-projections. Movement is supra-intentional, more "in the event" than in the body, more of the field of potentials and tendencies than of any given locality. Movement carries potentiality and envelops bodies in it; motion becomes an agency that brings forth a specific engagement with the virtual. The relations that emerge out of such motion are not relations between already established objects within a vacuous world but perturbations within the field of tendencies that travel across individuals to emphasise the complex interweave that the field is already becoming.

Here we deal with a directionality that plays itself out in the making. That is to say, the conditions for the establishing of a direction are laid out in the enaction of movement and not prior to it. The pull of potentiality has an equal if not greater say in how a movement is going to evolve than any concrete pre-established intention. An interweave of tendencies supersedes the mere concentration of attention within a single object. In fact, attention is always dispersed and fugitive. Its strength is not in the focus and the single-mindedness of purpose but in its expansive, all-encompassing quality. This is a new type of "attention" that is broader in scope than trivial "intentionality". This type of attention is not only non-purposive and supra-subjective but also capable of accounting for "the complex modalities attending, in the event, to experience in the making" (Manning 2016, 154). It is for this reason that instead of conceptualising a relation within the region of the virtual, we speak of engenderings and enmeshments to emphasise the expansive quality of attention and directionality. Conceptualising movement in this way allows us to remain in the mesh, in a regime of co-immersion whereby immersion is seen as "attentive interactions with diverse lifeways" (van Dooren et al. 2016, 6). Co-immersion is so expansive and prolific in its generation of virtualities that it verges on dissolution. At the same time, this dissipative quality of movement is where its generative zest lies.

This is not to say, however, that the movement and directionality of a body invariably evolves in concert with its environments and seamlessly reverberates with the virtual field. Dissonance is possible; movements and rhythms may not match; grades of speed and slowness may not always co-align effortlessly. Co-alignment is not necessary, however, nor is there any striving to readjust so that a body's rhythms can align with the movements of an environment. A body can move with increased slowness or at an intensified speed that is entirely in clash with other reverberations coming from within its field of interaction. At the same time, this movement is not "corrected" so as to adjust to the various surrounding speeds and slownesses of the field. One such movement is the very particular *inflection* that a body introduces to the virtual field and is valuable as such not only in and for itself but also in its correlation with the remaining regions of the field's network. The virtual field does not aim to unify—it continually complicates. A non-aligning body is welcome within its domain as it brings forth ever more varied co-compositions. As nothing within the field is shaped in advance, there is also no sense of a "correct" speed or a "proper" slowness; a body's partaking in an enmeshment may take place in ways which are non-harmonious. An engagement with the virtual, then, can also trigger processes that show how a body's levels of intensity can be different from those of its surroundings. These processes equally partake in the becoming of the virtual.

We arrive at a definition of a body that does justice to a body's entanglements with various environments within and without the permeable boundary it shares with a world. With this definition, we turn to a concept of "life that is both absolutely singular and connected to other bodies" (Philippopoulos-Mihalopoulos 2015b, 207) so that "every body is fleshed out by the singularity of a life and, as such, flourishes into the position of a lively agent, whether animate or inanimate" (ibid., 207). A body is primarily composed of gestures, that is, micro-openings towards the virtual. The virtual permeates a body and a body is always already susceptible to the pull of the virtual. How do we get there?

Organism and the Field of Potentiality

When we speak of potentiality as a "system" or a "network", and even when we evoke the concept of ontogenesis in discussing the virtual, one is invariably inclined to think that there is an underlying holism, a concerted togetherness of parts. And when we speak of a theatre of the virtual, one still has, albeit at the back of one's mind, the old concept of organism that allows us to see performance pieces—regardless of their level of complexity, abstraction, or disintegration—as structured wholes. Further still, when we evoke the concept of the theatrical as a "living system" in continual ontogenesis, the comment that immediately comes to mind is that "the ontogeny of a living system is the history of maintenance of its identity through continuous autopoiesis in the physical space" (Maturana and Varela 1972, 98). In what follows, the concept of organism will be addressed to show how a theatre of the virtual offers another way of looking at organisation, structure, and whole.

The vernacular concept of organism goes like this:

> (1) An individual organism is walled off from the environment; (2) An individual organism has a complete set of the same genes in every cell in its body; (3) It is immunologically self-recognizing, self-accepting and other-rejecting; (4) It is a behavioral unit, with a CNS and co-ordinate limbs that 'makes decisions' as a unit.
>
> (Wilson 2014, 23)

One such definition draws a picture of an organism as an "egotistic" category—a conservatively acting entity wherein each node is entirely and fully focused on the perseverance and survival of the system at hand. Organisms, seen in this way, are supreme examples of biological individualism. They wall themselves off against an environment and draw a clear boundary between themselves and others, focusing on perseverance in their own being.

Deeply rooted in dichotomist thinking, the concept of organism thrives on the delineation of an expansive outside (environment) and a region of interiority (inner life of the body). Even more so, the concept of organism is traversed by a wealth of micro-conceptual scenarios that determine its being. For one, it relies on the division of form and matter—the high-level orderliness of an organism being possible because of the organising function of form. Here a fully functional division between form and matter and a foregrounding of the organisational capacities of form imply that matter cannot initiate its own genesis out of its own resources. And the mattering of an organism is additionally punctured by the concept of entelechy—the ontogenetic program that is ingrained in bodily matter.

Also, the vernacular concept of organism is tied to the notion of a holistic design. This is a type of design that is ordered, structured, and sustains complex relationships between parts and a whole: an organisation. An organism, then, is a system wherein each part is ordained a specific place and function that contributes to the perseverance of the whole. At the same time, an organism is a networked entity—each part is inextricably related to all others and to the whole in such a way that its function is vital. There is a reciprocity between the different parts as each part works together with all others in order to realise the entelechy of the whole: "the passive effect of preceding, external causes, and something that is actively, immanently self-caused and self-generating" (Shaviro 2010, 140). An organism, then, is a heterogeneous integrated teleological system wherein each part works for the perseverance, development, and self-actualisation of the system in its entirety. In this sense, organisms are ontogenetically "persisters" (Smith 2017).

Even more so, we could go as far as to see organisms as ontologically prior to bodies. Here I make an allusion to Aristotle's belief that "communities are ontologically prior to the individual, because human beings can only flourish in a community and not alone" (Crespo 2017, 128). According to this logic, bodies can only persist as organisms and only as such do they become capable of flourishing within an environment. An organism is the condition of possibility for a body as a body can precipitate its becoming through and by virtue of its pre-established inherence as an organism. Only by being an organism does a body sustain a level of organisational unity that allows it to be both withdrawn from an environment and inextricably interwoven with it. The concept of organism becomes the ground for negotiating the politics of the outside and wrestling of an enclave of interiority from the public sphere. The enabling condition of a body, then, is the complex interweave of "agency, habit, and institutions" (Crespo 2016, 867) that we call an organism. The foregrounding of such properties has led to the formation of the machinic concept of organism derived from Leibniz and gaining popularity within the Cartesian tradition. The notion of organisms as mechanistic entities defined in terms of discreteness, functionality, teleology, and whole-part reciprocity still persists in the cultural imagination as the most viable definition of the term. But even more so, the machine concept has imbued the concept of organism with an atmosphere of unwavering cooperation. Because of a system of checks and balances based on agency, habit, and institutionalised practice, an organism can only infallibly work in one's favour.

There is no wonder, then, that the cultural imagination draws a mechanistic concept of life—the procedural force operating in a living organism—as a struggle for survival, a battle for resources, and a competition among organisms where only the most capable ones can truly retain their integrity and achieve their "purpose". This teleological and individualistic concept of organism is reinforced by the mammalian notion of organism as an entity with a certain kind of intentionality. Here we observe a heightened sensitivity towards other organisms that manifests itself as a reflective capacity. But most significantly, and in spite of the dominance of mechanistic metaphors, we have a departure from the inorganic and an almost absolute alignment of "organism" with the "living". And then again, this philosophising of the organism as "life" brings forth a troubled genealogy.

This troubled amalgamation of machine metaphors and notions of "the living" within the concept of organism is mirrored in the persistent distinction between natural and artificial organisms. Following the *Physics* and *De Anima*, the former has internal purposiveness—its final cause is found within.

The latter is externally purposive—as in the case of most automata, an externally purposive organism is used for something external to itself and serves a goal that is external to its own being; its functionality exists in relation to something other than the organism itself. Recent work has showcased the distraught divide between animate and inanimate, organic, and artefactual:

> The inanimate does not simply fall away, vehicled by mechanism, into the category of nonlife but continues to operate as an uncanny force across the divide that supposedly protects and defines life. If life emerged in contrast or opposition to the inert machine, it was to develop as another form of machine called a program. And if the living organism were to be defined as automotive and autogenerative, that was possible only within a more general and less categorically defined structure of automaticity.
>
> (Wills 2016, 1–28)

There is an ongoing debate in the philosophy of biology about the concept of organism as a discrete entity within a world. The question is whether we can reliably determine the boundaries of an organism, delineate its domain, or demarcate its field of interaction. Whereas it is acknowledged that "organisms are federations of organism-like entities which may themselves be only loosely integrated, and they in turn form parts of larger organism-like entities" (Wilson 2014, 33), the existing definitions of organism fail to account for a being's capacities for auto-genesis. Even more so, there is little to no consideration of a being's variegated engagements with environments both within and without the nominal border of a body. The vernacular understanding of the term rather speaks for the "deep genealogies of colonial violence" (Stark et al. 2018, 24) that permeate the organism–environment divide.

And we continue to deal with the exclusivity of an organism as capable of exceeding materiality, that is, as a special bearer of intelligence and purveyor of various practices of immateriality that have the surpassing of "the human condition" as their goal: "We urgently need to overcome the still pervasive idea that the value of human reason, meaning, knowledge-making and creativity lies in rising above our worldly ... existence" (Anderson and Perrin 2015, 11). In the special case of anthropos, the concept of organism has also vicariously contributed to the development of concepts such as "humanity" and "the human". To wrestle with this troubled heritage, we now have the stance that "we have never been human" and that, by proxy, any vocabulary associated with an upholding of "the human" is already obsolete: "The mourning of humanity, the accusations that 'we' have not attended sufficiently to our inhuman others, the extension of human rights or personhood to nonhumans: all these Anthropocene gestures are modes of generating a humanity that never was" (Cohen et al. 2016, 11).

Still, in foregrounding the pervasive materiality and enmeshment of things, research in the philosophy of biology has already put forward the proposition that "organism" may be a relic concept. Such complexities allow us to question the solidity of the term:

> 'Organism', we should conclude, is a vague concept, like that of 'material object'. A rock, a teacup, a railroad car, even a skyscraper—these are all material objects. But what about a mountain peak ... a plume of smoke, a continent, a wireless network?
>
> (Wilson 2014, 34)

In recent work, the very fact of the organism has been complicated as an "ontological problem" (Huneman and Wolfe 2010, 151). This requires an approach that allows for "a form of estrangement" (Hickey-Moody 2015, 804) to settle in. But even more so, it requires "that our critical and creative activities also be responsive ones" (Cunniff Gilson 2014, 87). The introduction of a relative rigidity within the concept of organism has left its reverberations across the entirety of the spectrum of definitions of a self. In this way, the concept of organism has become vicariously responsible for the proliferation of moral concepts such as integrity, virtue, individual, personhood, and perhaps even the concept of legal ownership:

> The early modern conception of the organism as a well circumscribed, self-maintaining and self-repairing locus of power and vulnerability was accordingly a discovery of some important features of plants, animals, and microorganisms. At the same time, it was projective, a transcription of an emerging introspective or reflective sense of the self as a fortified individual, deserving of recognition and respect, and entitled to further protection. The integrated and well-defended self underwrote and continues to underwrite a set of ethical stances and social movements, from rugged individualism and self-ownership to human rights ... Moral integrity and entitlement are seen as closely related to physical inviolability.
>
> (Wilson 2014, 33)

As much as it sustains the entwinement of power, that is, "the construction of the paradigmatic liberal political and legal subject" (Grear 2016, 44), and "selectively stigmatized" (ibid., 44) debates on dependency and vulnerability, the concept of organism becomes increasingly porous. An organism is embodied and embedded in a world as a "vulnerable subject ... radically particular and differentially experienced" (Grear 2015, 306). Being a body, in the vernacular imagination, coincides with being an organism—exposed, at the sway of forces, but also an enclave of autonomy and self-propelled action. But the question remains as to whether the concept of organism remains a viable one and what exactly do we gain by insisting on its preservation.

Diaphanous Organismicity

We saw how the concept of organism is distilled out of a tradition rooted in classical antiquity and perceiving organisms as living beings with their own micro-organisational activity that, however, operate as discrete entities clearly delineated within a spatiotemporal continuum. An organism, first and foremost, is a system that is "living" and "self-sustaining", enjoying a certain degree of "functional closure" (Toepfer 2014, 59), capacity for cooperation with things other than itself, and a strong sense of isolated self-propelled agency. Given the complexity of one such concept of organism and the suggestion that one should consider degrees of organism-hood, Toepfer proposes the concept of "organismicity" as a "state variable" instead of that of an organism. Organismicity would designate "a property of systems that comes in degrees" and that expresses the gradient nature of various aspects of the organism's way of being, in particular, the following six: (1) the transition from organised systems in nature to organisms, (2) the beginning and ending of an organism in time, (3) the spatial limits of individual organisms in cases of clonal growth, (4) the existence of various levels of organisation within an organism, (5) the often vague boundary between organism and environment, and (6) the occasionally gradual transition from individual to community (Toepfer 2014, 60).

One such definition allows for an enhancement of the existing concept in introducing nuances and degrees. Whereas the traditional concept of organism entails an integrated system whose distinguishing condition is functional closure, with "organismicity" we have a multitude of degrees of organisation, degrees of system-hood, and degrees of openness. And while an organism that foregrounds the machinic and entelechial aspect is an Aristotelian–Cartesian concept—a typical reference is Descartes' *Passions of the Soul* (1649), a work that marked the beginnings of later mechanistic, functional, and organisational accounts of biological entities—"organismicity" could be called Simondonian–Deleuzian in that it remains at the sway of degrees of freedom and thresholds within the virtual.

Linking the concept of organism to the functional closure that is entailed by the concept of organisation is perhaps one of the most persistent residues of the Aristotelian–Cartesian tradition. This is a co-composition that is purposive inasmuch as it works towards its own perseverance and perpetuation. An organism, therefore, may be a networked entity composed of myriads of interacting nodes, but this relational quality is first and foremost subsumed to the workings of a sealed whole that operates with an eye towards its own personal entelechy. Here we have the concept of the machine coupled with the concept of organisation at its best—a holistic system that precipitates the emergence of complex phenomena out of the concatenation of subordinated interlinked functions. We have a unity that emerges out of the complex intra-activity of interlinking and co-determining. This activity, however, invariably takes place within the closed interiority of a system without extending to the milieu. Further still, the system is composed in such a way as to subsist in competition with its milieus.

The concept of organism as a holistic system sustained by interdependent parts is just one step away from the definition of a machine as a purposive organisation composed of complex interlinked units of varied capacities. The interactionist component remains tied to the interiority of the system; the guiding principle remains that of closure. Even more so, the agency aspect of an organism is equally linked to the system's interiority, aligning a capacity to act with the capacity of being a structured complex whole closed off from an environment. So, we have not only a system that subsists in separation from its milieu, marked by contiguity, and endorsing interiority but also a system that works through the productive interlinking of co-dependent and individually indispensable parts.

The concept of organismicity is a quasi-organismic aggregate that subsists in varying degrees of organism-hood and is predominately defined in terms of degrees of functional and systemic closure, levels of spatiotemporal delineation including the delineation of a region of interiority, layers of self-preservation and self-continuation, grades of organisation operating in concert with one another to inform a whole, and an existence in opposition to an environment that, however, at times extends the organismic into the milieu. For example, one product of an organism's continual interaction with an environment is the creation of ecological niches, that is, something that virtually stretches out an organism's boundaries to the extent that it leads to the coagulation with a given environment. Adding this refined definition of organisms as organismicities to the vantage of the virtual, we observe how the boundaries of an organism become diaphanous. We arrive at a place wherein closure is no longer necessary—the focus is on degrees, extensions, and coagulations. Working with the virtual allows us to disentangle bodies from the rhetoric of "struggle" and "against" in favour of an engagement with an "attunement" and "toward".

When one such concept of organismicity—allowing of degrees and thinking in terms of gradients—is opened to the virtual, we have a dimension added to the concept. Now, a productive interlinking of co-dependent and individually indispensable parts takes place all the way within and all the way outside the porous nominal boundaries of an organism. Because of its becoming-the-field, an organism sheds its clear delineation; the "internal" contiguity becomes a reverberation that operates not only within but also across the field of potentiality; and interiority is downplayed. The vantage that opens up with an attunement to the virtual allows us to think beyond the model of the "walled-off, immunological self-recognizer, other-rejector, and behavioral unit" (Wilson 2014, 35). When thinking in terms of the virtual, we see that which was previously an "organism" as an extended self stretching out infinitely and permeating the entirely of the networked environments it builds in interaction. Yet this does not lead to a withdrawal of materiality. Rather, we make an entrance into a region of "eco materialism" as both "a philosophy ... and a code of conduct" (Weintraub 2018, 10–19), that is, a region of attunement and co-inhabiting. One such postorganismic concept of organism begins to see the body as a playground for political inclusion. A body becomes "a heterogeneous political space" that makes us question "whether the conception of political space as exclusively human is capable of attending to issues of ecological justice where the well-being of humans and ecosystems is inextricable" (McCullagh 2019, 142).

We deal with an enaction that is environmental. The environmental "expands from a focus on the natural ecology to an entanglement with technological questions, notions of subjectivity and agency... and a critique of such accounts of rationality that are unable to talk about nonhumans as constitutive of social relations" (Parikka 2015, 36). From this vantage, one becomes particularly aware of subjects as arbitrarily assembled, as "an after-effect—or residuum—of a process that is oblivious to that subject" (O'Sullivan 2012, 169). This definition of the environment is not only extended but also comprehensive inasmuch as it gives "an expansive sense of the earth and cosmos as the volatile ground of human and other creaturely life" (Clark 2011, 23). Within such enmeshments, there is no pattern, nor is there any component that could guarantee or work towards the self-preservation of a system. Rather than that, we have constant expressive activity from within enmeshments and levels of attunement co-aligning in ways that evade prediction. There is nothing to guarantee that the practice of world-making through encountering and enacting would be a success. In fact, there is no definite entity any place within an incessantly individuating field and no world as such is actually made.

Another possible objection to the "spontaneity" of the virtual would not come from proponents of the concept of organism but from those who favour a concept of the machine:

> We are thus saying that what defines a machine's organization is relations, and hence that the organization of a machine has no connection with materiality, that is, with the properties of the components that define them as physical entities. In the organization of a machine, materiality is implied but does not enter *per se*.
>
> (Varela 1979, 9)

The proposition here would be to abandon the concept of organism as it unites matter and organisation and to turn to the concept of the machine as it foregrounds the organisational component. The appeal to an intrinsic design would be retained as it would be the functionality and realisability of the overarching organisation that would matter most. But the virtual is not machinic inasmuch as it does not primarily consist of organisation. The situation is quite the contrary: the virtual is of matter and of continual "refleshings" (Palmer 2016, 507). If there is any detectable organisation effect, it would be a secondary phenomenon—a by-product of the practices of the networked enaction of mattering.

Mattering is a way of being in a world whereby a given world is experienced as a comprehensive milieu. An experience of networked enaction is prior to any distinction between subject and object, animate and inanimate, living and non-living, and human and non-human. Mattering operates beyond "a fetishized notion of matter that attributes properties to the nonhuman, which arise from human activity" (Levant 2017, 260) and distances itself from discourses that attempt to attribute "liveliness" to what is construed as otherwise "non-living" matter.

One such experience does not take place in opposition to but *alongside* the experience of being an organism. How does this happen? The concept of organism introduces division. We have a walled-off self-preserving entity set apart from an environment. This entity operates in a mode of coming to terms with an environment only to the extent that the environment can become instrumental in realising the organism's own entelechy. All the while, we also have a different mode of operation at work. According to the terms of this other mode of operation, the networked enaction of matter populates a world with spectral entities—individuating virtualities—things and extra-ontological inherences all of which are of the spectrum of the living, and all of which are of agency and personhood. We have a scenario wherein entities formerly known as "objects" take on subject positions. Further still, from this vantage, it even becomes difficult to think of an object position as such and, even less so, to assign positions "premised on the centrality of the 'invulnerable' subject" (De Lucia 2020, 334). As we are plunged within a milieu of co-individuation, it is difficult to tell which entity exerts an influence on which as we have to do with practices of co-mingling and reciprocal interactivity. Objectifying, establishing items of knowledge, identifying reality conditions, and walling off enclaves of interiority cannot take place from within a vantage of networked enaction because we simply do not have a unified ordering position. In another sense, however, everything within the field of potentiality is a position—albeit with nothing to objectify.

Organism and Machine

Just as the concept of the machine has pervaded the concept of organism (Nicholson 2014, 162–163), so has the machine concept been diminished in its alignment with the notion of an organic system. Machine metaphors abound when it comes to theorising the concept of organism and, equally so, organicist allusions come to the fore as a theoretical resource for conceptualising automata. The machine metaphor as a "constrained system" has been instrumental in the development of contemporary biology and has offered a conceptual basis for the development of an analytical program in the life sciences (Marques and Brito 2014, 77–79). At the same time, with the machine metaphor, we have an infusion of the inorganic uncanny—those non-human non-biological yet highly organised entities that "exert their recalcitrant and inhuman condition" (Tironi et al. 2018, 188). And, when we get to conceptualising "living" forms from the vantage of the virtual, the machine metaphor and its lively incarnation, the concept of organism, prove to be simply insufficient.

Having its peak with the emergence of the mechanistic philosophies of the seventeenth century, the machine metaphor aligns with the époque's ambition to create a plausible overarching account of nature. The matter-form dichotomy provides a ground for the creation of a distinction between inert materiality and organisational activity, turning the concept of "life" into a function, a peculiar type of mechanism. Here the difference between living forms and automata is one of degrees and levels of complication that nevertheless share the same mechanistic principle. The mechanical paradigm developed during this époque builds upon Aristotle's *Physics* and specifically on the concepts of functionality and purposiveness. Herein the entelechy of things serves as an inextricable component of reality that pervades the natural world. According to this logic, a living proof of the impersonal pervasive force of entelechy is, for instance, the observed tendency of living beings to grow, develop, adapt, and regenerate—a tendency that is perceived as natural inasmuch as it is believed to express the principle of nature in its entirety. So together with the immediate materiality of living beings, we have the additional organising function of form supplied through the teleology principle—not mere living beings but organisms. What appears to be at work here is an "inhuman condition", marked by "the persistence of the post-metanarrative of development" (Woodward 2016, 3), mixed with forces that the vernacular imagination construes as "natural".

The power of the machine metaphor to account for the natural world lies in the perception that both biological and machinic organisms are constrained material systems yet capable of growth and learning. Notwithstanding their complex, non-atomic character, or the high level of internal heterogeneity that they enjoy, organisms are, at the same time, highly ordered wholes whereby each part expresses the system in a different way while contributing to the perseverance of the whole. Again, in the vernacular imagination, biological and machinic organisms share this organising principle: we have an undercurrent of materiality punctured by the matter-forming principle of entelechy. Both biological and machinic organisms are material systems that are organised around a final cause. Both biological and machinic organisms are internally heterogeneous but operate as structured wholes; each functional element within the system works towards the continuation of the system as such. Biological and machinic organisms operate through coordination and regulation; both systems are first and foremost marked by a pervasive functionalism.

While one such vantage vicariously foregrounds the relational and interactionist component in the building of the machine metaphor (the organisation, or the form), we also have the complete priority of the autonomy principle at play. The autonomy principle aligns organisation (disembodied form, entelechy as a principle) and structure (matter, the material realisation of an organisation) to make them work together towards the independent self-preserving activity of a system. In looking at the concept of autonomy and the conceptual goal of naturalising teleology through potentiality, however, an organism would no longer be a pre-formatted entity but a "transversal" one (Murphy 2016, xx), an "ontological go-between" (Wolfe 2014, 151). Equally so, a machine would become a boundary concept that is fugitive and unsettled. When we speak of biological and machinic organisms, then, we would, in fact, speak of thresholds of enhanced virtualisations of matter.

This would be a study of the organisational principle in the abstract, apart from its expression in things, life as separate from its manifestations in the living, substance as separate from its expressions. And abstraction, rather than a negative process, is "a simultaneous affirmation and negation" whereby "the processes of affirmation and negation go in opposite directions at the same time" (Palmer 2014, xxi). This approach exposes the contingent nature of the relation between life and living forms, an organism, and the particular materiality of its parts.

The concept of organisation relies on the notion of constraint: organisms are theorised as sets of constraints operating in concert and, in one way or another, constraint is incorporated into the concept of organisation in order to make explicit the specificity of living beings (Kauffman 2001; Mossio and Moreno 2010; Deacon 2012). "Degrees in constraint" (individuality) is also the underlying concept that makes it possible to theorise the very difference between organic bodies and artefacts (Symons 2010).

The introduction of the concept of autonomy brings an inflow of emergence into biological and machinic organisms. We have organisms that are believed to emerge spontaneously from within, without external intervention or "exterior assembling". So at times of change, we have a unity that uniformly and harmoniously evolves into another unity of a different order. The process of differentiation that takes place in organisms is believed to be that of internal ordering as we have a unity established in advance and safeguarding the functioning of a system notwithstanding the integration of the new. Change takes place against the backdrop of a pre-established integration and is ingrained in the prior history of the organism. At the same time, change also works projectively as an extension into the future of an organism, creating conditions for expansion. Simultaneously, we have processes of productions of components coming from without; these are themselves the result of other external processes bearing no direct reference to the system at hand and having no direct impact on the way it evolves. So it seems that in terms of production, machines would generate something different from themselves, something that is pre-established by the external processes of production of components.

Maturana and Varela place this distinction at the core of their argument. In saying that in autopoietic machines (living beings) we have a coincidence between operation and fabrication (the machine fabricates itself through its own functioning), they also say that the so-called allopoietic machines (e.g. automata) are initially non-autonomous. In the latter case, we have a gap between the external and internal processes of production of components as well as a gap between functioning and fabrication. Autopoietic machines (e.g. organisms) are autonomous ways of being, their goal being "to produce and maintain" (Johnston 2008, 188) themselves. They are identity-preserving and identity-maintaining, and are autonomous because they are capable of generating their own dynamics. Allopoietic systems, on the contrary, cannot enjoy this level of autonomy as they are isolated on both ends—in terms of the pre-established systems of constraints and in terms of the concrete production that invariably remains external to their being. Yet autopoietic unity can emerge spontaneously within allopoetic systems, in the presence of a catalyst, via linkages such as composition, concatenation, and disintegration (Varela 1979).

From the vantage of potentiality, however, such distinctions can no longer be made. There is no longer a difference in kind between autopoietic and allopoietic; instead, we have a mattering of purposely "vulnerable systems":

> And just as one can talk about vulnerable human bodies … in the same way one can talk about vulnerable (or fragile) systems … The very need to invisibilise the materiality continuum that brings all operations together, exposes systems to the vulnerability of a constant battle of differentiation against dedifferentiation. … This is the autopoietic meaning of vulnerability in its most foundational sense: to be thrown into the material continuum …
> (Philippopoulos-Mihalopoulos 2015a, 456)

The generative capacity of vulnerability pervades the entirety of a system in its materiality including the products of its functioning and the pre-established constraints, that is, the ordering systems that precondition its work:

> … this sense of a constitutive vulnerability … needs to take into its compass a susceptibility of bodies not only to each other but to their surrounding environment. … in every encounter, the ones who confront each other are not only bodies composed through their exchanges with other bodies, but are also made up of the elemental flows they have learned to live with, the materials and life forms they have strained to associate with, the forces that have lured or repelled them.
> (Clark 2011, 210)

This increased dissipation and even a "decentring" of nature (Aretoulakis 2014, 172) into vulnerable systems might make us think of posthumanism. Even more so, one is reminded that "with the Anthropocene there is no nature that stands outside human impact: earth systems are seen to be decidedly 'post-natural'" (Braun 2015, 107). The very concept of nature as something allowing us to sustain the human–artefact distinction becomes increasingly uneasy. Yet bringing in the concept of posthumanism here would not be of help as it would not do full justice to organisms and machines as radically extra-human, that is, neither human nor non-human, maximally abstract and intensely virtual subsistences: "When matched by a lack of reflexivity, post-humanist discourse risks re-enacting epistemic violence against Indigenous and other nondualistic onto-epistemological traditions" (Margulies and Bersaglio 2018, 104). Accordingly, posthumanism brings forth troubled discussions on the more-than-human and intensifies the type of epistemic silence that makes "post-humanism complicit in re-producing a colonial intellectual tradition that problematically appropriates, erases, or invalidates other ways of being and knowing" (ibid., 104). When we speak of autonomy, then, what is meant is not a "human" or a "machine" autonomy as our habitual understanding of the terms would imply—an autonomy that entails agency and tangible action that exerts its presence upon a world. Autonomy, rather, is a conceptual region of immersive virtuality that retains a maximal capacity for a recomposition of the given.

Within this region, both biological and machinic organisms operate as vulnerable dissipative systems enjoying an equal level of continuity between pre-established constraints, self-organisation, and concrete production. Like entropic systems, they welcome "a dissipation of the existing orders of energy forms" to become "a device for unlimited speculation" (Colman 2006, 178) arranged within the same field of potentiality, enjoying various degrees of spontaneous emergence. Both biological and machinic organisms undergo self-organising processes whereby we witness the emergence of unprecedented dynamics, the establishing of new constraints, and the proliferation of organisational openness. This aligns with Simondon's thinking from *The Mode of Existence of Technical Objects* wherein openness is the mark of a machine. An open machine is characterised by a "margin of indeterminacy" (Simondon 2017, 147). Even more so, openness is necessary as the margin of indeterminacy allows a machine to form alliances and enter into information exchanges with other systems, persisting in a regime of perpetual connectivity and perpetual alignment to the rhythms of others.

If we accept the vantage of potentiality, we have to abandon the idea that biological and machinic organisms are primarily defined in terms of their organisation, complexity, or level of autonomy. There is no talk of highly evolved machines or less evolved organisms. The gradients introduced with the concept of organismicity are not about hierarchy but about thresholds of repotentialisation. Organisms, just like machines, are ontogenetically and essentially "persisters", that is, ecological entities "constitutively embedded in their worlds" (Smith 2017, 7). Whereas we might still deal with pre-established material structures that function as organisational constraints, we can no longer differentiate between categorically open (non-established, plastic, capable of spontaneous emergence, encouraging mutation) and closed (pre-established, rigid, non-emergent, built to prevent mutation) systems. What we call living organisms and machines can equally partake in the virtual. They may express a certain degree of order and stability, but those would be the precarious order and stability of the metastable state.

From within the virtual, we cannot set a divide between the precarious and the stable. We no longer make a distinction between that which is the aftermath of the concatenation of processes or materials and that which is fundamentally plastic, the result of an engagement with thresholds of self-organisation. When we speak of biological and machinic organisms, the vernacular understanding of these terms compels us to imagine a wealth of pre-established constraints set up in such a way as to safeguard the organism from deformation or even the introduction of too much variety and novelty within the system. There is an emphasis on regularity and predictability. When we speak of biological and machinic organisms *through* the virtual, however, the emphasis is on dynamisms and disruptions. One is more interested in the anomalous influxes, the capacity for mutation, even the ability to jump out of an arrangement set for self-preservation. First and foremost, one sees biological and machinic organisms as dissipative systems that re-compose and revisit the conditions for their co-composition.

Let us transfer this arrangement to the realm of performing automata. Here we observe two things. First, we see how the pre-established constraints and the ongoing co-production of constraints safeguard the perpetuation of the whole and secure the co-dependence of parts. At the same time, this arrangement also has a virtual dimension where the introduction of each constraint generates an additional "atmosphere" of virtuality. This atmosphere of virtuality becomes "the excess of affect that keeps bodies together; and what emerges when bodies are held together by, though and against each other" (Philippopoulos-Mihalopoulos 2016, 90). So we can also think of biological and machinic organisms as concatenations of constraints and the affected virtual. An amalgamation of precarious conditions and predictability, dissipation and processes of construction, rigidity and the introduction of variation into the pre-established order are the aspects of biological and machinic organisms that make them capable of both self-preservation and a fundamental openness towards the virtual. And self-preservation is not built on closure but on the continual changes in the modes of production and reproduction that traverse organisms and machines.

Structural rigidity is the condition for delineation and distinctness; however, it is not to be aligned with autonomy. Within the virtual, the condition and mark of "autonomy" (albeit a different concept of autonomy almost unrecognisable as such) is the openness of a system. Autonomy is not so much the self-preserving aspect of an organism or a machine as its capacity for receptivity—that is, the ability to be responsive notwithstanding any consideration for the unity of one's own boundaries. Responsivity aligns the various components of an organism and a machine to attune them to the single activity of becoming receptive. As holistic organisational wholes, both organisms and machines exist as such when their components work in concert. The removal or the addition of a component would introduce entirely new dynamics into a system. We may even begin to think of the newly established re-composed system as an entirely novel organism or a machine. So each nominally distinct "part" exists and co-exists only within the networked environment of its activity "in a tangled web of mutual dependence and reciprocal causation" (Marques and Brito 2014, 110). Biological and machinic organisms, too, are such "organized systems of material aggregates, whose specific properties and functions depend on their particular form, which are subject to disintegration but are constantly repaired and replaced by the activity of material construction of the system" (ibid., 111). The intricate system of self-constitution and pre-established systemic unity, self-regulation and corrective construction, punctures the ways biological and machinic organisms persist in an environment. Whereas the virtual allows for a foregrounding of the constitutive and the downplaying of the regulative aspect of the genesis of organisms, we still take a look at organisms beyond another restriction—the constitutive role of the concept of pre-established organisation as such. The work of Sougwen Chung undermines even this very last domain to foreground the atmospheric, gestural, and response-driven motilities within systems of collaboration.

Omnia

And now is the time to ask "under which conditions can technological advances become emancipatory rather than disciplinary, and which social and political theory would enable this healing pharmacological dimension to emerge?" (Devellennes and Dillet 2018, 15). Against the backdrop of a decline of the concept of nature and novel dialogues on entanglement, the consolidation of technoecology as a conceptual realm is a direct aftermath of "the autonomization of the technical as it unfolded in the genesis of the technosphere and the enforcement of a technogeological paradigm of the earth" (Hörl 2017, 12). This signals "a turn to a generalised ecological paradigm, a geologic technoecology, a total technical milieu. And thus there is a need for an onto-ethics adequate to current socio-technical attachments of the body…" (de Freitas 2019, 88). We arrive at this onto-ethics by taking a plunge in the very mesh of things—in seeking, or better still, constructing the embodiment of those intensities in need of articulation.

Omnia per Omnia (2018) turns the kinetic flows of cities into drawing lines. Using the city of New York as a template, Sougwen Chung reinvigorates the tradition of landscape painting to see it as a collaboration between a(n human) artist, a robotic swarm of surveillance cameras, and the dynamics of human movements in urban space. *Omnia* vicariously delves into the possibility of encountering a wealth of ways of sensing. We have the perceptual apparatus of organic flows within the city but, at the same time, are allowed glimpses into the ways in which a machine perceives those surroundings. An interweave of organic and artefactual is displayed in a drawing performance where Chung works together with a swarm of custom-designed drawing robots on a single piece of canvas. The collaboration looks into the organismic quality of the collaborative process whereby we do not have a singular source of agency or intentionality. Rather, we are confronted with an expansive gesture that is ultimately "environmental"—encompassing the zest of a new type of plurality that involves both humans and artefactual agents.

Chung's work is concerned with combining the hand-drawn line and the intuitive gesture with the work of algorithms and computational technologies. Drawing becomes an excavation of the intricacies of human–robot collaboration, delving into the possibility of novel ways of dwelling and co-inhabiting based on egalitarian togetherness. Taking on debates on public safety and interaction in the public space, the resulting canvases are based on extractions from a multitude of public cameras, capturing the very movement that flows within a city. Extracting gestures and behaviours, Chung and the robotic swarm transfer crowds' movements to a drawing canvas. This is a closer look into the reactivity of crowds and the swarm-intelligence-like response patterns of people moving in large urban areas. The work plunges into the collectivity of a movement taken on by some to be expanded towards the entirety of a given stretch of environment.

With the help of video analytics mapping out the directedness of crowds, Chung collects and recreates what she calls "the biometrics of the city". Primarily, these are optical captures of the flows of bodily movements within a given pre-mapped urban area. This behaviour, then, is translated into a robotic movement that works as a gesturely motion on a painting canvas. One witnesses how both technology and bodies facilitate a form of art that manifests itself as a collective drawing of lines. We have bodies that we habitually designate as both robotic and non-anthropomorphic as well as bodies that are biological systems. Both artefactual and organic actors, however, partake in an expansive organism that, at the same time, undermines the very idea of the term. In this sense, the gesture of collaboration—which, as Chung notes, entails a high degree of vulnerability—becomes primary. We have a foregrounding of enmeshments and engenderings and not so much a work as an artistic object with its own materiality.

Once confronted with the very materiality of the drawing canvas, one is simultaneously taken into the vast cloud of virtualities surrounding the hand-drawn line. The drawing hand and the swarm of robotic units are triggers and facilitators that take us to the virtual existences of computational technologies and let us partake in the flows created by unwitting human and non-human collaborators traversing the city and forming their own spontaneous swarms. This connectivity puts on display the energies cutting through entities known as "human" and those known as "machines", the quasi-organismic quality of the interconnected map of flows, and the collaborative zest of the mere dwelling-with, the simple fact of moving together in a shared space. *Omnia* shows how an organism is created out of openness and flows—this is a reverse-engineering of the walled-off individualistic organism and an entrance into the expanse of movement. This expansive concept of organism—made palpable through an engagement with the virtual—allows us to conceive of novel ways of togetherness that primarily consider energetic exchanges, gestures, and a mode of continual interconnected flowing.

The performance collaborators are Sougwen Chung and D.O.U.G._L.A.S. (Drawing Operations Unit: Live Autonomous System). No distinction is made between human and artefactual agency, nor is there any discussion around the fact that one of the collaborators is a non-organic artefactual apparatus. Rather, the focus is on the collaboration as such and the capacity for invention entailed in any form of thinking with and sensing with. This gesture has already overcome the ethical imperative to witness technical objects as part of symmetrical relations,

> The specific mode of existence of technical objects relates back to their participation in life … . This specificity is the condition of possibility to entertain a symmetrical relation with the technical object as 'other.' It requires an epistemological and simultaneously ethical act.
> (Schick 2021, 4)

Instead of focusing on the symmetry or asymmetry of the relation, *Omnia* sets out to interrogate the practices and heuristic potential of the collaborative imagination, asking question such as "What does it mean to collaborate with the spaces we inhabit, the tools we build? Where does 'I' end and 'we' begin?" (Howard 2018, n.p.). The work, then, is only vicariously about that superfluous fascination with the work performed by intelligent artefactual agents but is more about creating modes of togetherness: the

> self-organising effects at the infraindividual scale can channel through the individual body, reverberating out to larger scales … the micro-ethnographic scale plugs into the trans-individual scale of the collective endeavour so that the task is 'a doing done through us'.
> (de Freitas 2019, 93)

Chung says, "In *Omnia per Omnia*, I collaborate through a drawing duet with machines to understand my own engagement to technological complexity, as articulated by a multi-agent body, and represent how these technological systems see in contrast to humans" (Chung 2018, n.p.). The resulting four canvases are called density study (40.761124, -73.999089), direction study (40.712848, -73.989411), dwell study (40.695045, -73.972466), and velocity study (40.722215, -73.992944), all in mixed media and in a 48in x 48in format.

In evoking the metaphor "biometrics of the city", Chung shows how the city of New York becomes the conduit for multi-causal robotic agency. The motion vectors extracted out of the city's multifarious motionscapes are linked to DOUG_LAS, triggering a swarm-intelligence-like painting act as Chung and the artefactual collaborators work on a canvas portraying flows of motion. The surveillance cameras of the city become conduits that capture these flows as Chung works with surveillance apertures to delve into the question of robotic perception. One shifts the attention towards the very ontological frame that we need to question in order to enable novel ways of envisioning robotic agents as participants in worlds seemingly dominated and orchestrated by human agency. The metaphor of "seeing" is also brought to the table, posing the question if there is a specifically robotic way of sensing that bypasses both the visuality and visibility tropes to arrive at a more expansive, motion-based type of sensing that can be aligned with the concept of attunement. Sensing via attunement is also related to the hive-intelligence quality of the robotic swarm, mixing the publicly available visual data (the panoptical) with the mode of interconnectedness that is the condition of possibility for attunement (the environmental). The expansive hive-intelligence apparatus gathers, in real time, information about the less tangible side of interconnected movement. It draws a map of density, directionality, and velocities within the city. The algorithm's "way of seeing" is one of drawing and mapping out the various attunement-enabling conditions within the motionscape.

The drawing canvas displays an "optical flow". However, this optical dimension is distilled out of virtual movement—exerted on a city that is continually in flux. The canvases show the very pressure of the virtual—supra-subjective, multi-causal, and moulded out of a wealth of enmeshments. What is captured is not simply a pattern that gives us a glimpse into crowd behaviour but also a way of sensing collectivity through the various acts of attunement that mould this ever-evolving pattern. One is radically exposed to and made aware of extra-human, extra-organismic sensing:

> ... outside any encounter with human perception, the electron, the mountains, the tree involve perceptions. They are perceptions in themselves: they *are* how they take account, in their own self-formative activity, of the world of activity always and already going on around.
> (Massumi 2011, 26)

This engagement with the extra-human, however, does not evoke the concept of allure inasmuch as allure entails two distinct ontological planes of inquiry that construe a constitutive distinctness between objects:

> An object is alluring when it not only displays particular qualities but also insinuates the existence of something deeper, something hidden and inaccessible, something that cannot actually be displayed. Allure is properly a sublime experience because it stretches the observer to the point where it reaches the limits of its power or where its apprehensions break down. To be allured is to be beckoned into a realm that cannot ever be reached.
> (Shaviro 2014, 42)

Rather, the inquiry takes place within the virtual and thereby eschews questions of access. It is entirely developed from within a cloud of potentialities, making the very virtual tangible as such.

In an earlier collaboration with Drawing Operations Unit: Generation 2 (2017), Chung dwells on the possibilities of robotic memory. Similar to

Omnia, this performance takes place on the drawing canvas, combining the hand-drawn line and input from a robotic collaborator. In the initial stages of the piece, the machine collaborator—a robotic arm—learns how to draw by mimetic processing of the drawing style of Chung's hand. Drawings are analysed with the help of a computer vision algorithms gesture by gesture, over time. During the learning process, the robot "demonstrates a style inspired by the artist's drawing gestures, trained on deep learning algorithms. A composite behaviour of human and machine develops" (Chung 2018, n.p.). Variations are introduced in real time as the robotic arm extracts its behaviour from neural networks trained on the basis of Chung's drawing gestures. What takes place during the performance is a drawing duet where the robotic hand has accumulated knowledge based on the study of gestures and the artist's previous drawings but ultimately offers an interpretation of those. As is typical of practices of collaboration, automation and autonomy coagulate to co-create novel patterns of behaviour for the collaborators. This collaborative mode of co-habitation is one of immersed togetherness, bringing forth a novel form of ontological awareness. Through the display of diaphanous organismicity, machinic collaboration paves the way for a "new materialist literacy" (Bühlmann et al. 2017, 47) towards becoming adept in responsive ways of attuning oneself to non-anthropomorphic ambience.

One can see why these are foremost an inquiry into the force of ecology. Ecology, within the pages of this book, is the science of ambiences and atmospheres. Unlike environments—the concrete milieus generated by a body, ecologies are the virtual atmospheres and spectral inflections that traverse bodies in motion. Rather than having interactions among discrete objects, *Omnia* shows us just that—the atmosphere within the cloud of potentialities enveloping a human–artefactual entanglement. And still, vicariously, the ethics developed out of the entanglement effects in these interactions becomes palpable just as well. This ethics of entanglement means something as simple as the call that we "respond, reimagine, and receptively approach the world with care in all its complexity" (Burke and Fishel 2019, 100). It invites us to be "accountable for our political position by unlearning imperial epistemologies and making knowledge production a means of collective transformation" (Sundberg 2015, 124). Entanglements, needless to say, are seldom unproblematic:

> A key aspect of our relationships with stuff is that they involve more than networks of humans and things, a symmetry of relations. Rather, our relations with things are often asymmetrical leading to entrapments in particular pathways from which it is difficult to escape.
>
> (Hodder 2016, 13)

Omnia plays with the expectation for asymmetrical entanglement and the conceptual complacencies that the vernacular imagination finds in human-thing collaboration. Finally, the work displays how the perceived inequality between humans and things construes and perpetuates "asymmetries in human–thing entanglements" (Hodder and Lucas 2017, 119) while also showing, in a most visceral way, a path towards being a being relating to others.

On the website showcasing Chung's work, we have the following declaration of egalitarian confluence taken from the Gutai Art Manifesto:

> … the human spirit and matter shake hands with each other while keeping their distance. Matter never compromises itself with the spirit; the spirit never dominates matter. When matter remains intact and exposes its characteristics, it starts telling a story and even cries out. To make the fullest use of matter is to make use of the spirit. By enhancing the spirit, matter is brought to the height of the spirit.
>
> (Yoshihara Jirō 1956, 202)

This passage vicariously showcases a view on togetherness as a confluence of disparate forces that equally partake in the making of worlds and in the co-shaping of being. A commitment to this confluence between crowd behaviour and artefactual sensing—through face-tracking and motion recognition apparatuses—is also replicated in the very act of the performance. We have a meeting of artefactual and biological sensing that co-shape an experience of imagination:

> Once the robots start moving and the music fades in, everyone turns quiet. The slow and seemingly purposeful movement of the robots, the traces of the blue paint they leave behind, the motion of Sougwen's brush and the expression of total concentration on her face create an atmosphere of a ritual, a spiritual action. …
>
> (Abraham 2018, n.p.)

Response: Against Communication

On seeking out a territory for gesture within the concept of organism, we arrive at the very nature of response. Unlike a solution to a problem, a response is not final and necessarily evades closure. A response is a problematising activity as it interrogates the very conditions of the emergence of a problem:

> with response, an answer is required that refers back to the problem not just as a difficulty to be managed but as a historically contingent and unique development, the very conditions of which are vital to comprehending how to respond. By responding, we speak directly to a problem by addressing its conditions.
>
> (Cunniff Gilson 2014, 88)

In being such, a response "expresses and gives voice to the problem itself, making the depth of the difficulty appear to us" (ibid., 88). Within a theatre of the virtual, the mode of operation is that of response.

The notion of response remains distant from a "rhetoric of branding and innovation" (Lemke 2017, 150). We do not have a radical reinvigoration or a rethinking of a concept, a significant shift, or a decisive dismantling. What takes place within a vantage of response is rather a change in inflection, an alteration in tone, and a subtle adjustment that makes things more exposed to potentiality. Thinking in terms of response does not by any means entail thinking in terms of communication or translation. The concept of translatability is alien to the field of potentiality as here each entity already subsists in immediacy and connection. At the same time, this is not a region that does not allow for any "privacy" of things. The various points of inflection within the virtual do not have to be completely and transparently intelligible to one another. Nor is there a need for "communication" as the "translation" of incongruent ideas. "Communication" is replaced by "attunement". And attunement is not so much a verbal or a cognitive phenomenon as an energetic one. "Understanding" takes place through a procedure of attunement that can be likened to a responsive change of vibration—aligning oneself to the perturbations created by others. Responsive alignment does not take place via language and is not achieved by linguistic means. Even more so, it does not have much to do with the cognitive faculties traditionally associated with understanding. This is not a matter of "reasoning". Nor is it a matter of the senses as such. One could liken responsive attunement to a *visceral tactility*, a kind of sensing that pervades the entirety of one's being and triggers understanding on a level that is pervasive—understanding and communicating by viscerally becoming an-other.

So when one operates from the vantage of the virtual, debates on the "impossibility of translation" become obsolete. Across ontological layers, a plenitude of entities and non-entities interweave in complex patterns and interact in ways that allow them to become an-other without sacrificing the integrity of their structure. Attunement makes it possible for them to understand and align to other entities and non-entities across the virtual field, form networks of interaction, and even dissolve. Attunement, however, is a type of interaction that does not become tangible to the observer. Attunement takes place strictly between and within the interweave of entities and non-entities, forces, and speeds. The field of potentiality "has nothing to say" in the strict sense of having to offer an account of itself. The virtual does not speak; potentiality does not explain itself; and response does not communicate.

Attunement brings forth a type of understanding that could be seen it terms of "affective tonality" (Manning 2013a, 166) as a pre-linguistic phenomenon that is before articulation and does not need articulation as such in order to thrive. It is a visceral phenomenon of co-composing. And attunement is not an event of communication but a practice of expression. Models of communication are replaced by the forceful folding and refolding of an existing composition to the point that novel textures and resonances are gleaned out of the activity of vigorous realignment. There are two constituents that are primary here: force and movement. Force is the very constitutive zest of matter itself. This is a function that is not coming from outside of matter (as the organising function of form), nor does it have its source from "within" (as the ingrained entelechy of an entity). A model within which an access to affective tonality is feasible is equally so a model that allows us to see matter as mattering—as auto-generative and precipitating its own auto-genesis without recourse to external organisation. Within a recomposition through affective tonality, force is the functional side of mattering. That is to say, mattering works through force—a potentiality that equally permeates the fabric of beings and extra-ontological entities. The force of matter is expressed by movement. In a manner of speaking, movement is the principle according to which matter expresses itself in that it begins to shift across various levels of potentiality and actuality. So affective tonality has force as its function and movement as its expression.

Affective tonality is gestural: it is a practice of invitation and ontological generosity as it allows us a glimpse into the plenitude of being and the creative zest of the extra-ontological. Affective tonality beckons towards recomposition in displaying novel ways of mattering and moving. But even more so, it offers novel ways of conceptualising matter and movement. Practising affective tonality is a plunge into the practice of encountering. Encountering, in turn, brings an inflection into matter, aligns with the ontogenetic force of mattering, and partakes in the proliferation of singular worlds within the virtual. Affective tonality works beyond regimes of iteration, progression, isomorphic mapping, and meaning production.

Surely enough, affective tonality is partly mimesis. Affective tonality vicariously builds isomorphic maps between experience, feeling, perception, and thought. In doing so, it makes us aware of the concerted efforts of an organism to realign and recompose by making all these various "compartments" of a body intelligible to one another. In a certain manner of speaking, then, affective tonality works with the given. However, and more significantly, affective tonality also has an aspect that is solely virtual. This is not an interrogation into genesis as such but an invitation to think across and beyond the concretion of a given ontogenetic flow towards the generative work of the virtual itself. This is the power of a thing "to beckon to the beyond of its genesis" (Manning 2013a, 182).

We arrive at a practice working towards the recompositions within an individuating body but also towards one's co-composition with environments. Just as the discrete becoming of a thing is guided by a productive realignment of thresholds of experience, feeling, perception, and thought, so is the scenic landscape surrounding a thing a playground for co-composing and re-composing. Here we deal with a particular style of being or an attitude towards being: that of a fundamental openness. A fundamental openness, however, does not imply a blind exposure to the forces of an "outside". This is a critical practice of realignment that takes the outside into consideration and actively invents ways of co-composing. Openness is a way of looking that considers the scenic landscape. However, this consideration is made not in utilitarian terms but in terms of the possibilities that the individuating zest of a thing-in-becoming can bring. And again, this practice is not about individual subjects and objects, nor is it about individual journeys of becoming. It is about entering the threshold of potentiality. The focus here is on the very interstitial gesture—the practice of alignment and realignment, the generative power of the in-between, and the repotentialising zest of the given. We emphasise the activity taking place at the threshold as a separate entity with its distinct *style* of being and capacity to bring forth a different inflection into the given. This practice at the interface of things is not so much about the participating individuals as about the event of alignment, about enabling and being able to rise to the occasion of a singular co-composition.

Co-composition is not a gesture of asymmetrical generosity whereby one constituent extends an abundance of relations towards another constituent that is "poorer" in terms of its capacities for relation-building and world-forming. Even more so, there is no instrumentality attached to the relation that is formed in co-composition. Rather, we deal with a confluence whereby relation-building is a composition taking place from within the resources of potentiality and through these resources. This is about aligning thresholds of being without attaching a statement about the exact relation capacities and degrees of freedom of its constituents. If there is something that is fundamentally generous and relation-bestowing, this is the virtual as such. Discrete entities nominally designated as "subjects" and "objects", that is, entities entering in relationships of realignment and mutual co-composition, partake in this plenitude and become conduits for the fundamental generosity of the virtual. It is not that the subject bestows something upon the object and it is not that the object is made instrumental in the act of bestowal. Such characterisations glide into one another and can only exist to the extent that they still delineate increasingly fluctuating boundaries. What matters here is the gesture of fundamental response: directed towards the virtual and drawing from the resources of potentiality in order to inform the given in novel ways.

What takes place in the interstitial region of the co-composition is an event. The eventual character of the alignment reveals a maximal exposure to the virtual. This is, among other things, an encounter with the impersonal force of something that is extra-ontological: "What the side of the element that is turned towards me conceals is not a 'something' susceptible of being revealed, but an ever new depth of absence, an existence with existent, the impersonal par excellence" (Levinas 1969, 142). Where thresholds of being are traversed and where degrees of matter enter in re-composition, potentiality and actuality are equally real. Both the potential—regardless of its degrees of actualisation and regardless of its status as a potentially potential or actually potential—and the actual—regardless of its status as a lesser or greater level of actualisation—are of the domain of being. They are existents and partake in the making of worlds as existents. At the other end of the scales, we have a supra-existent—the event. The event is an aspect of the virtual that does not have the status of an entity—it is inherent in things but does not have any being separate from this inherence. It purely subsists as an extra-ontological influx that permeates being (Deleuze 1990). This is how the complex relationship between the virtual, potentiality and actuality, and the event play themselves out at the threshold. Whereas potentiality and actuality are equally "real", that is, equally of "being", there is an additional aspect of the virtual that is evental. This is a supra-existent region in that it does not have a reality of its own but subsists in and catalyses the realities of potentialising and actualising entities within the theatre of the virtual.

And it is no wonder that the event becomes somewhat more palpable exactly within the interstitial region of maximum potentialisation. The event is written into the relation with the virtual as the conduit that precipitates movement across thresholds of being. An evental influx alters the conditions for the emergence of the new as well as the conditions of the re-composition of matter. As an event is distilled at the brittle border between regimes of being, the extra-ontological aspect of the virtual begins to permeate these co-aligning systems of determination. The result is a "mutation" of the real that is practically unpredictable as it is virtually impossible to foresee the various movements of coagulation and realignment that will transpire in the complex—always differently accentuated and always multi-directional—interweave of potentiality and actuality.

Now, let us go back to *Omnia* where humans and artefacts work together to expose the brittle threshold between actual and virtual. These continue the work of bridging the mimetic with the emergent, that which is of being with the extra-ontological. The event propels the conditions for the emergence of novel recompositions and repotentialisations of the given; it guarantees a constant influx of the virtual into the given world region. This exchange between being and the extra-ontological is not one-directional but takes place interchangeably and pervasively. The extra-ontological region colours existence with the force of abstract potentialisation while the being-aspect of the virtual secures the ongoing play of potentiality and actuality. In the former case, we deal with mutant emergencies without prefigured outcomes; the latter takes us to a scenic landscape that displays not so much the work of discrete individuating entities as the generative zest of matter itself.

In both cases, we have dynamic responsive enmeshments that foreplay movement as such. Even more so, movement becomes an onto-genetic category in its own right. As movement is entwined with the work of the virtual—even in its minor aspect as a precipitator of the event—the virtual and movement are both recast in their mutual enmeshment. Movement—the co-creation of a tracing within the given—becomes increasingly engaged in practices of repotentialisation, whereas the virtual becomes overwhelmingly involved in practices of reconnecting actuality.

This engendering of the new is not mimetic only. It is an affective singularisation that has its source in an exposure to the virtual. Encountering the virtual is a singular expressive practice anchored in movement. And movement is so well suited to account for one such encounter precisely because of its capacity for affective tonality. Movement brings forth the receptive alignment that runs through the spectrum of epistemological accesses—making thought and experience intelligible to one another—but, at the same time, maintains a connection with the extra-ontological region of the event.

From this vantage, again, we no longer have discrete entities undergoing alterations. We have a movement that partakes in the variegated inflections of the real, altering world regions where it encounters and recomposes more or less discrete entities. The work of the theatre of the virtual is an expression and an account of this movement. The perturbations traversing bodies on the verge of becoming are articulated and made palpable. What we encounter is not merely a tendency to recompose but a more deeply ingrained connection with the virtual and the generative force of movement. We encounter a force within the virtual that is compositional. It has the capacity to bring forth a structure within an encountered entity, precipitate unprecedented mutation, and even cause entities to shift entirely towards the extra-ontological, making them infra-virtual.

Unlike the virtual, which is still an existent and of the order of the real, the infra-virtual will be of the order of the event—a mutant singularity that has undergone a refolding towards the maximally saturated virtual. The infra-virtual is not an ontological entity any longer—it has gone one step further than any potentiality in that it has shifted towards an infra-existential subsistence, a region of the recalcitrant "fragility of things" (Connolly 2013, 400). So here we do not even have categories and degrees of being but an overwhelming and pervasive co-composition that permeates the entire scenic landscape. This extra-ontological region works in favour of being. It has the capacity to catalyse the processes of potentiality and actuality. The extra-ontological strikes a chord that begins to reverberate across the entirety of an environment. One is no longer above, beneath, or outside of the scenic landscape, one is no longer a subject and an entity, but equally a movement and equally the scenic.

Why response? "Response" offers a level of attunement that is expansive and involves all constituents within an ecology, that is, it is the *collectivisation of responsivity*. It brings forth a kind of responsibility that is not necessarily related to the organising gaze (as is the case with the scenario offered by Levinas), nor does it pertain to human subjectivity, invariably creating a subject–object relation (as is the case with Buber). Our concept of response (Dimitrova 2017, 173) replaces such linear understanding of responsibility. Response is understood as an all-encompassing attunement that thrives on permeability. Similar to plastic waste and climate change, response is pervasive: "viscous" inasmuch as it can "stick" to beings that are involved with it, "nonlocal" as it reverberates across the entirety of a field of potentiality, entails "profoundly different temporalities than the human-scale ones", and manifests its effects "interobjectively" (Morton 2013, 1–10) and transobjectively, across and through things.

Within diaphanous organismicity, the porous boundary of a body acts as a sensing organ that anticipates regimes of attunement. A body always already, constitutively, remains in contact with the co-emergent ecologies that surround it. Its ongoing activity is that of response: it does not choose or calculate its position but unites and reactivates relations. Unlike responsibility, a response is not the creation of an exclusive relation to another (a non-self). When we think with the virtual, everything is a response and one cannot but respond. Response is always already in position and about to take place. There is nothing proprietary about it, and the relations it forms are persistently inclusive—unlike relations created in I-Thou exclusivity.

Response, at the same time, is choreographic in its character. Response works through an ecology of rhythms and decisions that themselves are part of a plenitude of potentials. The plenitude of potentials is distributed in such a way that its ecology is dispersive yet network-oriented. Each node and component is part of the field of potentiality and thereby is an expression of the field. At the same time, nodes and components resound with and through one another, creating duration out of expression and distilling spatiality out of the various reverberations across the field. As they echo and resound across the nodes of a quasiverse of movement, they precipitate qualitative shifts in the composition of other forms. These shifts, in turn, engender further singularities. In this way, we have a field of potentiality entirely defined in terms of the politics of response—empathetically receiving a motion or an impulse, taking it in, making it one's own, transforming it and then handing it over somewhere further across the reverberating nodes.

A politics of response thrives on openness and permeability. A politics of response creates the ground for and weaves the atmospheres of "collective self-invention in the interstices of existing political formations" (Saldanha and Stark 2016, 437). This is why response is choreographic—it is a motion that aligns itself to the variety of ecologies within and outside of its perimeter of action. Such ecologies can both be felt and hypothetical, viscerally experienced and maximally speculative. What matters most is the capacity for openness, which is the privilege of remaining in the mesh. Along these lines, Manning proposes the concept of "mobile architectures" (Manning 2013b) as a way of thinking the choreographic in its capacity to give us insight into the force of the virtual. When the philosopher speaks in terms of mobile architectures, the focus shifts towards the event of movement as something that does not take place within and for a discrete body. Rather, we witness an ontogenetic architecting of environments in movement.

The procedural part of response is this perpetual resounding, attunement, and alignment to the ecologies of others. Response anticipates the gestation of singularities. The presence of singularities, in turn, safeguards a constant "supply" of emergencies, a cloud of repotentialised expressions that continue to imprint the pressure of the virtual upon a given stretch of reality. In this way, components within the field of potentiality—to the extent to which we can think of discrete entities at all—stretch outside their nominal boundaries to incorporate the ecology in its entirety as well. Further still, singularities within the field retain all expressions of the virtual that have shaped them across their various stations and residences as forms within an environment. In this way, the field of potentiality always already remains an invitation to enter in composition with others. Response is the field's procedural side, and response can be said to be choreographic in such a way that it allows us to think of the field in terms of both orchestration and arbitrariness. This is a design that remains continually in motion and refigures its constituents with every step. Prefiguration and emergence work together to expose the texture of the new.

Response is not about the body but about the flow of potentialities that makes itself palpable through movement and attunement. It is this progression of rhythms and decisions that can be best described as response. And a take on response as choreographic allows us to conceive of ecologies—in the sense of politics—that are generative and self-composing. It offers us access to the field of potentialities and allows us to gain insights into potentiality as a procedure for response. Looking at the procedural character of potentiality, in turn, allows us to perceive the connections and conditions that underline phenomena such as attunement and alignment. Attunement and alignment are the two forces of the virtual working within the politics of response; responsive receiving is the key activity of a functioning ecology.

A politics of response may have a body as its starting point but surpasses the sole engagement with a discrete body to stretch towards more comprehensive if not global ways of alignment and attunement. As *Omnia* has shown, responsivity allows us "to think transversally, to interlace the mechanosphere, the social sphere, and the inwardness of subjectivity" (Graafland 2017, 48). A politics of response extends an invitation for the creation of techniques of ecologising, the practice of partaking in a field of potentialities whereby each entity reverberates across the entirety of the virtual field. In this sense, response is both a politics—in opposition to a politics of power—and a practical philosophy—in opposition to hierarchical politics of generosity, hospitality, I-Thou. While having a body—a relatively discrete object within a relatively established world—as its point of departure, response shifts to interstitial regions such as movement and extra-ontological constituents such as the event while still reinstating the question of its "carnal insistence" (Bolt 2013, 10).

In fleshing out the formal constituents and conceptual atmospheres surrounding the theatre of the virtual, we arrived at the concept of organism. Habitually, bodies are invariably perceived as organisms—self-preserving and other-rejecting discrete entities walled-off from environments, primarily seeking to persevere in their established form. Yet the concept of a body that we had crafted so far can no longer sustain an organismic interpretation. So we began to speak of diaphanous organismicity to do justice to the porous, permeable, and spectral body that inhabits the theatre of the virtual. Diaphanous organismicity allows for degrees and thinks in terms of gradients beyond delineation; a body becomes an expanse as it reverberates and attunes. It is this dispersal of the organism that we encounter in the work of Sougwen Chung.

Diaphanous organismicity is gestural. And gesture is a compositional force within the virtual. Gesture has the capacity to bring forth a structure, precipitate alteration, and even cause shifts towards the extra-ontological event. So this compositional force within the virtual brings forth both ontological and extra-ontological regions that co-compose in continual attunement. Here we speak of a visceral attunement that is dispersive and thrives on pre-linguistic affective tonality. We described the operations of attunement that take place through affective tonality as operations of response. Within the pages of this book, response is not a communicative event but a question of style; a practice of expression and realignment that manifests a deep connection with the virtual. It is through response that organisms and machines loosen up any existing pre-formatting to become co-generative. Whereas, across specificities, communication is mimetic and inherently linguistic, response is a sensing practice of engendering through attunement.

A response evades closure and works through the logic of inflections within the given to make things more exposed to potentiality. But we do not stop here. Apart from all this, a practice of perpetual response exposes us to the infra-virtual, that is, a non-real region that surpasses the virtual as it allows entities to pass into infra-existence. Here we no longer argue that the virtual and the actual are both real. Nor do we still struggle to demonstrate, within the limitations of argumentative thought, how movement, potentiality, and gesture constitute the given. Rather, we pass into regions of exuberant non-reality. What we witness within these regions are not simply choreographies of openness and permeability but performances at the very frontier of existence.

Works Cited

Abraham, Irina. 2018. "What Happens When Tech Engineers and Artists Collaborate? 'Only Human' Curated by the New Museum's NEW INC and Nokia's Bell Labs at MANA Contemporary." *Whitehot Magazine*, May 2018. https://whitehotmagazine.com/articles/bell-labs-at-mana-contemporary/3966.

Anderson, Kay and Colin Perrin. 2015. "New Materialism and the Stuff of Humanism." *Australian Humanities Review* 58: 1–15. http://australianhumanitiesreview.org/wp-content/uploads/2015/09/AHR58_01_AndersonPerrin.pdf.

Aretoulakis, Emmanouil. 2014. "Towards a Posthumanist Ecology. Nature without Humanity in Wordsworth and Shelley." *European Journal of English Studies* 18: 172–190. https://doi.org/10.1080/13825577.2014.917005.

Aristotle. 1984. Physics. In *The Complete Works of Aristotle: The Revised Oxford Translation*, edited and translated by Jonathan Barnes. Princeton, NJ: Princeton University Press.

Bolt, Barbara. 2013. "Introduction: 'Toward a New Materialism' Through the Arts." In *Carnal Knowledge: Towards a 'New Materialism' Through the Arts*, edited by Estelle Barrett and Barbara Bolt, 1–13. London and New York: I. B. Tauris.

Braun, Bruce. 2015. "From Critique to Experiment. Rethinking Political Ecology for the Anthropocene." In *The Routledge Handbook of Political Ecology*, edited by Tom Perreault, Gavin Bridge and James McCarthy, 102–114. London: Routledge.

Bühlmann, Vera, Felicity Colman and Iris van der Tuin. 2017. "Introduction to New Materialist Genealogies: New Materialisms, Novel Mentalities, Quantum Literacy." *The Minnesota Review* 88: 47–58. https://doi.org/10.1215/00265667-3787378.

Burke, Anthony and Stefanie Fishel. 2019. "Power, World Politics, and Thing-Systems in the Anthropocene." In *Anthropocene Encounters: New Directions in Green Political Thinking*, edited by Frank Biermann and Eva Lövbrand, 87–108. Cambridge: Cambridge University Press. https://doi.org/10.1017/9781108646673.005.

Chung, Sougwen. 2018. "Omnia per Omnia." Accessed August 1, 2021. https://sougwen.com/project/omniaperomnia.

Clark, Nigel. 2011. *Inhuman Nature: Sociable Life on a Volatile Planet*. London: Sage.

Cohen, Tom, Claire Colebrook and Hillis J. Miller. 2016. *Twilight of the Anthropocene Idols*. London: Open Humanities.

Colman, Felicity. 2006. "Affective Entropy: Art as Differential Form." *Angelaki: Journal of the Theoretical Humanities* 11 (1): 169–178. https://doi.org/10.1080/09697250600798060.

Connolly, William. 2013. "The 'New Materialism' and the Fragility of Things." *Millennium – Journal of International Studies* 41: 399–412. https://doi.org/10.1177/0305829813486849.

Crespo, Ricardo. 2017. *Economics and Other Disciplines: Assessing New Economic Currents*. London: Routledge.

Crespo, Ricardo. 2016. "Aristotle on Agency, Habits and Institutions." *Journal of Institutional Economics* 12 (4): 867–884. https://doi.org/10.1017/S1744137416000059.

Cunniff Gilson, Erinn. 2014. "Ethics and the Ontology of Freedom: Problematization and Responsiveness in Foucault and Deleuze." *Foucault Studies* 17: 76–98. http://dx.doi.org/10.22439/fs.v0i17.4254.

De Freitas, Elizabeth. 2019. "Love of Learning: Amorous and Fatal." In *Posthuman Ecologies. Complexity and Process after Deleuze*, edited by Rosi Braidotti and Simone Bignall, 87–105. London: Rowman & Littlefield International.

De Lucia, Vito. 2020. "Rethinking the Encounter Between Law and Nature in the Anthropocene: From Biopolitical Sovereignty to Wonder." *Law and Critique* 31: 329–349. https://doi.org/10.1007/s10978-020-09281-9.

Deacon, Terrence. 2012. *Incomplete Nature: How Mind Emerged from Matter*. New York: Norton & Company.

Deleuze, Gilles. 1990. *The Logic of Sense*. Translated by Mark Lester and Charles Stivale. Edited by Constantin V. Boundas. London: Athlone.

Devellennes, Charles and Benoît Dillet. 2018. "Questioning New Materialisms: An Introduction." *Theory, Culture and Society* 35 (7–8): 5–20. https://doi.org/10.1177/0263276418803432.

Dimitrova, Zornitsa. 2017. "Robotic Performance. An Ecology of Response." *Performance Philosophy* 3 (1): 162–77. https://doi.org/10.21476/PP.2017.3135.

Graafland, Arie. 2017. "A Research into Human-Machine Technologies—Architecture's Dream of a Bio-Future." In *Critical and Clinical Cartographies: Architecture, Robotics, Medicine, Philosophy*, edited by Andrej Radman and Heidi Sohn, 21–61. Edinburgh: Edinburgh University Press.

Grear, Anna. 2016. "Vulnerability, Advanced Global Capitalism and Co-symptomatic Injustice: Locating the Vulnerable Subject." In *Vulnerability: Reflections on a New*

Ethical Foundation for Law and Politics, edited by Martha A. Fineman and Anna Grear, 41–60. London: Routledge.

Grear, Anna. 2015. "Toward New Legal Futures? In Search of Renewing Foundations." In *Thought, Law, Rights and Action in the Age of Environmental Crisis*, edited by Anna Grear and Evadne Grant, 283–315. Northhampton, MA: Edward Elgar.

Hickey-Moody, Anna Catherine. 2015. "Beside Ourselves: Worlds Beyond People." *British Journal of Sociology of Education* 36 (5): 802–813. http://dx.doi.org/10.1080/01425692.2015.1043187.

Hodder, Ian and Gavin Lucas. 2017. "The Symmetries and Asymmetries of Human–Thing Relations. A Dialogue." *Archaeological Dialogues* 24 (2): 119–137. https://doi.org/10.1017/S1380203817000137.

Hodder, Ian. 2016. *Studies in Human-Thing Entanglement*. http://www.ian-hodder.com/books/studies-human-thing-entanglement.

Howard, Lindsey. 2018. "Sougwen Chung on Prototyping Human-Robotic Collaborations." Interview by Lindsey Howard. *NEW INC*, April 20, 2018. https://www.newinc.org/archive/sougwen-chung-only-human-2018-k34sf.

Hörl, Erich. 2017. "Introduction to General Ecology. The Ecologization of Thinking." In *General Ecology: The New Ecological Paradigm*, edited by Erich Hörl and James Burton, 1–75. London: Bloomsbury.

Huneman, Philippe and Charles Wolfe. 2010. "The Concept of Organism: Historical, Philosophical, Scientific Perspectives: Introduction." *History and Philosophy of the Life Sciences* 32 (2–3): 147–154. https://www.jstor.org/stable/23335070.

Johnston, John. 2008. *The Allure of Machinic Life: Cybernetics, Artificial Life, and the New AI*. Cambridge, MA: The MIT Press.

Kauffman, Stuart A. 2001. *Investigations*. Oxford: Oxford University Press.

Lemke, Thomas. 2017. "Materialism without Matter: The Recurrence of Subjectivism in Object-oriented Ontology." *Distinktion: Journal of Social Theory* 18 (2): 133–152. https://doi.org/10.1080/1600910X.2017.1373686.

Levant, Alex. 2017. "Smart Matter and the Thinking Body: Activity Theory and the Turn to Matter in Contemporary Philosophy." *Stasis* 5 (2): 248–264. https://doi.org/10.33280/2310-3817-2017-5-2-248-264.

Levinas, Emmanuel. 1969. *Totality and Infinity*. Pittsburgh, PA: Duquesne University Press.

Manning, Erin. 2016. *The Minor Gesture*. Durham, NC: Duke University Press.

Manning, Erin. 2013a. *Always More Than One: Individuation's Dance*. Durham, NC: Duke University Press.

Manning, Erin. 2013b. "Mobile Architectures." *Performance Paradigm* 9. https://www.performanceparadigm.net/index.php/journal/article/view/134/133.

Margulies, Jared and Brock Bersaglio. 2018. "Furthering Post-human Political Ecologies." *Geoforum* 94: 103–106. https://doi.org/10.1016/j.geoforum.2018.03.017.

Marques, Victor and Carlos Brito. 2014. "The Rise and Fall of the Machine Metaphor: Organizational Similarities and Differences between Machines and Living Beings." In *The Notion of Organism. Historical and Conceptual Approaches*, edited by Andrea Gambarotto and Luca Illetterati. Verifiche 43 (1–4): 77–113.

Massumi, Brian. 2011. *Semblance and Event. Activist Philosophy and the Occurrent Arts*. Cambridge, MA: The MIT Press.

Maturana, Humberto and Francisco Varela. 1972. *Autopoiesis and Cognition: The Realization of the Living*. Dordecht: Reidel Publishing.

McCullagh, Susanne. 2019. "Heterogeneous Collectivity and the Capacity to Act. Conceptualising Nonhumans in Political Space." In *Posthuman Ecologies. Complexity and Process after Deleuze*, edited by Rosi Braidotti and Simone Bignall, 141–159. London: Rowman & Littlefield International.

Morton, Timothy. 2013. *Hyperobjects: Philosophy and Ecology after the End of the World*. Minneapolis: University of Minnesota Press.

Mossio, Matteo and Alvaro Moreno. 2010. "Organisational Closure in Biological Organisms." *History and Philosophy of the Life Sciences* 32 (2–3): 269–288. https://www.jstor.org/stable/23335075.

Murphy, Patrick. 2016. *Persuasive Aesthetic Ecocritical Praxis: Climate Change, Subsistence, and Questionable Futures*. Lanham, MD: Lexington Books.

Nicholson, Daniel. 2014. "The Machine Conception of the Organism in Development and Evolution: A Critical Analysis." *Studies in History and Philosophy of Biological and Biomedical Sciences* 48: 162–174. https://doi.org/10.1016/j.shpsc.2014.08.003.

O'Sullivan, Simon. 2012. *On the Production of Subjectivity. Five Diagrams of the Finite-Infinite Relation*. Basingtoke: Palgrave Macmillan.

Palmer, Helen. 2016. "Rewritings/Refoldings/Fefleshings: Fictive Publics and the Material Gesture of Defamiliarization." *Continuum* 30 (5): 507–517. https://doi.org/10.1080/10304312.2016.1210724.

Palmer, Helen. 2014. *Deleuze and Futurism: A Manifesto for Nonsense*. London: Bloomsbury.

Parikka, Jussi. 2015. *The Anthrobscene*. Minneapolis: University of Minnesota Press.

Philippopoulos-Mihalopoulos, Andreas. 2016. "Milieu, Territory, Atmosphere: New Spaces of Knowledge." In *Knowledge-creating Milieus in Europe*, edited by A. Cusinato and Andreas Philippopoulos-Mihalopoulos, 79–95. Berlin/Heidelberg: Springer.

Philippopoulos-Mihalopoulos, Andreas and Thomas E. Webb. 2015a. "Vulnerable Bodies, Vulnerable Systems." *International Journal of Law in Context* 11 (4): 444–461. https://doi.org/10.1017/S1744552315000294.

Philippopoulos-Mihalopoulos, Andreas. 2015b. "Lively Agency: Life and Law in the Anthropocene." In *Animals, Biopolitics, Law. Lively Legalities*, edited by Irus Braverman, 193–209. London: Routledge.

Saldanha, Arun and Hannah Stark. 2016. "A New Earth: Deleuze and Guattari in the Anthropocene." *Deleuze Studies* 10 (4): 427–439. https://doi.org/10.3366/dls.2016.0237.

Schick, Johannes. 2021. "On Technical Alterity." *Foundations of Science*: 1–7. https://doi.org/10.1007/s10699-020-09771-0.

Shaviro, Steven. 2014. *The Universe of Things: On Speculative Realism*. Minneapolis: University of Minnesota Press.

Shaviro, Steven. 2010. "Interstitial Life: Remarks on Causality and Purpose in Biology." In *The Force of the Virtual: Deleuze, Science, and Philosophy*, edited by Peter Gaffney, 133–147. Minneapolis: The University of Minnesota Press.

Simondon, Gilbert. 2017. *On the Mode of Existence of Technical Objects*. Translated by Cécile Malaspina and John Rogove. Minneapolis, MN: Univocal.

Smith, Subrena. 2017. "Organisms as Persisters." *Philosophy, Theory, and Practice in Biology* 9 (14): 1–16. https://doi.org/10.3998/ptb.6959004.0009.014.

Stark, Hannah, Katrina Schlunke and Penny Edmonds. 2018. "Uncanny Objects in the Anthropocene." *Australian Humanities Review* 63: 22–30. http://australianhumanitiesreview.org/2018/12/01/__trashed/

Sundberg, Juanita. 2015. "Ethics, Entanglement, and Political Ecology." In *The Routledge Handbook of Political Ecology*, edited by Tom Perreault, Gavin Bridge and James McCarthy, 115–126. London: Routledge.

Symons, John. 2010. "The Individuality of Artifacts and Organisms." *History and Philosophy of the Life Sciences* 32 (2–3): 233–246. https://www.jstor.org/stable/23335073.

Tironi, Manuel, Myra J. Hird, Cristián Simonetti, Peter Forman, Nathaniel Freiburger. 2018. "Inorganic Becomings: Situating the Anthropocene in Puchunenacaví." *Environmental Humanities* 10 (1): 187–212. https://doi.org/10.1215/22011919-4385525.

Toepfer, Georg. 2014. "Organismicity and the Deconstruction of the Organism: From Substantial Forms to Degrees of Cooperation, Closure and Agency." In *The Notion of Organism. Historical and Conceptual Approaches*, edited by Andrea Gambarotto and Luca Illetterati. *Verifiche* 43 (1–4): 59–77.

van Dooren, Thom, Eben Kirksey and Ursula Münster. 2016. "Multispecies Studies: Cultivating Arts of Attentiveness." *Environmental Humanities* 8 (1): 1–23. https://doi.org/10.1215/22011919-3527695.

Varela, Francisco. 1979. *Principles of Biological Autonomy*. New York: North Holland.

Weintraub, Linda. 2018. *What's Next? Eco Materialism and Contemporary Art*. London: Intellect.

Wills, David. 2016. *Inanimation: Theories of Inorganic Life*. Minneapolis: University of Minnesota Press.

Wilson, Catherine. 2014. "The Concept of 'the Organism' in the Philosophy of Biology." In *The Notion of Organism. Historical and Conceptual Approaches*, edited by Andrea Gambarotto and Luca Illetterati. *Verifiche* 43 (1–4): 15–39.

Wolfe, Charles. 2014. "The Organism as Ontological Go-between: Hybridity, Boundaries and Degrees of Reality in Its Conceptual History." *Studies in History and Philosophy of Biological and Biomedical Sciences Studies* 48: 151–161. https://doi.org/10.1016/j.shpsc.2014.06.006.

Woodward, Ashley. 2016. *Lyotard and the Inhuman Condition: Reflections on Nihilism, Information, and Art*. Edinburgh: Edinburgh University Press.

Yoshihara Jirō. "Gutai Art Manifesto." Translated by Reiko Tomii. Originally published as Jirō, Yoshihara. 1956. "Gutai bijutsu sengen." *Geijutsu Shinchō* 7 (12): 202–204.

Yusoff, Katherine. 2014. "Geologic Subjects: Nonhuman Origins, Geomorphic Aesthetics, and the Art of Becoming Inhuman." *Cultural Geographies* 22 (3): 383–407. https://doi.org/10.1177/1474474014545301.

Conclusion

The main ontological category throughout this book is motion. In looking at the theatrical as a motion that does not cease, this book examined the concept of the virtual as key to constructing theatrical practices of radical engendering. An intensive engagement with the virtual reveals an ongoing genesis of forces that shoot through the given—not simply social and environmental conditioning forces but also visceral intra-bodily processes that determine the very material constitution of things. A focus is the generative zest of the virtual itself—the coming together of tendencies and operations of energetic entwinement. Hereby the entire virtual field is seen as a kinetic system—a system entirely composed of motion. The virtual field is inhabited by ontological regions such as gradients of potentiality and actuality as well as by extra-ontological inherences such as the event.

The concept of a theatre of the virtual developed throughout the pages of this book is manifold. It is conditioned on a fundamental attunement to the ontological and extra-ontological forces that skirt the given but systematically evade actualisation. Further still, it allows us to enter into regions that are supra-rational, that is, indifferent to the strong logicality of argumentative thought. These regions are open to infinite engendering. An attunement to these regions, in turn, allows us to see existence as prolific, self-generative, and flowing forth in continual self-renewing performance. That is to say, we enter cosmoi of persistent mattering without vacuous regions in need of relation. An awareness of one such mode of openness—viscerally, through an exposure to the genesis of forms, through touch and affective tonality—may call for a realignment of our stance and conduct, for new systems of valorisation. That is to say, it may call for a new ethics. Ethics in and for itself, however, has nothing to do with the theatre of the virtual. Nor is the theatre of the virtual to be aligned with the construction of an ethical paradigm. The theatre of the virtual does not tell us how to live. Rather, this—not *the* theatre of the virtual but *a* theatre, indicating that there are many—is a question of an attitude, an inflection upon the given, a question of *feeling*. This is a question that is first and foremost ontological. It signals the opening up to a dimension within the theatrical that is yet to be thoroughly conceptualised.

DOI: 10.4324/9781003231080-6

Within the pages of this book, we have made our first attempts, using the means available to us, to create accounts of the virtual as a theatrical force.

So what is a theatre of the virtual? We have answered this question by looking at some of its multifarious gradients. In doing so, we adopt the stance that gradients and ontology are inextricable from one another, take shape simultaneously, and continuously inform one another through their co-individuation. Further, we work from the assumption that the ontological portrait of a work undergoes continual individuation; this is a performatively constituted flux of grades of potentiality and actuality. The work of the theatre of the virtual, then, is that of continual fluxional engendering. It co-generates its ontology as it traverses both ontological and extra-ontological (evental) regions.

What is primary here is the inextricability and bi-directionality of the movement. Just as bodies perform their mattering so is matter that which performs bodies. And then again, matter takes its course in ways that cannot be predicted. Specificity branches out unexpectedly; novel variance is introduced with each juncture within individuation. Once we enter the virtual, we have an exuberance of indeterminacy that plays itself out within a complex interweaved motion of potentiality and actuality. What is gained from an engagement with the virtual is nothing less than a repotentialisation of the given. These operations of continual engendering are maximally abstract, yet inextricable from the material practices that carry their motion and zest so that "matter and ontological practices are really co-constructed and entangled in the interminable movements of their performances" (Gamble et al. 2019, 127).

The four chapters of this book look at different types of engendering the virtual. We started out by looking at grades of interweaving potentialities and actualities to construct a theatrical ontology that is non-purposive, kinetic, and self-constituting. That is to say, we looked at the very ontology of form as it comes to be. We reasserted motion as our primary category—motion as having its own being and a reality in its own right. We introduced the concept of the virtual as the counterpart of the actual—a clandestine actor that is equally real and equally capable of informing the given. And we made our entrance into conceptual regions that are speculative and characterised by high degrees of indeterminacy. These regions, we sought to emphasise, are exuberantly impractical. Nothing is determined in advance; the concatenation of motion and action bring forth novel indeterminacy at every step. Finally, we defined the virtual as extra-anthropomorphic, meaning indifferent to anthropomorphic inscriptions and removing the distinction between the living and the non-living.

We saw how in postdramatic theatre, motion does not have the exhaustion of potentiality as its end but leads to the proliferation and dispersal of potentiality in infinite directions, precluding linearity and irreversibility. We no longer deal with fully actual entities but with gradients of the virtual, each leaving its singular inflection upon the given. And whereas the focus is on the interweave of potentiality and actuality, postdramatic theatre still retains a connection with entelechial theatrical ontologies and defines itself in alignment with these, subsisting in the tension between the mimetic and the extra-ontological (the event). But we also became aware that shifting our focus to potentiality allows us to see how a work makes palpable its very ontological scaffolding and how high degrees of contingency begin to traverse it. It is here that we first alluded to another vital function of the virtual: its capacity to create inflections within the given and engage with questions of *style*. In being such, the virtual is not a question of being but a style of being.

In looking at Theo Jansen's *Strandbeest*, we witnessed the very dynamics of a becoming-with, a radical confluence with an environment that becomes an ecologising practice. One is exposed to the generative zest of matter itself, the dynamics of metastability that define an individuating shape, and a dispersal of the body towards bodies–environments within a scenic co-individuating milieu. Along these lines, our concept of the theatre of the virtual was further refined as a radical exposure to the spectrality of things, foregrounding a logic of ecological attunement.

It is here that we shifted one step further than postdramatic theatre towards a generative theatrical ontology that is multi-centred and capable of engaging in manifold individuations. This focus on the dynamic morphogenesis within the given allowed us a glimpse into the various reverberations between gradients of potentiality and actuality, not only within a discrete entity but across ecosystems. Building on the event in postdramatic theatre as a discrete event structure, we expanded on our preliminary concept of the extra-ontological event. Rather than an encroachment and a fissure within being, we chose to position the event as pervasive and co-individuating.

We also saw how "synthetic" bodies became co-extensive with their milieus, drafting out expansive fields of potentiality in their interactions with seemingly discrete environments. This is where potentiality became gestural, showing itself in motion and in manifold acts of relating. In this way, we reaffirmed the capacity of matter to form enmeshments infinitely and veer towards spectral atmospheres of radical openness and movement. In building bodily peripheries, gesture within a theatre of the virtual exposes the environmentality of bodies and thrives on a certain logic of the threshold that signals not simply a lack of resolve but a readiness to dwell in the cloud of potentialities that envelop bodies. Bodies, in turn, become interstitial, that is, they become transducers where virtual and actual coalesce.

Shifting towards intensive bodily entwinement to explore the work of violent conditions, we arrived at another point of inflection within the field of potentiality—that of the event. In *Pindorama* by Lia Rodrigues, touch was introduced as an operation for the engendering of an event that repotentialises matter. Herein engendering does not presuppose a system's radical alteration. Rather, this is an operation that introduces inflections within a system, safeguarding a fundamental readiness to receive the extra-ontological event. We continue to speak of bodies–environments of increasing grades of spectrality. Within this atmospheric interweave of interpenetrating bodies and their milieus, touch carries forward the conditions of the new. It reinstates a connection to the virtual and infuses truncated lives with novel practices for the creation of enabling conditions. As a repotentialisation technique, touch safeguards a sufficient resource of the virtual within a system to secure the interweaving of potentials within the metastable state. This way, touch is nothing less than an ontogenetic operation and an engine for bodily engendering. The touch-event does not invade a body from without but precipitates change immanently.

It is at this juncture that we also encounter the practice of bodily becoming-environment, that is, a moulding of climates and atmospheres that surpasses individuals. Instead of bodily individuality, we have quasiversal motilities—expansive environments wherein bodies and movement cannot be distinguished from one another. To account for the permeability of the passage between virtual and actual as a locale of perpetual matter-forming, we introduced the concept of *feeling*. An entrance into *feeling* opens us to a level of perception that is more attuned to the virtual as a speculative reality. This gives us a heightened sense of the processual pervasiveness of connection and foregrounds the expansiveness of being. *Feeling* is both visceral and conceptual, constituting a threshold between ontological and extra-ontological regions. And finally, *feeling* is a fundamental affinity towards the force of the virtual.

Within a theatre of the virtual, we witness how a body is primarily composed of gestures and atmospheres. This is no longer the self-preserving, other-rejecting biological unit called an organism but a cloud of virtualities. The virtual permeates bodies and bodies are maximally open to the pull of the virtual. The boundaries of an organism become diaphanous. Instead of closure, we seek degrees, expanses, and coagulations of otherwise disparate ontological layers. A theatre of the virtual, then, effectively erases the difference between organism and machine, biological and non-biological, and living and non-living. Once we accept the vantage of potentiality, we need to abandon concepts such as organisation or stability—these cannot work once entities are no longer discrete. Rather, we speak about thresholds of re-potentialisation. What was previously a mesh of living organisms, machines, biological and non-biological apparatuses, artefacts, and "natural objects" are now continually individuating bodily atmospheres. If there is any organisation and stability, this is the brittle stability of the metastable state. Bodies overcome their stature as self-preserving organisms within an environment to open themselves to dynamisms of various incongruous textures. Entering the virtual means accepting a mode of fundamental openness and a readiness to become part of the refigurations of the given.

When exposed to the performance collaborations in Sougwen Chung's *Omnia per Omnia*, we witnessed an invigorating practice of response that allowed us to think outside of the concept of organism. In constructing a theory of expansive selves, stretching out infinitely, and permeating the entirety of the networked environments built in interaction, we arrived at an ontoecology of response—a practice of energetic attunement that co-creates a mode of ontological abundance, an overflow of repotentialisations. Response precludes the need for communication or translatability because it is based on attunement—an energetic supra-linguistic phenomenon that can be likened to a capacity for visceral tactility. Here bodies become expansive sensing organs and their sensing activity is pervasive. Communication is replaced by practices of visceral realignment. In being maximally open to the virtual and making themselves thresholds for the passages of potentiality, bodies thus create techniques for new forms of ecologising fully indifferent to designations such as human and artefact, and living and non-living.

And now, we arrive at our final question. Why do we need a theatre of the virtual? What are its promise and theoretical force? Trivially, this is nothing less than the promise that another world is possible. A shift towards virtual processuality makes palpable the plenitude of anthropomorphic and supra-anthropomorphic forces stretching out within and without an individuating entity. A theatre of the virtual sets out to do justice to these forces—to aid in tracing their conditions of emergence and the significance of their co-articulation. A logic of spectrality settles in—not so much entities as atmospheres, not so much a being as a style of being, and not so much a body as multitudinous milieus of varied interactions. We have enabling practices of mattering and relating, a body that becomes a sensing organ and ceases to be a gaze and strategies for the repotentialisation of the given. As a result of all these, we arrive at new forms of attention. What these new forms of attention deliver to us are bodies that actively engender the conditions for their flourishing, bodies that become diaphanous, and bodies that give us a heightened sense of a co-constituting ecological expanse. In short, we arrive at a collective invention of the given.

Works Cited

Gamble, Christopher N., Joshua S. Hanan, and Thomas Nail. 2019. "What Is New Materialism?" *Angelaki* 24 (6): 111–134. https://doi.org/10.1080/0969725X.2019.1684704.

Glossary

Genesis is an operation of ongoing constitution within the virtual that permeates the fabric of the given and continually alters existing shapes. These existing shapes, in turn, are surface effects emerging out of the dynamics of an incessant engendering. A theatre of the virtual expresses this as individuation—the interweave of forces and the traversing of thresholds of matter—whereby the level of the fully actual is less pronounced. A theatre of the virtual seeks cleavages and points of remodulation within the theatrical whereby one becomes acutely aware of an engagement with a constitutive movement. An individual, to the extent that one such entity can be discerned at all, would invariably be in a state of metastability—a transversal bundle of forces punctured by a plenitude of infra-individual inherences. In this sense, a theatre of the virtual rather speaks of a 'trans-dividual', an actuality that makes palpable its inextricable bond to an ontological region of ongoing constitution. This region is entirely defined by movement. We have an interweave of energetic multiplicities, entangled systems of metastability, emergent singularities on the brink of entering the actual.

Gestural potentiality is a term illustrating the movement-quality of the virtual. A gesture is the adoption of a movement. Movement is the principal ontological category within a theatre of the virtual. A focus here is the spectral plenitude of relations entailed in any given entity, and the expansiveness of the field of interaction within which every entity partakes in the given. Potentiality is gestural in the sense that it is entirely an opening and an expression of this opening. We do not speak of directionality but of the continual excess of themselves that entities are. This excess is expressed through the figure of the gesture: a threshold between a body and an environment wherein we rather deal with bodies-environments. A stretching out into an expansive habitat, gestural potentiality signals the coalescence of bodies and milieus in a motion without closure. This is an operation of dispersal, that is, an extension of the periphery of a body across a continuum covering the entirety of an environment. Gestural potentiality is not purposive. Further, this movement-quality does not possess an entity-hood. Gestural potentiality inheres as an attitude and an ambience: not a being but a style of being, not a body but a surrounding.

Feeling is a bodily capacity that makes palpable the very pressure of the virtual. As such, it is categorically different from the epistemologically informed operation of sensing. Unlike experiential sensing, feeling is conceptual, speculative, and incorporeal. The atmospheres and perturbations created in the reordering of forces within the virtual are made palpable not through sensing but through feeling. Rather than operating through the gaze and relying on the spectating capacity of a body, sensing is visceral. Herein the entire body is utilised as a sensing organ in entering the actual, making a body exposed in its full ontological vulnerability. Just like sensing is an experiential capacity tending towards the actual, so is feeling a speculative capacity oriented towards the virtual. Feeling is the conceptual counterpart of sensing that makes possible a connection to the virtual. Whereas sensing is tactile and has a clearly definable trigger in the outside world, feeling is abstract. Feeling is a signal that we have reached a threshold between disparate ontological layers. As a speculative reality, the virtual can only be felt. That is to say, the virtual can be made palpable through the recalcitrant persistence of a feeling body that, because of this feeling-capacity, safeguards the possibility of its articulation.

Touch is a concept that expresses the pressure of the virtual within a vantage of potentiality. This is an abstract capacity that is not to be conceived as something adjacent to bodies or co-extensive with bodies. Rather, touch is an incorporeality that engenders an event. This is an ontogenetic operation taking place immanently and primarily belonging to the virtual region. As such, touch incorporates both feeling as a speculative capacity and sensing as an epistemological practice. Because of its unmediated relation to the virtual and capacity to engender an event, touch becomes an operation for the potentialisation of matter. While not of the body, touch carries the shift occurring within bodies, the changes in tonality, the alterations in inflection. Touch is the conduit for the transductive activity of bodies, transmitting change towards an ecology. Through touch, a body-transducer makes its entanglements expansive and global. A virtualising touch bears justice to the vulnerability of the metastable state. In doing so, touch shows how bodies are in excess of themselves, embroiled in continual re-constitution and a plenitude of engenderings. Because of its relation to the virtual, touch can be likened to a machine for the generation of potentialities.

A body becomes a *transducer*, that is, a conduit and a linkage between the ontological layers of the virtual and its actualisation within a world. In this sense, a body becomes interstitial—it carries the impulse of the virtual within the domain of the actual, transmits potentiality and makes it available to the region of formed entities. In partaking in the actual, a body engenders novel virtualities, widening the field of potentiality.

This transmission is multi-causal and evolves in a plenitude of directions, causing the entirety of a field to reverberate with the tensions of a bodily gesture. A gesturing body makes the virtual palpable, enhances its power, and introduces novel potentials within its field. This is the meeting ground of two different—albeit equally real—ontological layers. A body becomes their point of juncture, the singularity distilled out of their encounter, the point of reaching a surplus—an excess of oneself that becomes a gesture and by dint of this becoming, repotentialises the given. A body simultaneously incorporates the force that enables a becoming and is the very environment of the becoming as such. Because of this linkage to the virtual, the transducer carries the capacity to engender novelty. A body incorporates the pressure of the virtual and the elusive quality of the actual, the reversibility of the movement from actual to virtual as well as the gesturing of potentiality towards the actual.

Organismicity allows for variations between states and degrees within a nominally defined organism. Rather than conceived as structural and functional closure, organismicity is multitudinous in incorporating degrees of organisaiton, degrees of system-hood, and degrees of openness. The concept of organismicity is defined in terms of transversal layers and grades that exceed an organism, add a touch of spectrality to it, and make its nominally established boundaries spill over a milieu. Organismicity—the affective compound incorporating permeable ontological layers, multidimensionality, and an extension towards a milieu—is closer to the productive zest of potentiality. It moves across levels and degrees, works with extensions and coagulations. With the continual refleshings taking place within organismicity, we have a cross-linking all the way within and across a diaphanous organismic multitude. Levels of attunement ascertain the continual reverberations across bodies-environments shaping the organismicity of the virtual. The experience of the networked enaction of mattering takes place alongside the experience of being an organism. While partaking in the life of a terrestrial biome, a body-environment is shot through by a plenitudinous spectrality—these are the individuating singularities of the virtual that continually repotentialise their fields of interaction.

Environmentality is the becoming-environment of a body, that is, a body-environment. This expansion is not local and does not pertain to dimensionality. Rather, we have the involvement of a body-environment in an expansive yet clandestine co-alignment whereby a body stretches out to incorporate the entirety of its milieu. An individuating body-environment is generated by movement. While foregrounding the incorporeality of movement, environmentality also makes felt the permeability of a body and a world. A body-environment foregrounds movement as an ecologising force repotentialising the crosslinked porousness of any actual shape. This is the very moulding of climates and atmospheres whereby bodies expose themselves as multitudinous motilities across layers of being, differing in speed and intensity, traversing incongruent ontological landscapes. A body-environment evokes a feeling of permeability, dissipative expressivity, an expanse encompassing disparate milieus and non-aligning ontological layers, tonalities and inflections. Environmentality is the ever ongoing excess of itself that a body presents with its very positing. This is the meeting point of environments—the concrete milieus generated by a body—and ecologies—the virtual atmospheres and spectral inflections that traverse bodies in motion.

Response is the conceptual counterpart of communication within a theatre of the virtual. A response is a bodily operation of openness—not comprehension and understanding but a visceral alignment with the forces of the virtual. Put simply, a response is this perpetual resounding and attunement to the ecologies of others. In bringing forth a dimension of visceral attunement, response engages all constituents within an ecology, and thus works towards the collectivisation of responsivity. Responsive receiving and repotentialising is the very mode in which an organism operates within potentiality. The alterations carried by a response are subtle—we have changes in inflection and alterations in tone that however make things somewhat more exposed to the pressure of the virtual. Response is enmeshed in the energetic enfleshings within a world, is fully engaged in the corporeal insistence of bodies-environments. And in doing so, a response does infinite justice to the virtual entanglements that puncture bodies across the continuum of the living and the nonliving. A visceral tactility replaces understanding as an epistemological operation. We have recompositions within an individuating body and co-compositions with environments. Even more so, in its capacity to appeal to a maximally open repotentialisation, the response brings forth an aspect of the virtual that is evental. Once co-aligning systems of determination are perturbed by an event, we witness a realignment that engenders real novelty within the interweave of potentiality and actuality.

Ethics of enmeshment. If there is a guiding trope throughout this book, this is the figure of the enmeshment. Enmeshment is pervasive and encountered at every level of inquiry, within each conceptual encounter offered on these pages. This gesture is simply demonstrative: things persist in regimes of interweaving. In being such, things are not simply co-extensive with their environments but are inextricably woven into milieus and shot through by relations. An ethics of enmeshment foregrounds the co-presences, the entanglements, the co-habitations, and the regimes of co-constitution that permeate being and non-being. The virtual and the actual operate the way they do because of the possibility of their perpetual enmeshment; bodies and environments are weaved into one another. Within a theatre of the virtual, an exposure to this perpetual enmeshment allows us to witness how organisms become multiple organismicities. Touch becomes a transducer and an operation for engendering the virtual. Individuation takes place at the fault lines of varied enmeshments between ontological regions of different textures (virtual and actual) and the extra-ontological region of the event. Ecological response also has enmeshment as its enabling condition. An ethics of enmeshment prompts us to be accountable and do justice to these atmospheres of trans-permeation. This is a call to relate through response, engender the virtual through attunement, eschew violence through the repotentialising force of touch, and partake in individuation through safeguarding a sufficient amount of openness through every system we traverse.

Index

action (*kārya*) 7, 142; depletion of potentiality 9–14; principles of 8; stages of 16
active potentiality 28
actual: connectivity of virtual and 94; interweave of 96; perpetual encroachment of 85
actualisation 10, 14, 24, 26, 27, 31, 32, 40, 41, 49, 50, 81; touch of 90
actualisation engine 64–65
actuality 7, 8, 22, 26, 62, 63, 142; of first order 31; of potentiality 11; and virtual 22–27
affective intensity 73
affective tonality 129, 130, 132, 136, 141
Agamben, Giorgio 61
alignment 117, 135; evental character of 131; perpetual 121; practice of 131; responsive 129
allopoietic machines 119–120
ambience 58, 61; non-anthropomorphic 127
anagnorisis 10, 14, 21
Anthropocene gestures 112
anukaraṇa 17, 18
Aristotelian–Cartesian concept 114
Aristotelian drama 19
Aristotelian ontology 8
Aristotelian system 2, 24
Aristotle 6, 7, 9, 11, 100, 111; concept of action 55; hylemorphism 36; *Metaphysics* 9, 12, 14; *The Nicomachean Ethics* 86; *Physics* 7–10, 12, 14, 24, 118; *Poetics* 7, 9, 10, 12, 14–19, 24, 29; principle of entelechy 67; views on nature and dramatic plot 12
art 25–26
atmosphere 8; of ontological constitution 8; of potentiality 9, 32; conceptual 42, 43, 85; spectral 60, 68; of violence 85; of virtuality 122
attainment 7, 11, 13, 15, 16, 59–61
attention 108–109
attunement 126, 129, 135, 141, 145
autonomy 108, 113, 119, 120, 122; human/machine 121
autonomy principle 118–119
autopoietic machines 120

becoming 37, 47–49, 66–67
being 37, 47–49
Bene, Carmelo 24
Bharata Muni: *Nāṭyaśāstra* 14–19
biological organisms 118, 119, 121–123
Blue Kettle (Churchill) 21–22
bodies–environments 64, 81, 99
bodily becoming-environment 100–104, 144
body 4, 28–29, 63, 133–134; actualisation engine 64–65; become dissipative within theatre of virtual 66; destruction of 81–82; of drama 16; movement and directionality of 109; movement-bodies 88–89, 104; notions of 2; perturbed by touch 73; system for generation of worlds 90; as transducer 67, 98
Butler, Judith 86

Chung, Sougwen: *Omnia per Omnia* 123–128, 136, 144–145
Churchill, Caryl 24; *Blue Kettle* 21–22; *A Mouthful of Birds* 20–21
classical drama ontology 54
classical dramatic theory 6–7, 20
communication 145; contact and 80; problem of 81; response against 128–136

comprehensive receptivity 88
confluence 128, 131
consistent forms, individuation of 38
constraint 88, 104, 119, 120; organisational 121; pre-established 122
contact and communication 80
continual engendering 80, 89, 104, 142
continual ontogenesis 110
continuity 16, 31
counter-actualisation 25–27
counter-effectuation 25
creation 23–26

"degrees in constraint" 119
Deleuze, Gilles 20, 24, 29, 30, 48, 83, 91, 98
De Lingua Latina (Varro) 60
Descartes, René: *Passions of the Soul* 114
determinism 7, 37
Deuber-Mankowsky, Astrid 11
devastation 84
diaphanous organismicity 114–117, 127, 133–136
dichotomist thinking 110
Diodato, Roberto 58
directionality 108; of body 109
dispersive virtuality 66
drama (*nāṭya*) 7; body of 16; classical ontology of 12; formal unfolding of 14; outcome of 10; principles of action and motion 8; Sanskrit notion of 16–17
drama of potentialities 19
Drama Studies 19
dramatic theory 7, 10, 19
dynamic individuation 36

ecology 5, 54–56, 103, 127; notions of 2; supra-anthropomorphic concept of 55; of virtual 88
ecosophy 55, 56
emotion, "proper purgation" of 13
emotive entelechy 13–15, 17
energeia (being-at-work) 13, 14, 20, 27, 28
engagement: politics of 88; receptive 89; with virtual engenders 90
engendering practice 98–104
enmeshment 2, 43, 54, 56, 116; dynamic responsive 132; of individuating networks 51; mutual 63, 132; perpetual 1, 35
entanglement: ethics of 127; human–artefactual 127
entelechia (being-at-an-end) 13, 14, 27

entelechial goal, of tragedy 13, 15
entelechial motion 11, 13, 24, 40
entelechial plot 15, 21, 25
entelechy 10, 13; emotive 13–15, 17
entities 65, 68, 107, 124; build bridges between 108; organism-like 112
entity-hood 102, 103
environment 4–5, 50, 116, 127; engendering practice 98–104; milieu and 46; notions of 2
environmental ethics 81
environmentality 61, 98–104, 143
ethics 141; of entanglement 127; environmental 81; of response 97
event: and sense 103; touch and 90–94; touch-event 89, 104
extra-anthropomorphic ontologies 42
extra-human sensing 126
extra-ontological knowability 97–98
extra-ontological region 6, 9, 12, 24, 32, 132, 133, 136
extra-organismic sensing 126

feeling 44–45, 53, 68, 72, 79, 82, 101–103, 141, 144
field of potentiality 109–113, 129, 134
force 129–130
form 19–22, 36, 43; genesis of 141; potentiality-driven 30
Fossils (Jansen) 41–42, 44
fundamental openness 8, 30, 130

Galtung, Johan 83, 88
genesis 2, 32; of enaction 55; of forms 141; principle of 67
geomorphic aesthetics 107
gestural potentiality 57–64, 68, 80, 81, 90, 94, 97, 99; conceptual milieu for 64
gesture 2, 3, 68, 107, 136; of asymmetrical generosity 131; dramatic theory and 19; of fundamental response 131; pre-constituted region 102; politics of 97
Greek tragedy 13; definition of 17
growth: in *Nāṭyaśāstra* (Bharata) 14–19; in *Poetics* (Aristotle) 14–19
Guattari, Félix 24, 55, 56; ecologies of virtual 88
Gutai Art Manifesto 128

Haeckel, Ernst 5
hamartia 10
happiness 86
Heidegger, Martin 85

Index   155

"the human" 112, 124
human–artefactual entanglement 127
human–environment interactions 101
humanity 112
hylemorphism 35, 36

immersive virtuality 121
inactive potentiality 28
indeterminacy 6
indeterminism 37, 39
individuation 6, 8, 21, 24, 29–32, 37, 46, 49; of consistent forms 38; dimensions of 38–39; dynamics of 36, 40; threshold of 38
inflection 2–3, 109, 136, 143
infra-virtual 133
intensive engagement 8, 31, 72, 99, 141
interfusing 46–52

Jansen, Theo: *Fossils* 41–42, 44; *Strandbeests* 41–46, 51, 143

katharsis 13–15
kinetic sculptures 41–46
kinetic system 31, 35, 141
Kosman, Aryeh 10

legal ownership 113
Lehmann, Hans-Thies 20, 50, 51

machine 124; organism and 117–123
machine metaphor 117, 118
machinic organisms 118, 119, 121–123
Manning, Erin 134
matter-form dichotomy 118
matter/mattering 36, 49, 82, 94, 110, 116–117, 120, 130; confluence of 45; defined as 35; force of 130; potentialisation of 95–96; repotentialisation of 95–98; of trans-subjective ecology 88
meaning 91–92
Merleau-Ponty, Maurice 11
Metaphysics (Aristotle) 9, 12, 14
metastability 9, 35, 36, 41, 47
metastable system 43, 95; transducer in 97
milieu 48; and environment 46; of interaction 56
mimesis 8, 15, 17, 22, 49, 130; Greek notion of 17
The Mode of Existence of Technical Objects (Simondon) 121
mono-causal system 39, 73
mono-local progression 65

motion 3–4, 7, 142; cessation of 8; depletion of potentiality 9–14; of individuation 31; in *Nāṭyaśāstra* 14–19; ontological portrait 32; in *Poetics* 14–19; principles of 8; processuality of 107; self-annihilation of 59–60
A Mouthful of Birds (Churchill) 20–21
movement 100–101, 108, 130, 132–133; of body 109; inextricability and bi-directionality of 142; radical openness and 143
mutual enmeshment 63, 132

Nancy, Jean-Luc: *The Sense of the World* 91–93
Nāṭyaśāstra (Bharata): motion and growth in 14–19
networked enaction, of mattering 116–117
New European Drama 8
The Nicomachean Ethics (Aristotle) 86
non-aligning body 109
non-purposive gestural potentiality 90

Omnia per Omnia (Chung) 123–128, 144–145
one-directional progression 65, 73
ontogenesis 39–40, 73
ontogenetic procedure 96–98
ontological horizon, potentiality as 27–32
ontological problem 113
ontological vulnerability 97–98
ontology 4, 6; of form 19; of *Poetics* 2; of theatrical 53
openness 7, 8, 23, 58, 60, 121, 122, 124, 141; fundamental 130; radical 53, 60, 143
organisational constraint 121
organism 144; as holistic system 115; and machine 117–123; notion of 111; of potentiality 109–113; teleological and individualistic concept of 111
organismicity 114–117
organism-like entities 112
originality 54
ousia 9

Passions of the Soul (Descartes) 114
pathos 13–15
Performance Philosophy 19
Performance Studies 19
performing space 76, 82, 96
peripeteia 10, 54

156   Index

perpetual enmeshment 1, 35
pervasiveness 93, 101
Philosophia Rationalis (Wolff) 10
philosophy 25, 26; of biology 112
Physics (Aristotle) 7–10, 12, 14, 24, 118
Pindorama (Rodrigues) 74–79, 82, 96, 104, 143
plastic principle 89
plot 9; action-driven 19; extra-ontological 12; and functions 10; junctures of 16; stages of 16
plot as motion (*kinêsis*) 14, 27–28
plot elements 16
plot structure 14
Poetics (Aristotle) 7, 9, 10, 12, 24, 29; motion and growth in 14–19
postdramatic theatre 8, 20, 22, 26, 50, 51, 142–143
potentialisation, of matter 95–96
potentiality 6, 7, 26, 53, 142; atmospheres of 9; depletion of 9–14; exhaustion of 8; exposure to 59; extinguishment of 7; field of 129, 134; gestural 57–64, 68, 80, 81, 90, 94, 97, 99; as ontological horizon 27–32; organisational and forceful 66; organism and field of 109–113; of second order 31; self-annihilating quality of 40; threshold of 131; types of 28
potentiality-driven forms 30
praxis 13, 14, 29
precarity 76, 107
pre-constitution 89, 102
pre-established constraint 122
pre-individual 38, 39, 43, 46, 48–51, 102
pressure of the virtual 101–103
primitive technical object 53
principal aesthetic moods (*rasa*) 17
processuality, of motion 107

radical openness 53, 60, 143
realignment 129–132, 136, 141
reality 42, 48, 94; multitudinous ontological and extra-ontological layers of 73; of theatrical 54
receptive engagement 89
relation 47, 96–97
relationality 47, 51, 57
relation-building 131
repotentialisation 144, 145; of bodies 104; continuous mutual 96; of matter 72, 96, 98; practices of 132; thresholds of 121, 144

repotentialising matter 95–98
response 145; against communication 128–136; ethics of 97
responsivity 122, 133, 135
Rodrigues, Lia 87; *Pindorama* 74–79, 82, 96, 104, 143
Ruprecht, Lucia 63

sahṛdaya 18
Sanskrit drama 16–18
science 25–26
sense 92–94; event and 103
The Sense of the World (Nancy) 91–93
sensing 72, 78, 82, 96, 126
shortening lives 86
Simondon, Gilbert 9, 32, 35, 36, 52, 53, 65; *The Mode of Existence of Technical Objects* 121; theory of individuation 50
singularity 24, 29–31, 42–43, 48, 134; production of 65
slow violence 45
spectacle, elements of 17
spectators 74–78
spectrality 32, 48, 63, 64, 103, 143–145
Strandbeests (Jansen) 41–46, 51, 143
structural rigidity 122
style 108, 131, 143; intervention of 107
synthetic bodies 45, 143

technical object 52–57
technicity, of touch 79–82
teleology 10
theatre of individuation 37
theatre of the virtual 9, 26–29, 31, 32, 50, 51, 55, 56, 62, 101, 141, 142, 144; body become dissipative within 66; as kinetic system 35
theatrical ontology 8, 51, 142
Thomist tradition 35
Toepfer, Georg 114
touch 2–3, 72, 141; as actualisation 62, 90; bodies perturbed by 73; and event 90–94; experience of 99; gestural dimension of 74; land of palms 74–79; subterranean politics inherent in 99; technicity of 79–82; violence of 80, 81; violent conditions 83–90
tragedy, definition of 13–15
trans-dividual 40, 67–68
transducer 64–68; body as 98; in metastable system 97
translatability 129
trans-subjective ecology 88

transversal individuality 66
truncated life 84, 86–87

Varro: *De Lingua Latina* 60
vernacular concept, of organism 110
violence 83–90; atmosphere of 85; definition of 83; events of 87; oppression employ 90; question of 85, 86; topos of 91; of touch 80, 81
violence-enabling ontological systems 83
violent conditions 83–90
virtual 32; actual and 22–27; connectivity of actual and 94; ecology of 88; interweave of 96; as theatrical force 1–3
virtual–actual interweave 26
virtual body 58, 103
virtual ecology 86

virtual entanglements 51
virtual field 58, 64, 65; defined as 53–54
virtualisation 50, 119
virtuality 1, 4, 27, 45, 48, 49, 87; atmosphere of 122; cloud of 44, 90, 124, 144; co-composition of 89; dispersive 66; immersive 121; potentials and 43, 49, 50
virtual self 56–57
vulnerability 124
vulnerable systems 120

Weil, Simone 23, 87
Wolff, Christian: *Philosophia Rationalis* 10
world concept 85, 92, 93; interchangeability of 102–103; world-forming 79, 93, 131; world-making 24, 86–87, 116

Taylor & Francis eBooks

www.taylorfrancis.com

A single destination for eBooks from Taylor & Francis with increased functionality and an improved user experience to meet the needs of our customers.

90,000+ eBooks of award-winning academic content in Humanities, Social Science, Science, Technology, Engineering, and Medical written by a global network of editors and authors.

TAYLOR & FRANCIS EBOOKS OFFERS:

- A streamlined experience for our library customers
- A single point of discovery for all of our eBook content
- Improved search and discovery of content at both book and chapter level

REQUEST A FREE TRIAL
support@taylorfrancis.com